Olympic Sports and Propaganda Games

Olympic Sports and Propaganda Games

Moscow 1980

Gardner Webb College Library

Baruch Hazan

Transaction Books
New Brunswick (U.S.A.) and London (U.K.)

Library of Congress Catalog Number: 81-7447
ISBN: 0-87855-436-x (cloth)
Printed in the United States of America

Library of Congress Cataloging in Publication Data

Hazan, Baruch, 1942-
   Olympic sports and propaganda games.

   Includes index.
   1. Olympic Games (1980: Moscow, R.S.F.S.R.)
2. Sports and state—Soviet Union.   I. Title.
GV722 1980.H39   327.1'4   81-7447
ISBN 0-87855-436-x   AACR2

CONTENTS

Come to me in my dreams, and then
By day I shall be well again.
For then the night will more than pay
The hopeless longing of the day.

Matthew Arnold

Foreword

Baruch Hazan is on the faculty of the Institute of European Studies in Vienna, Austria, a neutral country between East and West and member of the United Nations and of many other international organizations, is by its very geography and history a privileged location for East/West studies. It is no accident that the Institute of European Studies was founded in Vienna over thirty years ago, at a time when the city was still divided into the American, British, French, and Soviet zones of occupation. Since 1950, the institute, which has over seventy-five U.S. universities and colleges as affiliates and associates, has served over ten thousand students wishing to study at the very seam where East and West meet. The institute's faculty is uncommonly diverse and especially strong in the area of East-West studies. Several nationalities are represented; the background of some faculty members is in the West, of other in the East. It is not surprising, therefore, that neither the view that the U.S. boycott of the Moscow Olympics was necessarily a good thing, nor the conviction that the games as a whole should be considered a propaganda victory for the Soviet Union is shared by all.

The matter is by no means clear-cut, and propaganda can often be a double-edged sword. Those who opposed the boycott of the 1980 Moscow Olympics, both in the United States and in other Western countries, most commonly argued that sport and politics should be kept separate. It is often overlooked that the origin of the modern Olympic games was political at heart. Its founder, Pierre de Coubertin, was convinced tha the lack of physical education in French schools had been the fundamental cause of France's defeat against Germany in 1870, and international sport competitions were to help set this right. As this book shows in detail, there is a close connection in the Soviet Union between sport and politics. Baruch Hazan suggests that many an American who freely expressed his opinion in favor of participation despite the U.S. government's call for a boycott stood in grave danger of unwittingly becoming a tool of Soviet propaganda. While that may have been the case on one level, on another the fact that Western democracies can afford to have their citizens publicly criticize their policies in the very heart of the Soviet Union may, in the long run, turn out to have a much more profound impact.

The question remains: for all the resources it had at its disposal, did the Soviet propaganda effort described so comprehensively in this book make a lasting impression on either its own citizens or on others? Hardly anyone in the West or the Third World would consider sports achievements as reflecting the superiority of an entire political system. As for Soviet citizens themselves, did they really need to be impressed by this fact? Is the government there any more secure after the games than it was before? Could it be that the entire propaganda effort was an exercise in futility?

Avery Brundage once said, "Failing to recognize that sport like music and other fine arts transcends politics, they [i.e. political powers] sometimes attempt to use it as a tool or weapon for political purposes" (*The Speeches of President Avery Brundage, 1952 to 1968*, Comite International Olympique, p. 67). This statement and similar ones by Lord Killanin—quoted and criticized in this book—may seem naive at first, but they have at least two frames of reference that are not immediately obvious. On one level this stubborn insistence upon the fiction of the separation between sport and politics is related to the entire status of the Olympic movement as representing only amateurs. As long as athletes from the East are labeled as amateurs—and given political realities there, no alternative seems possible—amateur sport organizations in the West, in their desire to compete with the East and in their struggle to avoid being assimilated into professional organizations, will continue to insist upon this separation as a matter of survival. Figure skating is probably the clearest example of this predicament.

What international sport officials really appear to be defending in the separation between sport and politics is their attempt to channel international competition into an area that is not under the all-encompassing jurisdiction of politicians—in the East as well as the West—but of a transcending independent, metapolitical international organization. That would be in line with Pierre de Coubertin's original vision, and it, too, may be naive. Maybe the fact that the IOC was able to move the Soviet Union to such unprecedented gratuitous propaganda efforts of indeterminate effectiveness—to what can be seen as an exercise in pure *l'art pour l'art*—vindicates Avery Brundage after all and represents the true victory of sport over politics.

Rudolf Schier
Director

Institute of European Studies
Vienna Center

Prologue

The decision fell in the morning hours of October 23, 1974. The decor was appropriate: the sober majesty of Vienna's neo-Gothic Rathaus. The occasion: selecting the site of the XXII Olympic Games. The procedure was unusual. While it was the International Olympic Committee, which—as usual—was to select the site of the 1980 Olympic Games, this time, unprecedently, the decision would be made by secret ballot. Hundreds of reporters, commentators, and various officials who had come from all over the world filled the corridors of the noble building with noise and excitement, while in one of the festive halls, behind closed doors, the sixty-one members of the International Olympic Committee began the ritual. With solemn dignity the two oldest members of the committee—David George Brownlow Cecil Lord Burghley, sixth Marquess of Exeter, and His Highness Prince-Regent Franz Josef von Liechtenstein—collected the ballots.

Twenty-two minutes later the doors of the hall opened and Michael Morris, third Lord Killanin, president of the International Olympic Committee, addressed the breathless audience: "The XXII Olympic Games will take place in Moscow, in 1980." He declined to disclose the figures for the voting. The excited journalists who attacked the phone booths paid no attention to the IOC official who quietly left the building carrying a sealed envelope in which the torn up ballots had been placed. His mission was highly unusual: the torn up ballots were to be thrown in the Danube. No official explanation for this strange procedure was ever given, but then there was no need: the voting reflected much more than a mere preference for a particular site for the Olympic games, and the IOC members were eager to preserve the anonymity of their choice.

Introduction

For ages the arsenal of instruments used by states in conducting foreign policy suffered from chronic meagerness. There were only two patterns of international association: diplomacy and war. Both patterns are related and have been pursued both simultaneously and separately, the failure of the one usually triggering the introduction of the other. Invention of the printing press was the first indirect step toward widening the range of foreign policy instruments. It enabled the spread of knowledge on a much larger scale and the use of preconceived information. It put an end to parochialism and tribalism in space and time by producing an explosion which extended people's minds and voices to reconstitute the human dialogue on a world scale.

A new world emerged. The printed word became a means for stimulating people's minds through knowledge and developing political (and other) awareness. As people became literate and more civilized, the printed word came to play an increasingly important part in spreading opinions and forming emotional attitudes. The spread of knowledge, facilitated by printing, combined with the democratization of some political regimes and the resulting possibility of influencing the selection of national leaders, produced a tremendous growth of the social strata relevant to the conduct of foreign policy. Whereas in the past international political contacts were the realm of a chosen few (royalty, heads of states, ambassadors) and the opportunity of giving advice and exerting influence was reserved to a limited number of trusted advisors and relatives, the spread of education and free elections significantly increased the number of people capable of influencing the country's behavior on the international scene, both by participating in the election of decision makers and expressing preferences and opinions with a view to influencing the decision-making process.

The emergence of newspapers further strengthened this tendency and soon leaders were to learn the power of the press (and opportunities presented by this power). Napoleon went on record saying that "three hostile newspapers are more to be feared than a thousand bayonets." It was not long before newspapers were used as instruments of domestic and later, international propaganda. Although attempts to mold and change opinions are as old as recorded history and propaganda has always existed, the advent of radio brought in its wake international propaganda on a large scale. Beginning as a means of entertainment, radio readily became a source of information and subsequently, especially in countries with politi-

4

cal regimes capable of monopolizing broadcasting, an opinion-forming instrument.

The printed word and newspapers broadened people's horizons and sharpened awareness of events in distant lands, as well as recognition of national interests, characteristics, and policy. In a way they were catalysts of nationalism. The radio reversed this process. It developed a new pattern of human association by overcoming distance and shrinking the world. Events everywhere were brought into the listeners' living room. Reports were followed by explanations about how events are to be understood and interpreted, and soon by recommendations about specific action to be taken. Whole nations were subjected to group persuasion and collective stimulation through the new mass medium.

The development of science and technology since World War II and the sophistication of the ways in which people can exterminate each other (thus proving their political credo right), has turned the conduct of a major war into a suicidal affair for any nation, to be contemplated, planned, simulated, mentioned as a possibility—but resorted to only seldom, with great restraint and on a scale limited in time and place. As a result, the value of international propaganda as an instrument of foreign policy has distinctly increased. Although it has never been a surrogate for military strength, national resources, or skillful policy, it has successfully supplemented all these factors and sometimes even compensated for the lack of one or more.

In an age of conflicting ideologies, propaganda has given politicians the power to persuade and manipulate people without resorting to physical force. Development of this third major instrument of foreign policy reversed the way in which the other two have been used. Instead of talking to leaders and fighting the people, technological sophistication has rendered it more effective (and less dangerous) to talk to the people and direct them to influence their leaders to suit the interests of the propaganda source. The increasing value of international propaganda prompted many countries to invest much thought and effort in developing new propaganda instruments and increasing their effectiveness. For political regimes striving to spread an all-embracing political ideology and committed to serving as an example to other countries, international propaganda has become the most important instrument of foreign policy. In two previous books[1] I described and analyzed the Soviet propaganda apparatus, its major instruments, techniques, and goals. These books presented sport as one of the most effective instruments of the Soviet propaganda machine, and briefly discussed its use and effects. Soviet authorities, never late to discern a good opportunity for a large-scale propaganda campaign, soon discovered the propaganda potential of hosting the Olympic games. Henceforth no effort or expenditure was to be spared in the attempt to become the host of the great sports gala and explore its propaganda value. The purpose of this study is to examine the propaganda aspects of Soviet sport in general and the 1980 Moscow Olympic Games in particular.

Note

1. Baruch Hazan, *Soviet Propaganda: The Case of the Middle East* (New York: Wiley, 1976); id., *Soviet Impregnational Progaganda* (Ann Arbor: Ardis, 1982).

1

Propaganda: Definition, Elements, Process

Every study of human behavior is a subjective venture, involving one's values, beliefs, prejudices, and preferences. This is all the more the case in the study of propaganda. A highly emotional and controversial area, the study of propaganda has always been characterized by lack of conformity, starting with the very definition of the concept, the attempt to isolate it from other factors affecting human behavior, describing and analyzing its activity, and culminating in the frustrating endeavor to evaluate its effectiveness.

The word *propaganda* comes from the Latin *propagare*, which describes the gardener's practice of putting fresh shoots into the ground to produce new plants, or simply—dissemination. Pope Urban VIII is usually credited with having attributed sociological connotations to the agricultural term by using it to describe the organized and deliberate spread of ideas which would not otherwise have taken place. In 1633 he organized a committee of cardinals in charge of the church's foreign missions: Congregatio de Propaganda Fide, or The Congregation of Propaganda.

The congregation's activity involved much more than influencing others or manipulating their behavior. In an organized and preconceived manner it engaged in spreading ideas to change the lives of those who embraced them. Its activity was continuous and its sphere large—entire nations being

7

considered as potential targets. The members of the congregation were the first real progagandists. It was only in the twentieth century that propaganda became a major weapon of political warfare. The spread of rigid all-embracing political ideologies of a missionary nature, claiming to possess all the answers and a clearly outlined plan for the future, on the one hand, and the development of modern mass media on the other, were instrumental in the development of propaganda.

It was not only propaganda—as a political instrument—that developed, but also the practice of dismissing ideas, values, opinions, and beliefs with which one disagrees or opposes as "propaganda." The concept soon acquired sinister connotations and a derogatory character, implying an unethical and generally unpleasant process involving lies, suggestive ideas, exaggeration, brain-washing, and the presentation of selected, censured, and manipulated information. The entire subject of propaganda quickly turned into a sensitive matter charged with emotion and surrounded by an aura of suspicion and mistrust. This impedes and confuses the study of propaganda and complicates the attempt to define it.

There is agreement that propaganda involves behavior manipulation by influencing opinions, barring the use of force. Since people have always tried to influence each other's behavior without resorting to force, one can maintain that propaganda has existed since human speech developed. This is a simplistic view, implying that any attempt to persuade others or manipulate their behavior is propaganda. We would like to offer and analyze the following definition of propaganda:

> Propaganda is the carefully planned, systematically conducted, centrally coordinated and synchronized process of manipulating symbols, aimed at alerting human response and engendering uniform behavior of large social groups, behavior expected to produce immediate and effective results, compatible with the specific political interests and goals of the propaganda source.

Propaganda as process. Modern propaganda is a complex matter involving a great variety of instruments, techniques, and agents, having a permanent presence and involvement in the international arena. It is not a random collection of articles and broadcasts on some topical international issue, but rather a process formed by an interplay of changes, susceptible of categorization and analysis into unchanging or systematically changing elements, which might themselves be complex subprocesses or patterns of action—arranged into a specific structure, governed, at least partially, by discoverable laws. The elements, participants, and currents involved in the propaganda process will be described and analyzed immediately following this elaboration of elements comprising the above definition of propaganda.

Propaganda as planned activity. There is nothing desultory about modern propaganda. While certain unexpected and importunate international events sometimes require a certain degree of improvisation on the part of the propaganda apparatus, the bulk of propaganda activity is carefully planned and preconceived. The ultimate goal of international propaganda is to facilitate the implementation of foreign policy goals. Since long-term national interests and subsequent foreign policy goals only seldom undergo major permutation, it is only natural that a country's basic propaganda activities maintain both their continuity and character. The planned character of propaganda is further enhanced by the structure of its apparatus. In almost every country today there is an administrative organ in charge of propaganda. Regardless of its denomination, one of its basic functions is always long-term planning of its activities.

Propaganda as systematically conducted, centrally coordinated and synchronized process. Implementation of any plan requires a system. All the more so when implementation involves the activity of numerous instruments and communication media aimed at influencing world events by producing the ultimate combination of integration and uniformity in the audience's behavior, as sought by the progaganda source. If international propaganda is to be effective, it must not only be carefully planned, but also systematically conducted. The profusion of interconnected instruments of propaganda, the complexity and multiplicity of decisions, preferences, and calculations, and the diversity and intricacy of the factors involved demand a rigid, skillful, and effective organizational structure capable of conducting, coordinating, and controlling the propaganda process, evaluating its effectiveness and adjusting alternatives and timing.

Coordination and synchronization of propaganda activity is a precondition of effective performance. A propaganda apparatus whose instruments reveal discord, employ wrong language and style, disregard differences in audience characteristics, or express different if not contradictory ideas cannot hope for effective results. Coordination and synchronization of propaganda instruments does not guarantee success. The propaganda process involves numerous and diverse elements and participants which can determine its effectiveness and outcome. Nevertheless, coordination of propaganda instruments facilitates the achievement of propaganda's ultimate goals.

Propaganda effectiveness depends largely on the structure of the society using it as a political weapon. Coordination and synchronization of propaganda instruments to produce a uniform message is only possible under political regimes capable of exercising total control over mass media. While every state employs propaganda as a foreign policy instrument, authoritarian states have elevated it to an art. Democratic regimes, unable to control mass media—which present the varied and contradictory opinions and beliefs prevailing in democratic societies—are seldom a match for authoritarian states' propaganda apparatus.

Propaganda as symbol manipulation. Since there is no agreement about what propaganda is, there can be no agreement about whether a certain event or message is propaganda. Drawing up a list of propaganda instruments seems an impossible task, simply because everything and anything can be used as an instrument of propaganda. Drill two holes in a simple shirt, daub some red substance liberally on it, and you have "the shirt worn by Comrade X before he was executed by the oppressors." Take a doll, mutilate skillfully, publish its picture in several hundred newspapers under the headline "Their Bombs Did Not Even Spare Children's Toys." Therefore the definition uses "symbol manipulation" as the only characteristic of the propaganda instruments.

Propaganda and the alerting of human response. This aspect of propaganda will be discussed at some length later, when we analyze the process of propaganda in general and the functions of the absorption screen in particular. The ultimate objective of propaganda is to facilitate implementation of certain goals. Since we are analyzing a process, it would be incorrect to concentrate on its final outcome without considering some preliminary stages. Before opinions can be formed and uniform behavior engendered, the audience must be alerted to the issue. Ringing the bell, indicating the problem, defining it, indentifying the adversaries, in short, stimulating awareness of the fact that there is a problem on which (later on) a position or opinion are to be found, is one of the preliminary goals of the propaganda process.

Propaganda aimed at large social groups. While prompting human awareness of an issue is an important preliminary goal of propaganda, alerting the individual to the fact that he has been subjected to propaganda is a misfortune the propagandist tries carefully to avoid. The unavoidable result of such a mishap is activation of the individual's alarm system, arousing his suspicions and making his views on the matter inflexible and stubborn—which makes it very difficult if not impossible for the propaganda message to sink in.

People are more susceptible and less alert when addressed as a group and their credulity is reduced to the lowest common denominator. An efficient propaganda apparatus cannot take into consideration characteristics of every individual. Such concern for detail is time consuming, useless, and technically impossible in any event. What is meticulously taken into account are common characteristics of large social groups, defined in terms of attitudes, emotions, motivation, common history, traditions, language, and so forth. Reducing the individual to an average member of a large social group, approaching him as part of a much larger entity, and utilizing this entity's collective emotions, beliefs, values, and interests is a basic characteristic of the propaganda process.

Propaganda and the engendering of uniform behavior. Regardless of the propagandist's preliminary or intermediate goals, the ultimate aim is to instill preconceived attitudes leading toward predetermined action. Prompting human response is the propagandist's initial goal. Instilling, modifying, and influencing opinions is the next step, and the ultimate goal is to engender uniform behavior, instrumental to the furtherance of foreign policy goals. Emotions, thoughts, opinions, and attitudes are useless (for the propagandist) so long as they are not translated into predetermined behavior. If this behavior is to have any effect in influencing the political decision-making process, it has to exhibit uniformity of thought and action on the part of the masses.

Propaganda aimed at anticipated and effective results. The propagandist knows exactly what his goals are. The entire propaganda campaign is planned to achieve specific results intended to affect the political issues involved. When this campaign revolves around an acute and urgent international development, the propagandist expects immediate results. This was the case with the campaign conducted by the Soviet propaganda machine is 1979 against the production and deployment of the neutron bomb by the United States, and the U.S. campaign against the Soviet invasion of Afghanistan in 1980.

Sometimes results are expected to be of a long-term nature. This is the realm of impregnational propaganda, a subject we will come to in due course. No matter how distant anticipated results may be, they always display the same basic characteristic: they are expected to smooth the path for implementation of the foreign policy of the country issuing propaganda.

Propaganda in the furthering of political goals. The political nature of issues involved distinguishes propaganda from advertisement, which often employs similar means, techniques, and instruments. International propaganda is the province of governments, state institutions, and professional propagandists. Regardless of its declared or ostensible goals, its nature is political and the issues it deals with are related to topical political developments on the international scene. The real goals sought by propaganda are purely political.

So much for the elements comprising the definition of propaganda. Let us turn now to the process itself. A simplistic approach to propaganda accentuates only four factors: the propagandist, the message, the audience, and the outcome (if any). Such analysis ignores several crucial factors which determine final results. The following all have a part in the propaganda process:

THE MAIN POLITICAL DECISION-MAKING BODY

Since international propaganda belongs to the realm of politics and is intended to facilitate implementation of foreign policy objectives—basic decisions involving initiation, activation, intensification, or reduction of the intensity of a propaganda campaign are made by the organ responsible for political decision making. Both propaganda and foreign policy emanate from the same sources—the international situation, national goals, domestic factors, and sometimes a political ideology—and both pursue the same ultimate goal: furtherance of the country's national interests as seen by the decision-making organ at any given moment. Whereas the conduct of propaganda is the responsibility of the propaganda apparatus—control, supervision, and evaluation of the propaganda campaign is done by the decision-making organ.

THE PROPAGANDA BODY

This is where preparation of the propaganda campaign is organized by professionals. It is also the organ directly responsible to the political decision-making body for the campaign's success. Its activity involves decision making on the content and form of the propaganda message and execution of these decisions, as well as decisions previously adopted by the policymaking body, involving the fundamental tasks of propaganda. The main propaganda body also determines what is to be said or shown, to whom, where, when, how, and at what intervals. In short, it constructs and conducts the propaganda campaign on the basis of decisions and instructions of the political decision makers.

The main propaganda organ is composed of politicians and top-level professional propagandists who seldom participate personally in the propaganda process. Some politicians may also belong to the main political decision-making organ and serve as a link between the two. The main propaganda body of the Soviet Union is the CPSU Central Committee Department of Propaganda, headed by Evgeniy Tyazhelnikov. It is amenable to the CPSU Central Committee Politburo, which is the main Soviet political decision-making organ. Although the specific areas of responsibility of Politburo members have never been officially disclosed, there have been indications that Pavel Demichev, candidate-member of the Politburo and Soviet minister of culture, and Mikhail Suslov, CPSU Central Committee secretary and Politburo member, also considered the party's chief ideologist, are the Politburo members in charge of propaganda policy. Both often chair meetings of the CPSU Central Committee Propaganda Department. (Suslov subsequently died on 25 Jan. 1982.)

The main propaganda body conveys specific instructions to the administrative organs of various propaganda instruments, such as the State Committee for Television and Radio Broadcasting (chairman—Sergey Lapin), the State Committee for Cinematography (Filipp Yermash), the Union of Soviet Writers (Georgiy Markov), the Committee for Physical Culture and Sports (Sergey Pavlov), and leading organizations responsible for "spontaneously" organizing most demonstrative propaganda activities such as public rallies, demonstrations, solidarity weeks and days, and so forth. Among the most prominent front organizations are: the Committee of Soviet Women (chairwoman—Valentina Nikolaeva-Tereshkova), the Soviet Committee for the Defense of Peace (Yevgeniy Fedorov), the Soviet Committee for European Security (Aleksey Shitikov), the U.S.S.R. Committee for Solidarity with Asian and African countries (Mizra Ibragimov). The main propaganda body synchronizes their activities and coordinates their operations to achieve uniformity of the propaganda message. It also evaluates the effectiveness of propaganda activities, striving to improve their impact and extend their application. Final evaluation of the propaganda effect in terms of contributing to the achievement of foreign policy goals is reserved to the political decision-making body.

THE PROPAGANDA MESSAGE

Propaganda is an aggressive and manipulative process aimed at controlling human behavior. Its instruments are innumerable: anything capable of influencing a person's emotions and behavior can be used as a vehicle of the propaganda message. The "classic" instruments of propaganda—printed and spoken word, films, television—represent but a fraction of the arsenal of propaganda weapons. Regardless of the number of propaganda vehicles, the message itself always displays the same characteristics:

1. All propaganda messages conform to the initiating country's foreign policy and are subjected to its needs and goals.
2. While some propaganda messages convey information, it is usually manipulated and manipulative information, designed to stir the audience in a certain direction.
3. Propaganda messages are usually adapted to their audiences. Differences in accent, customs, religion, etc., are carefully taken into consideration by the sophisticated propaganda apparatus.

So far we have dealt with elements of the propaganda process related to the propaganda source. Let us turn now to elements related to the audience. It is here that the most important part of the propaganda process takes place. While many of the audience's characteristics (language, education, values, experience, tradition, customs) affect the content of the propaganda message and the way the propaganda vehicles deliver this message, it is the absorption screen that serves as the first point of contact between the message and the audience.

THE ABSORPTION SCREEN

Everyone is equipped with a finely tuned mechanism for distinguishing and classifying information, including propaganda messages. This mechanism represents an abstract reflection of one's personality and immediate environment and serves as a filter determining whether the propaganda (or any other) message is to be immediately rejected as incredible, false, irrelevant, uninteresting, or absorbed and processed. This is the absorption screen. Absorption of the propaganda message does not necessarily lead to an opinion favorable for the propagandist, let alone action conforming to the propagandist's goals. What happens to the propaganda message after absorption is the realm of the personality screen. The absorption screen merely absorbs the message and conveys it to the personality screen. Penetration of the audience's absorption screen depends on several technical and rational factors.

The technical factors are related to the message's physical dimensions. For radio broadcasts the technical factors are clarity of reception, strength of signal, language, broadcast quality, and in the case of printed propaganda—typescript, color, layout, and so forth. Their common denominator: they have nothing to do with the content of the message. A propaganda message conveyed in unintelligible language, a broadcast jammed by other stations, a photograph obscured by more interesting material—will fail to attract attention and induce penetration. The importance of technical factors has declined as a result of technological progress and sophistication of the propaganda apparatus. Still, some countries attempt to counteract other states' propaganda by artifically creating technical factors to hinder that foreign propaganda. Jamming radio broadcasts, censuring foreign press, banning the import of certain magazines and books fall in this category.

Rational factors determining absorption of the propaganda message are related to three elements of the propaganda process: the propagandist, the message, and the audience. Characteristics of the propaganda source, such as credibility, intentions, past record, interests, aims, and motives, as perceived by the audience, affect the operation of the absorption screen. These characteristics qualify or disqualify a propaganda source and determine the chances of its message penetrating the absorption screen.

Characteristics of the propaganda message are more important at a later stage when the processing of the message takes place. Yet even at the absorption-screen stage, some of the message's characteristics are instrumental to its advance: its ability to touch emotional strings and trigger associations, past images, or better, stimulate specific emotional states (love, fear, hatred, pleasure), facilitates penetration of the absorption screen. Other characteristics of a more technical nature, such as dramatization of presentation and background effects, also increase chances of penetration.

Personal characteristics of the audience also determine whether the propaganda message is absorbed or rejected. While some of these characteristics are of a technical nature and immune to propaganda conditioning (deafness, blindness), most are a result of a person's education, intelligence, personal interests, preferences, curiosity, need for information, degree of sophistication, and the effect of previous propaganda. Some follow from belonging to a certain social group or identification with some value system or moral code. Others result from a person's experience, mental acumen, and psychological factors.

If a propagandist wants to facilitate penetration of the absorption screen by his message, he must not only take into consideration characteristics of his audience and adapt his message accordingly, but also attempt to influence at least some of his audience's characteristics. Here we reach the most important point of the propaganda process: impregnational propaganda and its instruments. While influencing his audience's opinion and stirring their action is propaganda's final output and the propagandist's ultimate goal, penetration of the absorption screen is a precondition (but not a guarantee) for achieving these goals. Conditioning the audience's outlook (of the propagandist's credibility, intentions, and motivation) is an important aspect of propaganda and a factor improving its chances of success. This activity may be defined as *impregnational propaganda*, as distinct from conventional propaganda related to specific international developments, which may be termed *operational propaganda*.

Impregnational propaganda has little to do with international issues. It is a sophisticated long-range process aimed at evoking good will toward the propaganda source, arousing interest in further information provided by the source, and developing positive attitudes such as admiration, benevolence, and affection toward the propaganda source—thus facilitating a positive human response to the operational messages, which in turn aids penetration of the absorption screen. Impregnational propaganda aims at conditioning the audience's absorption screen for successful penetration by operational propaganda messages. It impregnates the absorption screen or drills holes in its shield by creating strong interest in the propaganda source, developing admiration for its successes and evoking a positive atittude and credibility toward the social system it represents.

Impregnational activity comprises a large part of Soviet international propaganda. Every possible channel of human communication is being utilized in this effort. Soviet art, music, cinematography, theater, literature, and most of all sport are mobilized by the Soviet propaganda apparatus as agents for improving the Soviet image, promoting interest in Soviet life, evoking admiration toward Soviet achievements, and ultimately facilitating penetration of the absorption screen by painting it red. Soviet impregnational propaganda, long before the eruption of acute international crises and introduction of operational propaganda messages, is charged with improving operational propaganda's chances of success by conditioning or weakening the audience's absorption screen.

THE PERSONALITY SCREEN

This is the response-producing unit of propaganda. It processes propaganda messages which have penetrated the absorption screen, synthesizing them with the specific values, beliefs, opinions, attitudes, stereotypes, and images of the individual subjected to propaganda. This is the laboratory producing the propaganda output—opinions and action. There is mutual interdependence and influence between the propaganda message and the personality screen. While the personality screen rearranges, simplifies, and classifies the message according to its existing stereotypes, combines it with previous opinions, tendencies, interests, inclinations, and motives, and finally incorporates it into its value system (or completely discards it), the message itself may weaken or strengthen the personality screen components, enrich them, modify them, alter their priorities, and sometimes even rearrange the entire structure of the personality screen.

OUTPUT: OPINION AND ACTION

The propaganda effect is the last link of the propaganda process (feedback is also a possible contender for this honor). Yet we shall not dwell on the propaganda effect, because it is impossible to isolate it from other factors, some of which we may not even know exist. For instance, when a propagandist strives to stimulate certain action and his target audience behaves according to his expectations, it is impossible to prove that propaganda was the sole factor influencing that behavior. Let us conclude discussion of the elements of the propaganda process by examining its output—opinions and action.

When propaganda succeeds in influencing opinions, the opinion conditioned by propaganda may either be that prescribed by the propagandist or combine some of the message's elements with the personality screen's components. In both cases the opinion produced is of little value to the propagandist unless it leads to the anticipated behavior. The propagandist usually strives to assure the audience that its action will have significant influence on the political issues involved. Propaganda is tantamount to a mass leader defining the issues, stands, and adversaries, recommending the necessary course of action and promising positive results if such action is pursued. A side effect sought by the propagandist is conditioning of the audience's personality screen so that its response to operational propaganda may be foreseen, easily stimulated, and effectively directed.

There are three currents running through the propaganda process. First, the *instruction and control* current, flowing from the main political decision-making body to the main propaganda organ, and from the main propaganda organ to the administrative organs of the various propaganda instruments. Second, the reciprocal current of *report*, the heads of administrative organs managing propaganda instruments, usually reporting to the main propaganda organ and sometimes directly to the political body. Finally, the current of *evaluation* and *feedback*, stemming from the propaganda effect (as seen by the propagandist and the political body) and flowing to the main propaganda organ and the main political decision-making body.

We shall now turn to the propaganda functions of Soviet sport, mainly (but not exclusively) as an agent of Soviet impregnational propaganda. As such, sport has several characteristics which set it apart from all other impregnational propaganda instruments. No other instrument of propaganda commands such a huge audience. It is not only a question of the number of spectators who may attend an event, but the hundreds of millions who watch major sports events on television. The Olympic games command greater audiences than any other international event. The 1972 and 1976 Olympic games were watched by almost two billion people. What other event, let alone instrument of propaganda, can evoke similar interest throughout the world? The importance of these huge audiences is underscored by the skimpy audiences garnered by other instruments of Soviet propaganda. How many people abroad regularly purchase (or read) Soviet newpapers, listen to Soviet broadcasts, or attend Soviet exhibitions and concerts?

Sports spectators are easy prey. While aquiring a permanent audience is a difficult, continuous, and complicated endeavor for all other instruments of propaganda, the sports audience is always there, eager and willing to switch the television set on. The sportsman's excellence is a captivating and attractive force which needs no further promotion. No other instrument of propaganda creates such a sense of personal participation and emotional involvement as does sport. A good article or an effective broadcast can impress, influence opinion, or even stir to action. A concert, a painting, a film, or a book can envoke awe and respect, touch deep chords, move to tears, enrich one's spiritual world, and even fill one with admiration for the composer, writer, or painter and the specific cultural milieu that has produced him. But show me the painting, book, film, or melody that can set one jumping up and down, hugging and kissing the person sitting in the next seat—a person whom one does not even know.

Consider the following story: In 1963 a U.S.-Soviet track and field competition took place in Moscow. At that time the competition was an annual affair, the two countries' best athletes taking part. As always in direct U.S.-Soviet competitions, the political conflict between the two systems was influencing the background of the meet. During the same year the Soviet Union and the United States were engaged in a round of arms reduction talks, rumor having it that personal relations between Averell Harriman, leader of the U.S. delegation, and Nikita Khrushchev were strained, hindering negotiations. Still, the two leaders came to Moscow's Lenin Stadium at the very end of the competition to watch Valeriy Broumel, the great Soviet high jumper, try for the world record. It was getting dark and a light rain was falling. Broumel failed twice, and it was time for his last attempt. He sprinted toward the bar, leapt, and made it. For several seconds the stadium was silent, the 90,000 spectators waiting to see if the bar would topple. It did not and the volcano erupted. In the chairman's box, Khrushchev and Harriman were jumping up and down, screaming, hugging each other. Two old men. Enemies who spoke different languages and could not agree on a way to prevent the world from blowing itself up. Yet there they were, embracing like brothers at the simple act of a man jumping over a bar. What other instrument of propaganda can produce such an effect? There are other characteristics that make sport the most effective instrument of impregnational propaganda. In our complex and ambiguous world, sport remains one of the few areas in which the decision is almost immediate, unconditional, and final. There are no ifs and buts— one always knows who the winners are and who the losers. A sort of instant justice that also appeals to one's emotions. Also, the audience of a sports event is a visible group whose reaction to the events taking place can be recorded, tested, and processed for subsequent use by other instruments of propaganda. Sport is not merely just another instrument of impregnational propaganda. It is a medium that may simultaneously embrace billions of people, an unsuspecting audience whose absorption screen is exposed and vulnerable and whose mental defenses against propaganda are completely down. It is a means of attacking the audience's system, penetrating all defenses, engaging the audience emotionally, vocally, and physically. It is an instrument capable of evoking admiration for the winners and the social system that has produced them, and promoting further interest in other facets of this system. No other country understands that better than the Soviet Union.

2

Soviet Sport: History, Structure, Characteristics

In Imperial Russsia sports activity had no mass character. On the eve of the October Revolution there were in Russia 800 sports clubs and organizations, most consisting of very few members. The total number who took part in sports did not exceed 45,000 to 50,000 people.[1] Russian General A. Butovskiy was among the founders of the International Olympic Committee (16 July 1894). In his article "Olympian Games 1896," Pierre de Coubertin mentioned the contribution of the Russian representative to revival of the games.[2] Russia's participation in international sports was also limited before the revolution. Still the small team sent to the 1908 London Olympic Games was rather successful, its members winning one gold (N.A. Panin-Kolomenkin in figure skating) and two silver medals (N. Orlov and N. Petrov in free-style wrestling).[3] A bigger 169-member team sent to the 1912 Stockholm Olympic Games won only one silver and three bronze medals in wrestling, shooting, and sailing.[4] Today Soviet sources maintain that the poor show in Stockholm "was a result of the Tsarist government's disparaging attitude toward the development of mass sport."[5] Yet immediately after the games an investigating committee was appointed to find out the reasons for the defeat, and a new post—Chief Supervisor of Physical Development—was created. Its first head was Major General V.N. Voeykov.[6] The newly created sports authority soon organized several local and regional athletic and wrestling competitions.

Soviet sources now dismiss offhand the entire prerevolutionary period of Russian sport, maintaining that "only under the Soviet government, when leadership of the sports movement was transferred to the people, did sport become the cause of the people."[7] While this is true, the transformation did not take place overnight. The 1917 Revolution was followed by a long period of hesitation and indecision as far as sport was concerned. The radical transmutations that shook Russian society did not affect sport immediately. The regime's priorities lay elsewhere, and sport's obviously bourgeois overtones (in Imperial Russia) did not spur a positive attitude by the new authorities. The Civil War focused the regime's attention and it was only natural that various areas of social life were dominated by and subjected to the war effort. The first quasi-physical education organ by the Communist regime was clearly military.

On 7 May 1918 the All-Russian Central Executive Committee of the Soviets of the Workers', Soldiers', and Peasants' Deputies issued a decree establishing the VSEVOBUCH—a department of universal premilitary training, which had a special subdepartment of physical development and sport.[8] Lenin himself was said to have taken part in drafting the decree establishing the new organ.[9] The first All-Russian Congress of Workers in the Field of Physical Culture, Sport, and Pre-Military Training, which took place in 1919, stated that all physical culture and sports activity in Russia would be subject to the war needs, and emphasized that Soviet physical culture would be different from that in Western societies.[10] The first sports festival, organized on 25 May 1919 in the Red Square, had clear paramilitary overtones.[11] Gradually various sports events were organized, including ambitious national competitions. Such were the 1920 All-Russia Pre-Olympiads and the first Central Asian Olympics. The Pre-Olympiads were the first part of a nationwide festival of physical culture organized during the 1920 Second Congress of the Third International. Some 18,000 participants took part in the first mass sports event in Moscow's Red Stadium.[12]

The Tashkent Central Asian Olympics had a different and more important character. They lasted ten days in October 1920. More than 3,000 participants from Uzbekistan, Kazakhstan, Turkmenistan, and Kirgizia, along with other nationalities living in Soviet Russia took part in the games. The event's importance was twofold: it was the first time that several nationalities of the Soviet Union competed together,[13] and it was the first indication that Soviet authorities had begun to view sport as an instrument for integrating the various nationalities under the regime. This was recognized again in 1973: "The integrating functions of sport are great. This is of immense importance for our multinational state. Sports contests, festivals, and other types of sporting competition have played an important role in cementing friendship among the Soviet peoples."[14]

After the Civil War the importance of the VSEVOBUCH declined. Still, it controlled Soviet sport. There was no significant development in the structural or organizational framework of the nation's sports activities, not only because once again the regime's priorities lay elsewhere (this time, the New Economic Policy), but also because of rivalry among differing views of the place and function of sport in socialist society. The party attempted to deal with the rivalry at the highest level. The XII Party Congress (1923) outlined a policy by which physical culture was to be organized according to the production principle, and sports groups were to be organized directly in plants, factories, and offices.[15] The party congress' resolution also discontinued the activity of existing sports clubs and societies, many of which were based on prerevolutionary models.

A practical step toward implementing the congress' instructions was the establishment in 1923 of an RSFSR Supreme Council of Physical Culture, soon to be followed by the establishment of similar organs in the other republics. Lack of clearly defined rights, division of functions, and real organizational structure, as well as ambiguity of goals and objectives, caused renewed rivalry between the Komsomol and trade unions for control of physical education and sport. Party intervention at the highest level was imminent. On 13 July 1925 the party issued its first official document dealing exclusively with sport, titled "On the Tasks of the Party in Physical Culture."[16] The document set forth the functions and tasks of Soviet sport at the domestic and international levels.

Domestically, sport was expected to contribute to the improvement of people's health and physical fitness and to their character formation within the framework of general education, while preserving its close relation with military training. It was also expected to promote more intensive social and political participation on the part of Soviet citizens. Competitive sport was rehabilitated from an ideological point of view and pronounced "a valuable activity contributing to improving the people's health." Finally and most important, the resolution stated that "sports contacts between worker-athletes of the Soviet Union and other countries facilitate the further consolidation of the international workers' front."[17] This was the first official recognition by Soviet leadership of sport's political functions on the international scene. Subsequent resolutions at republican level invariably stressed sport as a contribution to educating youth and "fighting religion and natural disasters," and as a means of "protecting youth from the evil influences of the street, home-made liquor, and prostitution."[18]

The various resolutions issued in the mid-twenties did not prove very effective. That was a period of relative political instability following Lenin's death, and once again sport was not at the center of party attention. While there was a lot of domestic sport activity, including large athletics competitions and a good share of record breaking, Soviet sportsmen had no international contacts. Russia was not invited to the 1920 Antwerp Olympic Games or any subsequent games until 1952, as part of "an imperialist and bourgeois attempt to strangle or at least isolate the young Soviet Republic."[19] No Soviet Olympic committee existed, so one cannot speak of any clear Soviet effort to join the international sports scene. It was only after the formation of the Red Sports International (1920) by the Comintern that Soviet athletes appeared on the international scene, still within the framework of the Red Sports International.[20]

The First Five-Year Plan launched in 1928 opened a new period in the Soviet Union. One of its major characteristics was introduction of detailed planning to every aspect of life. Soviet sport, with its ambitious functions and tasks, unstable structure, and general disarray would sooner or later be affected by the organizational and social transformations shaping the new Soviet society. In September 1929 the party Central Committee issued a new resolution on physical culture.[21] It criticized "parallelism" and lack of coordination in the development and organization of physical culture; insufficient involvement of workers in sport; and the "record-breaking mania" which prevailed in Soviet sport. The resolution expressed the party's determination to raise sport to the level of other areas of national importance. A new top-level organizational organ was established—the All-Union Council of Physical Education, directly responsible to the U.S.S.R. Executive Committee. Similar councils were established at the republican level. The structural framework of the new organ resembled that of a regular ministry, and it was de facto a ministry of sport.

The new administration of Soviet sport started functioning in April 1930 and has not changed much up to the present. The all-Union council, which continued to function until 1959, organized Soviet sport along the lines of all Soviet state organizations: a rigid hierarchy, political soundness, strict control, and total subjugation to the ideological and political needs of the Communist party. Soviet sport as we know it today emerged in the thirties. It was then that some of the major Soviet sports clubs were created, among them Spartak (the militia's club), Lokomotiv (railroad workers trade union), Torpedo (car industry workers trade union), and so on. (The first Soviet sports club—Dynamo—had been created in 1923 under the patronage of the Ministry of Internal Affairs.)

Stalin's Constitution of 1936 changed the name of the supreme sports organ from All-Union Council of Physical Education to All-Union Committee of Physical Education and Sport. The change was merely semantic, not organizational or structural. In 1936 regular nationwide sports activities, such as soccer leagues and cups, were introduced. Existing clubs founded branches throughout the country, each club having its own membership rules and cards, colors, uniforms, badges, and so forth. Another development introduced in the thirties was establishment of a nationwide sports program for people of all ages—the GTO (Gotov k Trudyi i Oborone—ready for labor and defense)—which gave Soviet sport its mass character and provided a system for discovering and selecting potential "stars."

World War II and its aftermath terminated the political and ideological isolation of the Soviet Union and resulted in the creation of a bloc of East European countries identical to the former in political and social structure. A new situation emerged on the international scene. New prospects and opportunities opened, and the Soviet Union was perceptive enough to quickly grasp their significance. The value of international propaganda sharply increased and Soviet leaders were quick to understand the possibility of utilizing sport in that area. Yet if Soviet sport was to be assigned new international tasks something had to be done about increasing the skills of Soviet sportsmen and joining various international sports federations.

The first step in this direction was spontaneous (to the degree that anything in the Soviet Union is spontaneous) and somewhat perplexing: *Pravda* of 22 October 1945 carried on its front page a decree by the Council of Ministers prescribing monetary awards for setting records and winning championships. This is the only known case of official state professionalism in sport. The motivation for the decree was clear: to stimulate Soviet sportsmen to better their skills and increase their achievements. Also obvious was the ignorance and lack of experience of Soviet authorities in everything connected with distinguishing between professional and amateur sports and in dealing with such delicate matters without official decrees or similar documentation.

This situation did not prevail long. In July 1947 the U.S.S.R. Council of Ministers issued another resolution "On Compensating Soviet Sportsmen for Sports Achievement," which revoked the above decree on monetary awards and announced that the only awards for sports achievements, championships, and records were to be gold, silver, and bronze medals and insignia.[22] This resolution was clear indication that the Soviet Union seriously intended to join international amateur sports life. The party demanded quick results, and when they failed to materialize another decree followed, this time in the form of a resolution of the CPSU Central Committee in December 1948.[23]

The resolution severely criticized sport leadership for lack of control, vision, and prudence in developing Soviet sport. The immediate development of mass sport throughout the country was demanded. The resolution stressed that such mass participation would improve the skill of Soviet sportmen, "which should secure Soviet athletic supremacy in world championships in the immediate future."[24] The document also specified steps that would lead to its ambitious target: strengthening the organization of sport collectives; nationwide expansion of all sports; special attention to Olympic sports; improvement of sportsmen's manners; adaptation of the Master's and other rankings to international records; wide use of the press, radio, and cinematography to popularize sport among the public.

The December 1948 resolution amounted to Soviet application to join international sports and a declaration of its intentions in that field. Soviet yearning to join international sport was matched by Western ignorance of Soviet sport as well as apprehension and dismay in anticipation of Soviet sportsmen's inevitable appearance on the international arena. The prevailing fear of all things Soviet was reflected in the attitude of the international sports officials toward Soviet moves. Vague knowledge about the Soviet way of life combined with suspicion of Soviet goals produced reactions such as that expressed in a letter from Avery Brundage, IOC vice-president, to Sigfrid Edström, IOC president, regarding the possible participation of especially trained Soviet sportsmen in various international competitions: "The situation is charged with dynamite.... If we are to prevent the machinery of international sport from breaking up and the high standards of amateur sport from collapsing, we will have to watch things very carefully and stop all deviations from our regulations."[25]

The IOC made an attempt to uncover Soviet intentions regarding particpation in major international events. Thirty years after the October Revolution, the IOC finally learned something about Soviet sport and its organizational structure, as Edström wrote to Brundage:

> A newspaper in Switzerland now states that sport like everything else in Russia is organized by the state. There are no clubs like in our countries. It is a committee appointed by the state that runs everything with governmental money. The leader for the committee is consequently a paid man. His name is Nicolai Romanoff, and he rules the 600 stadiums, 14,000 other sport grounds, 6,000 ski-jump sites and 45,000 volleyball courts. All athletes competing in foreign countries are especially trained at the expense of the state and are taught to compete in a fighting spirit. Amateurism is not understood. Athletes who beat a world record get paid for it. What shall we do? Our young athletes all over Europe are crazy to have Russian athletes participate. I have time upon time sent invitations to Mr. Romanoff, but he does not answer. Perhaps he does not care, but he probably does not know that one should answer a letter.[26]

Correspondence between the two top IOC men continued, each letter revealing their growing concern about Soviet intentions. The behavior of

Soviet sport authorities did not help dispel IOC officials' fear. Whenever the Soviet Union applied for membership in an international sports federation it raised special preconditions. In 1947 the Soviet Union demanded that Russian be one of the official languages of each sport federation, that Soviet officials join the Executive Board, and that relations with "representatives of profascistic organizations of Franco's Spain be revoked."[27] Subsequent correspondence showed that the IOC had begun to grasp the new political reality that emerged after World War II and the necessity of admitting the Soviet Union and its East European satellites to the International Sport Federations. As Edström wrote to Brundage:

> There are three Olympic Committees at present asking for recognition, Poland, Hungary and Yugoslavia.... The political influence in said countries is now communistic as a communist minority has the political power in each country supported by Russia, but politics must not mix in with sports, therefore we cannot turn them down because the political influence in their country is communistic. We have even shown friendly tendencies toward Russia which is the most communistic country of all. I am against turning people down for political reasons. The greatest trouble will be to find men that we can have present in the IOC. I do not feel inclined to go as far as to admit communists there.[28]

Edström did not explain just how his reluctance "to admit communists" to the IOC tied in with his principle "against turning people down for political reasons."

The Soviet Union did not participate in the 1948 London Olympic Games. There was no Soviet Olympic Committee at that time, and no official request for recognition by Soviet sport authorities was received by the IOC. Soviet representatives attended the London games as observers. The Soviet Olympic Committee was founded in April 1951.[29] A request for recognition was immediately submitted to the IOC, which at its May 1951 session in Vienna approved the motion by thirty-one votes in favor with three abstentions.[30] Today Soviet sources attribute tremendous importance to their admission to the IOC and present it as a turning point and landmark in international Olympic history: "That event left its mark on the entire Olympic movement. A new historical stage began with it. The Soviet Union initiated a fundamental democratization of the Olympic movement and the development of equality and mutual understanding among sportsmen throughout the world.... By joining the Olympic movement we enriched not only Soviet sportsmen but the entire world."[31]

Another Soviet source presents the joining of the IOC by the Soviet Olympic Committee (established one month earlier) as a "well-deserved recognition of the Soviet Olympic Committee's constant struggle for democratization of the Olympic movement and its struggle to attract

TABLE 1
Medals and Points for XV Olympic Games in Helsinki[37]

country	total points	placing 1	2	3	3-4 *	4	5	6
		points 7	5	4	3.5	3	2	1
USSR**	494	22	30	15	4	25	14	13
USA	494	40	19	17	–	12	4	7
Hungary	258	16	10	16	–	5	5	7
Sweden	233.5	12	13	9	1	9	6	6
West Germany	173.5	–	7	16	1	11	14	10
Finland	144	6	3	9	4	3	12	4
France	136.5	6	6	5	1	7	8	4
Italy	136.5	8	9	3	1	3	2	7
England	107	–	2	8	–	11	14	4
CSSR	95	7	3	3	–	2	4	5

*Both semi-finalists in boxing receive bronze medals after their defeat.

**Despite the fact that the United States has won 40 gold medals, 18 more than the USSR, all Soviet sources using this table always place the USSR in first place.

sportsmen of many countries, recognition of its active steps against racial, political, and other kinds of discrimination, and its contribution to strengthening the friendship and cooperation of sportsmen throughout the world."[32] In the fall of 1951 the Soviet Olympic Committee decided to participate in the XV Olympic Games in Helsinki, "a decision greeted with great satisfaction by the entire world sports public."[33] The same source also notes the "hysterical statements" made by some Western sports reporters,

TABLE 2
Soviet Sportsmen at Olympic Games, 1952-80[38]

year	gold	medals silver	bronze	points	place
1952	22	30	19	494	1–2
1956	37	29	32	622.5	1
1960	43	29	31	682.5	1
1964	30	31	35	607.8	1
1968	29	32	30	590.8	2
1972	50	27	22	664.5	1
1976	47	43	35	788.5	1
1980	80	69	46	1219.5	1

presenting Soviet sports successes as "communist propaganda."[34] Another Soviet source accuses the "capitalist world" of inventing stories about Soviet sportsmen and "turning these stories into a political weapon against the Soviet Union and the socialist countries."[35]

Some 6,000 sportsmen from 69 countries took part in the XV Olympic Games. The Soviet Union sent an impressive delegation consisting of 381 members.[36] The games excelled in their standard. Eleven world and 47 Olympic records were broken, 2 world and 6 Olympic records by Soviet sportsmen. In the final account the Soviet Union won 22 gold, 30 silver, and 19 bronze medals, an impressive show indeed, especially compared with the achievements of other sporting powers (Table 1).

There is no official team point-system in the Olympic games. Nevertheless the point system used by the Soviet Union is universally accepted as the yardstick for judging "the winner" in Olympic games. Soviet participation in Helsinki became the first in a series of outstanding Olympic performances by Soviet sportsmen, which have made the Soviet Union the most successful country in post-World War II Olympic history and the world's leading sports superpower. The party postulate for achieving "world supremacy" in sport has been successfully fulfilled (Table 2).

For the first time in Olympic history the games were dominated by direct rivalry between the Soviet Union and the United States—destined to accompany the Olympic games and all subsequent major international competition. After 1952 Soviet sports underwent only minor organizational changes. Reorganization of the Soviet government following Stalin's death also affected the structure of Soviet sports organs. The All-Union Committee of Physical Culture and Sport was turned into a department of the Ministry of Health, its local branches becoming departments of the appropriate health organs at the respective levels.[39] The reorganization was apparently unsuccessful, because the old structure was soon revived.[40]

In January 1959 the CPSU Central Committee and the Council of Ministers issued a joint resoultion setting up a new organizational framework.[41] The all-Union committee was dissolved and its functions transferred to an ostensibly public organization—the Union of Sports Societies and Organizations. The main goals of Soviet physical culture, as indicated by the January 1959 resolution, included no innovations: sports organizations were expected to encourage and secure the involvement of the general public in regular physical activity; Soviet sportsmen's skills were to be furthered with a view to breaking records and achieving international victories; and the education of youths was to be in the spirit of devotion to the communist cause, the Communist party, and the communist state. In retrospect it is difficult to discern any specific political or professional reason for the 1959 resolution aside perhaps from the intention to ostensibly dissociate sport from the state and turn it into a public enterprise.

The October 1964 ousting of Khrushchev signaled the beginning of further reorganization of Soviet life. The turn of sport came almost two years later. On 11 August 1966 the CPSU Central Committee and the Council of Ministers issued a resolution "On Measures for Promoting Physical Culture and Sport"[42] which required of party and Komsomol organizations at all levels, as well as trade unions and sport organizations, that they improve the administration of sport to render it a more active means for society to influence people's moral outlook, encourage harmonious development and productive labor, strengthen and maintain good health to insure creativity until old age, and increase the people's ability to defend their country. A target of having 60,000,000 people actively and regularly engaged in sport was set for 1970. This was not achieved, for all Soviet sources throughout 1978-80 cite the total number of people actively and regularly engaged in sport at 52,000,000.[43]

All pretense of exclusively public or nonpolitical association was dropped in October 1968, when the Committee for Physical Culture and Sport, attached to the Council of Ministers, was created. The committee has the structure of a regular ministry, with organs at all federal levels. Its resolutions and decisions are binding on all ministries and public organizations.[44] The chairman of the committee, Sergey Pavlov, is actually the Soviet minister of sport. Pavlov's public career started in 1954, when he was elevated from being a boxing student at the Moscow Institute of Physical Culture and a minor Komsomol activist, to the position of secretary of the Moscow city Komsomol organization.[45] The same source attributes Pavlov's rapid rise to the impression he made on Khrushchev. In 1959 Sergey Pavlov was appointed secretary general of the Komsomol and in 1968, after a brief period of stagnation in his career, chairman of the U.S.S.R. Committee of Physical Culture and Sport. Later Pavlov became a member of the CPSU Central Committee.[46]

The U.S.S.R. Committee of Physical Culture and Sport is a huge organization of 20,000 full-time paid officials, who incidentally represent only 6.4 percent of all Soviet sports officials![47] Its annual budget is 12.5 billion rubles[48] or, as another source would have it, $35 million.[49] The committee supervises the activity of the tens of thousands top sportsmen (about 52,000,000), six million trainers and coaches, and various physical culture institutes producing 28,000 graduates annually, as well as construction and maintenance of stadiums and other sports facilities.[50] The total number of sports facilities in the Soviet Union varies slightly from one source to another, but differences are insignificant: "U.S.S.R. sports facilities comprise over 3,000 large stadiums with a total seating capacity of 11.4 million, over 66,000 gymnasiums, nearly 1,400 swimming pools, and more than 600,000 sports grounds of all kinds."[51] Other sources speak of "63,423 gymnasiums, 3,200 stadiums, and 1,344 swimming pools,"[52] and "over 3,000 stadiums and 1,200 big swimming pools."[53] The U.S.S.R. Committee of Physical Culture and Sport also supervises and evaluates the international activity of Soviet sportsmen, who participate annually in about 2,000 international competitions in 100 states.[54]

So much for the development and organizational structure of Soviet sport. This discussion was only intended to serve as background for the main subject: to describe and analyze the propaganda functions of Soviet sport. Since this topic will focus our attention on Soviet sport's international activities, many aspects of Soviet sport's domestic activities, important as they are, have been glossed over. The description of the structure and development of Soviet sport permits several general conclusions on the basic characteristics of Soviet sport, which shall be stated now and illustrated in the following two chapters.

Soviet sport is a state enterprise. This is self-evident and follows from the country's political system. Like every other facet of the society, Soviet sport is the concern of state authorities. It is subjected to and supervised by several party and state organs whose sole function is the direction and control of Soviet sport. At the party level sport and physical culture are the concern of the Section of Physical Culture and Sport of the CPSU Central Committee Department of Propaganda. Parallel sections exist at every party level, each party committee having departments or sections, or at least individuals in charge of physical culture and sport.

Routine daily coordination, control, and supervision is the realm of the Committee of Physical Culture and Sport of the Council of Ministers. It controls implementation of the sports budget, coordinates and supervises the activity of sports federations (each of the committee's departments being in charge of a separate federation), and carries ultimate responsibility for the international success of Soviet sportsmen. Its chairman, Sergey Pavlov, is also a member of the CPSU Central Committee and is presumably a member of the CPSU Central Committee Propaganda Department section of Physical Culture and Sport. Less important but nonetheless existing is the control at the legislative level. The Supreme Soviet Commission of Health, Social Welfare, and Physical Culture sometimes deals with matters which at least nominally affect Soviet sport.

In addition to specific administrative organs that deal with sport, the CPSU Central Committee and the Council of Ministers often show their interest in Soviet sport. The numerous decisions, resolutions, and decrees they issue, prompted by political and social considerations, leave no doubt about official concern with Soviet sport. Finally, there are the Soviet public and mass organizations such as trade unions and the Komsomol, which also have sports departments, instrumental to the development of Soviet sport.

Sport and sports achievements in the Soviet Union are not an end in themselves but an effective means of achieving ideological and political goals. These goals, mostly concerned with ideological penetration and propagation of certain ideological and political values and principles, make Soviet sport a political asset and an integral part of the Soviet political and ideological machine. Despite the Soviet propaganda counter-campaign against boycott of the 1980 Moscow Olympic Games urged by President Carter, whose main theme has been "sport has nothing to do with politics," the Soviet Union long ago dropped any pretense and officially declared that "whenever someone says that sport lies outside the framework of political relations, we feel their remark is not a serious one.... The Soviet people view sport as an instrument of peace. When for instance Soviet representatives call for the expulsion of the South African and Rhodesian racists from the Olympic movement, this is of course a political move. But this is a policy for the sake of peace.... When Soviet football players refuse to play a match at the Santiago stadium, where the ground is stained with the blood of Chilean patriots, this is also, of course, politics. It is a policy of struggling... against fascist regimes."[55]

Achievements of Soviet sport in the international arena are held up by Soviet authorities as proof of the superiority of the social system capable of producing such athletes. Soviet sportsmen are never allowed to forget it. In frequent seminars, meetings, and conferences they are constantly reminded of the far-reaching political consequences of their international performance. The candidates for the 1980 Olympic team were brought to Volgograd. After touring the city's industrial plants and enterprises they took part in a meeting titled "On the Tasks Connected with the Preparation of Soviet Sportsmen for the 1980 Olympics."[56] The sportsmen were addressed by former Olympic champions and by Sergey Pavlov, chairman of the Committee on Physical Culture and Sport, who "devoted a large part of his speech to the moral aspects of sports preparation and to the importance of educating sportsmen to actively take part in public life and stands on the issues of life, and of instilling high ideological convictions in them."[57]

After several similar speeches by party and Komsomol officials, the sportsmen took an oath on the site of the famous World War II battle and sent an appropriate letter-pledge to the CPSU Central Committee, the Supreme Soviet Presidium, and the Council of Ministers.[58] A similar event conducted by the Komsomol leadership was reported by *Sovetskiy Sport* of 14 December 1979. The titles of some of the reports read at the seminar were: "Lenin's Ideas: The Basis of Sportsmen's Communist Education"; and "On Further Improving the Work to Better Instill Communist Moral Ideology in Sportsmen in Light of the XXV CPSU and XVIII Komsomol Congresses." Other more effective means of motivating sportsmen will be discussed in the next chapter.

The unusual political and ideological importance attributed to sport by Soviet authorities is the reason for the unprecedented scope of Soviet sport's international contacts. The obvious line of thought is that an effective means of propaganda is to be used as much as possible. The numbers are impressive: "In 1975 alone, there were sports exchanges involving 30,000 athletes between the U.S.S.R. and other countries. Soviet sportsmen went to 67 countries."[59] In 1975 Soviet sportsmen maintained sports contacts with 87 countries in 54 kinds of sports. Some 1,048 foreign sports delegations visited the Soviet Union.[60] As declared by Sergey Pavlov, Soviet sportsmen participate annually in about 2,000 international events in 100 states.[61] The number of foreign sports delegations going to the Soviet Union has declined. According to a 1980 source "more than 700 foreign delegations come annually to the U.S.S.R."[62] At present the Soviet Union is member of 72 international sports federations; 126 Soviet representatives have been elected to the managing and technical organs of these federations, among them one president, 25 vice-presidents, and one secretary general.[63]

Moscow is interested not only in foreign sportsmen, but also in sports

TABLE 3
Final Unofficial Classification of States at XXII Olympic Games in Moscow

state	gold	medals silver	bronze	total	points
USSR	80	69	46	195	1219.5
GDR	47	37	42	126	829.0
BULGARIA	8	16	17	41	265.0
POLAND	3	14	15	32	241.0
HUNGARY	7	10	15	32	228.0
ROMANIA	6	6	13	25	204.0
GREAT BRITAIN	5	7	9	21	149.0
CUBA	8	7	5	20	142.5
CSSR	2	3	9	14	136.0
ITALY	8	3	4	15	121.0
FRANCE	6	5	3	14	109.5
SWEDEN	3	3	6	12	103.0
YUGOSLAVIA	2	3	4	9	71.5
AUSTRALIA	2	2	5	9	71.5
FINLAND	3	1	4	8	67.0
SPAIN	1	3	2	6	55.0
BRAZIL	2	-	2	4	40.0
HOLAND	-	1	2	3	35.5
DENMARK	2	1	2	5	35.0
NORTH KOREA	-	3	2	5	31.5
AUSTRIA	1	2	1	4	31.0
ETHIOPIA	2	-	2	4	25.0
SWITZERLAND	2	-	-	2	25.0
MONGOLIA	-	2	2	4	24.5
MEXICO	-	1	3	4	24.0
GREECE	1	-	2	3	17.0
INDIA	1	-	-	1	16.0

TABLE 3

state	gold	medals silver	bronze	total	points
BELGIUM	1	-	-	1	15.0
JAMAICA	-	-	3	3	13.0
TANZANIA	-	2	-	2	10.0
ZIMBABWE	1	-	-	1	7.0
UGANDA	-	1	-	1	5.0
IRELAND	-	1	-	1	5.0
VENEZUELA	-	1	-	1	5.0
LEBANON	-	-	1	1	4.0
GUYANA	-	-	1	1	4.0

officials, trainers—everyone even remotely connected with sport: "In 1979 many international congresses, conferences, symposiums, and seminars on matters of physical culture, theory, methodology and practice of sport, sports medicine, and journalism took place in the Soviet Union. Sports functionaries from the Federal Republic of Germany, Madagascar, Benin, France, Angola, Cyprus, Morocco, Tunisia, Zambia, and many other countries took part."[64]

Soviet sportsmen's international contacts are usually based on international treaties and agreements, signed by Soviet and other states' officials. In this area again, the Soviet Union has no peers. No other country bothers to base its sports contacts on a legal basis and official documentation. According to Soviet authorities these agreements and treaties "serve to strengthen the invincible movement for peace and security."[65] Ceremonial signing of such agreements is always an occasion for the Soviet mass media to publish statements made by the Soviet Union's Western and other partners at the time of signing the agreements. These statements usually endorse the Soviet view on the importance of maintaining sports relations with the Soviet Union, express enthusiasm and admiration for Soviet achievements in various areas, and so forth.[66] In line with its eagerness to increase the scope of its international sports contacts and provide more opportunities to use sport as an instrument of international propaganda, Moscow is always keen to obtain the right to host important international competitions. The long struggle to become the host of the Olympic games will be reviewed in a separate chapter. One of the most important characteristics of Soviet sport is its constant striving toward victory in the international arena. The entire political and ideological performance of Soviet sport is based on its being victorious.

Notes

1. F.I. Samoukov et al. (eds.), *Fizicheskaya Kultura I Sport V SSSR* (Moscow, 1967), p. 15.
2. A. Kiknadze, *Veter S Olimpa* (Moscow, 1978), p. 18.
3. N. Lyubomirov et al., *XVI Olimpiyskie Igri, Melbourn 1956* (Moscow, 1957), p. 7.
4. Ibid.
5. Ibid.
6. Kiknadze, p. 22
7. Lyubomirov et al., p. 7.
8. Samoukov et al., p. 18.
9. Lyubomirov et al., p. 8.
10. Samoukov et al., p. 49.
11. Lyubomirov et al., p. 8.
12. J. Riordan (ed.), *Sport under Communism* (Montreal, 1978), p. 19.
13. Ibid.
14. *Sport V SSSR* (no. 5, 1973), p. 9.
15. Samoukov et al., p. 43.
16. *Izvestiya Tsentralnovo Komiteta RKP/b* (20 July 1925), p. 1.
17. Ibid.
18. *Teoriya I Praktika Fizicheskoy Kultury* (no. 12, 1973), p. 13.
19. Lyubomirov et al., p. 8.
20. Ibid.
21. Samoukov et al., p. 70.
22. I.D. Chudinov, *Osnovnye Postanovlemiya Prikazi I Instruktsii Po Voprosom Fizicheskoy Kultury I Sporta, 1917-1947* (Moscow, 1950), p. 29.
23. *Naslednikam Resolyutsii, Dokumenti Partii O Komsomole I Molodezhi* (Moscow, 1969), pp. 380-86.
24. Ibid., p. 382.
25. Brundage to Edström, 26 October 1946, *Brundage Papers*, Box 42.
26. Edström to Brundage, 4 December 1946, *Brundage Papers*, Box 42.
27. Brundage to Edström, 4 March 1947, *Brundage Papers*, Box 42.
28. Edström to Brundage, 3 September 1947, *Brundage Papers*, Box 42.
29. Lyubomirov et al., p. 11.
30. A. Starodub, *Do Vstrechi V. Moskve* (Moscow, 1978), p. 13.
31. Kiknadze, p. 65.
32. Starodub, p. 15.
33. Lyubomirov et al., p. 11.
34. Ibid.
35. K. Gostka and K. Ulrich, *Olympisches Moskau* (Berlin, 1979), p. 23.
36. Lyubomirov et al., p. 12.
37. Ibid., pp. 16-17.
38. Kiknadze, p. 238.

39. N. Norman Shneider, *The Soviet Road to Olympus* (London, 1979), p. 25.
40. Ibid.
41. *KPSS O Kulture, Prosveshchenii I Nauke* (Moscow, 1963), pp. 254-60.
42. *Pravda* (25 August 1966), pp. 1-2.
43. *Sport I Lichnost* (godishnik) (Moscow, 1949), p. 41.
44. Riordan, p. 38.
45. Y. Brokhin, *The Big Red Machine* (New York, 1978), p. 115.
46. Ibid.
47. "Interview with the Minister." In Heinz Lathe, *Geheimnisse Des Sowjetsports* (Vienna, 1979), p. 256.
48. Ibid.
49. Brokhin, p. 114.
50. Lathe, p. 256.
51. Sergey Pavlov, "Sports for Everyone," *SPUTNIK* (English—no.7, July 1977), pp. 145-46.
52. Vladimir Kirilyuk, *UdSSR Heute und Morgen—Sport* (Moscow, 1978), p. 35.
53. Mezhdunarodnaya Kniga catalogue *Bücher über Sport* (Moscow, 1979), p. 1.
54. Lathe, pp. 259-60.
55. S. Popov and A. Srebnitskiy, *Sport in the USSR: Questions and Answers* (Moscow, 1979), quoted in *New York Times* (27 February 1980—Anthony Austin, "For Russia Olympics Aren't Fun and Games").
56. V. Snegiriev, "Kurs—Olimpiada," *Komsomolskaya Pravda* (2 October 1979).
57. Ibid.
58. Ibid.
59. Viktor Ivonin, "Sport and Physical Culture in the USSR," *Moscow News* (no. 31, 1972), p. 5.
60. Sergey Pavlov, "700 Iz 50 Milionov," *Sovetskiy Soyuz,* (no. 5, 1956), p. 14.
61. Lathe, pp. 259-60.
62. V. Vasiliev, "So wird es auch sein," *Sport in der UdSSR* (no. 1, 1980), p. 10.
63. D.I. Prokhorov et al. (eds.), *MOK I Mezhdunarodniye Sportivniye Obedineniya* (Moscow, 1979), p. 7.
64. Vasiliev, p. 10.
65. Report on ceremony of signing the FRG-USSR sports agreement, "Above All: Interests of Cooperation and Peace," *Sov. Sport* (30 March 1977).
66. Report on ceremony of signing the U.S.S.R.—Norway sports cooperation agreement, *Sov. Sport* (15 December 1979).

3

For the Motherland, for the Party, Get Those Medals!

The official Soviet view of sport is that "it is another sphere, another criterion for evaluating the advantages of the Soviet political system."[1] There follows from this the obvious political connotations: "Competitions are not just sports events. They carry a tremendous ideological and political charge, they demonstrate the aspirations of the Soviet people."[2] For Soviet authorities sport can best contribute to "the evaluation of the advantages of the Soviet political system" and make full use of its "ideological and propaganda charge" in one way only: by winning. A sports victory indicates not only better athletes but a better political system. The country that is victorious in the sports field is capable of victories in all other fields. Credit for victory goes not only to the athlete, but to the country he/she represents and to the social system that has produced him/her. Winning (or losing) on the sports field adds (and subtracts) points in the much more serious political game—this is the core of sport's impregnational value.

"One cannot isolate sport from society by erecting some sort of glass window for outstanding record-holders capable of winning several medals. Sport has come to belong to the masses and one automatically thinks of the social conditions in which it is developing, of society's attitude to sport.... Victories and defeats do form certain patterns, and that is where one

36

cannot avoid comparisons."[3] It is doubtful whether Soviet authorities have heard of Vincent Lombardi, but his maxim "Winning isn't everything, it's the only thing!" serves as a guiding light for Soviet athletes. In the Soviet press one often reads such statements as: "Points of course are not important, the main thing is that the score is in favor of friendship among sportsmen."[4] But the truth cannot be concealed: "Points, victories, medals... they are everything!"[5] Or the more matter of fact: "Sporting events... are social, political, and even economic events in which the number of medals, points, victories, and number of records are accepted by the world as signs of prestige."[6] Short and to the point: "Victory is what counts at the Olympics!"[7]

The importance of victories and medals is underlined by the great pains taken by Soviet authorities to record, tabulate, and publish the number of victories and medals won by Soviet athletes in international competitions. Statements like the following are frequently in the Soviet press: "Over the last ten years Soviet sportsmen have broken more than 80 European and world records and captured the lead in Europe. Our team won twice as many medals at the Mexico Olympics as it had done in Tokyo."[8] "During 1973 Soviet sportsmen participated in 2,500 international events. They successfully participated in 37 world championships and 42 European championships, winning 181 gold, 122 silver, and 82 bronze medals."[9]

When Soviet authorities make such tabulations and comparisons, they are careful to stress the performance of Soviet athletes against the background of U.S. athletes' performance, the ideological connotations frequently indicated: "In Munich Soviet sportsmen won 99 medals and got 664.5 points. In Montreal 125 medals (47-43-35) and 788.5 points. We were first in ten kinds of sports, the Americans, our constant opponents, in only six. They won fewer medals than our sportsmen and fewer points. As pointed out by Sergey Pavlov, chairman of the U.S.S.R. Committee of Physical Culture and Sport, the successes of the socialist community in Montreal (the GDR won 40 gold, 25 silver, and 25 bronze medals) constitute one of the most cogent arguments proving the superiority of the socialist system."[10] Soviet authorities apply tremendous efforts (and financial resources) to develop the skills of Soviet sportsmen and increase the effectiveness of their performance on the international scene. Training is basic, but not the only way Soviet sportsmen are prepared. The tremendous importance attributed to victory by Soviet authorities makes it imperative to seek it by all possible means, in addition to hard physical training. The most important among them: moral and psychological as well as ideological preparation, rewards for sports achievements, medical means, and a category of "special means" to be discussed at the end of this chapter.

MORAL, PSYCHOLOGICAL AND IDEOLOGICAL
PREPARATION

Soviet sportsmen are taught to compete as if they were on the battlefield, fighting for the honor of the Motherland, party, and people. The primary responsibility for conditioning sportsmen in this spirit lies with trainers:

> Trainers must pay special attention to breeding a motivation arising from the attitude to our socialist Motherland, the Soviet people, and the Communist party. At the basis of our sportsmen's achievements, however different in age, education, and character these sportsmen may be, lies the awareness of duty and a sense of great personal responsibility to the Motherland and the Soviet people. In performing their deeds and showing their willpower Soviet sportsmen are consciously following the norms and principles of communist morals. "In the name of the Motherland"—this is the main theme that inspires the demonstration of our sportsmen's skills, willpower, and mastery, leading to acts of sports heroism.[11]

This result is sought in several ways. First, there is indoctrination of sportsmen in the communist spirit:

> The education of Soviet sportsmen in the spirit of communist awareness is the leading principle of sportsmen's education.... Ideological-political work is of great importance in this aspect.... The duty of trainers is to educate not merely sportsmen—individualists, egoists, and nationalists—but people with a high communist consciousness, Soviet patriots defending the honor of their Motherland, irreconcilable to the enemies of socialism and communism. For this purpose, every sports enterprise, training, and competition must be skillfully connected with our country's communist construction and the idea of defending the sports honor of our Motherland.[12]

Trainers are made to study and then relay to sportsmen the CPSU program, the works of Marx, Engels, and Lenin, materials and decisions of the plenums and congresses of the CPSU and the Komsomol, and topical issues related to the domestic and international situation.[13] Party and Komsomol organs are called upon to cooperate with trainers in the ideological preparation of sportsmen.[14]

Lectures, speeches, discussions, methodological conferences, seminars, are the recommended means of increasing sportsmen's communist consciousness.[15] Among the subjects prescribed for discussion at these occasions: "Role of communists and Komsomol members in increasing the sports mastery of the the team"; "Personal example of Komsomol members"; "Implementation of personal duty by communists and Komsomol members"; "Socialist competition in the team"; "Are we doing everything we can for victory?"; "The CPSU and the government on the people's physical education"; "Duty, honor, and dignity of the Motherland during the Great Motherland War"; "Sport and heroism"; Sport and friendship"; "Sport and social progress"; "Sport and politics."[16]

It is the official Soviet view that such ideological preparation is impossible in capitalist society, where physical education is "permeated with bourgeois ideology and indoctrination."[17] As an additional incentive it is recommended to admit more sportsmen to the ranks of the party and the Komsomol on the eve of world championships and Olympic games, which would enhance "the defense of the Motherland's sports honor while competing, this task being viewed as a party duty."[18] This reminds one of the mass admission of soldiers to the party ranks during World War II, done with the same goals, which brings us back to the ever-present comparison Soviet sources make between sportsmen competing in stadiums and soldiers fighting on the battlefield. The idea that they are soldiers defending the Motherland is constantly inculcated in Soviet sportsmen. This is indicated by both the subjects recommended for ideological indoctrination and the statements of victorious sportsmen after competition.

A *Sovetskiy Sport* editorial published on the opening of the Lake Placid 1980 Winter Olympic Games is illustrative: "When the going gets tough our sportsmen remember the Motherland, which gives them strong wings for an eagle's flight." "'I mentally transfer myself to the siege of Leningrad, from the first day to the last,' says Lyubov Baranova, the renowned cross-country skier, cavalier of Lenin's order.... When the skiing got difficult, Lyuba remembered the blockade of the city on the Neva and said to herself: 'For the Motherland, Lyuba! For Leningrad!'" "The childhood of Vladimir Melanin was not easy. His father died in the front in 1941. He died so that his son—later an officer and cavalier of the orders of the Red Banner of Labor and Honor Insignia—could glorify the Motherland with his sports victories."[19]

This by no means exhausts the arsenal of means of enhancing sportsmen's ideological staunchness. Before major competitions Soviet sports delegations are taken to Lenin's mausoleum and the grave of the unknown soldier, "so that they can once agains feel the responsibility for defending the sports honor of the Motherland."[20] Sometimes they pledge victories at the sites of famous World War II battles, as was the case with the candidates for the team for the 1980 Winter Olympics, which in October 1979 took part in an ideological conference in Volgograd and took an oath at the site of the famous Stalingrad battle.[21] The Komsomol actively assists the party in the ideological preparation of sportsmen. Each sports team has its own Komsomol organization, which organizes regular activities usually related to improving sportsmen's performance. *Komsomolskaya Pravda* of 2 April 1980 reports a regular meeting of the Soviet Olympic teams' Komsomol secretaries. The report's headline is indicative of its content: "Komsomol Organizations Lead to Victory."[22]

Instilling a sense of duty continues throughout the competition. During the XX Olympic Games in Munich in 1972 the Soviet delegation regularly published a special "combat leaflet" called "For Our Victory." It included material related to the "achievements of the U.S.S.R., the working, revolutionary, and combat traditions of the Soviet people," etc. Prominent Soviet poets, composers, writers—Heroes of the U.S.S.R. and of Socialist Labor appealed to the sportsmen from the pages of the leaflet urging them to win. Some of the leaflet's regular columns were titled "Soldiers Tell of Their Past," "The U.S.S.R. Sports Character," and so forth.[23] During competitions sportsmen are bombarded with letters and telegrams from their countrymen urging them to "get that gold!" Such was the message sent by the Shachtiy coalminers to their landsman, the famous weight lifter David Rigert, during the XXI Olympic Games in Montreal: "You must bring to us in Shachtiy the winner's gold. We will add it to the black gold we dig, and this will be our joint contribution to the Tenth Five-Year Plan."[24]

There is also personal involvement of party and state leaders in the motivation-building process. Soviet marshals D. Ustinov and A. Epishev both took part in various ideological activities for Soviet sportsmen preparing for Montreal.[25] The entire delegation to the Montreal Olympic Games was greeted by L. Brezhnev, who personally urged the Soviet sportsmen to win.[26] Similar messages were sent by Soviet cosmonauts and other prominent personalities.[27] The reaction of Soviet sportsmen to this motivation-building ideological preparation is predictable. Their statements after victory are usually ideologically correct and sound.

Ice skater Irina Rodnina: "The general striving to increase our Motherland's glory, to do everything for her and to make one's own personal contribution is characteristic of U.S.S.R. sportsmen... as is the feeling that in this way sportsmen join in the great constructive toil of U.S.S.R. citizens."[28] *Sovetskiy Sport,* which carried Rodnina's statement, added a personal touch: "What is the main feature of Rodnina's character? There can be no mistake—a keen sense of responsibility to the Motherland and the great country of the Soviets.... Rodnina, member of the CPSU, cavalier of the orders of Lenin and the Red Banner, delegate to the XVIII Komsomol congress, is the embodiment of the best qualities of Soviet sportsmen and a real Soviet citizen."[29] Nina Panomaryova, discus thrower, the first Soviet athlete to win a gold Olympic medal (Helsinki, 1952): "What a happy thought—to present my Motherland with a second gold Olympic medal! How remarkable!"[30] Pavel Pinigin, wrestler: "There is probably no more beautiful moment than knowing you have vindicated the trust of your country and friends. For this alone it is worth toiling in the sweat of your brow and turning away from the many temptations of life. We three wrestlers from Yakutia were happy to have given our Motherland three Olympic medals at once—one gold and two silver."[31]

Only seldom is the reaction surprising, as in the personal story of Soviet basketball player and later coach Alachachian, describing the circumstances surrounding preparation of the CSKA basketball team for the European Cup match against Real Madrid, which it lost by 17 points:

> We started on the path to defeat long before ever going out on the court. The defeat began in Moscow. There was one meeting after another where they told us we were the first Soviet athletes ever to go to Franco Spain, reminded us that the whole country was counting on us not to disgrace the Motherland, assured us that everyone believed in us, asked us whether we'd be worthy of their trust, entreated us to fight like men, and asked us how they could help. I don't doubt for a second that the intentions of the prime movers of the meetings were the highest: every one of them wished us well. But what they *did* do flagrantly contradicted what they *intended* to do. When we returned to Moscow (down by seventeen points but assured a return game at home), they upped the number of meetings dramatically. Some of them criticized us, some supported us, some asked us to give our all in the return game, others told us not to worry. Still others proposed plays we should run to recoup the points. Again they all wished us well—and interfered with our really getting ready for the game. At the next meeting—the 10th straight I believe—I couldn't hold out any longer. When they asked what we needed for a victory in Moscow, I answered plain and simple: "No more of these goddam meetings!"[32]

REWARDS FOR SPORTSMEN

The importance Soviet authorities attach to sports victories is reflected by the lucrative awards, prizes, orders, medals, and other benefits awaiting the victors. Officially there is no professionalism in Soviet sport: "The social category 'sportsman' does not exist in the U.S.S.R. Sportsmen are students, workers, soldiers, and officers."[33] Nevertheless, Soviet sources are frank about the need to reward sportsmen after major international achievements: "Rewarding the sportsmen is very important because it demonstrates to him the objective significance of his deeds and achievements for society.... After receiving his award from the state, the sportsman reevaluates his behavior and begins to understand that his activity is necessary to the people and society. In addition, after receiving an award, the sportsman will strive to justify it and reach new heights in sport."[34]

There are two main ways of rewarding Soviet sportsmen: officially (medals, titles) and unofficially (various financial arrangements and awards). In the Soviet Union there is a special medal, Sportivnaya Doblest

(Sports Valor), awarded to Soviet sportsmen "who have demonstrated willpower and determination and have defended the honor of the Motherland."[35] This is only one of the lowest medals and orders bestowed on Soviet sportsmen who have distinguished themselves in sport. High party and state awards are frequently bestowed on leading Soviet sportsmen. The Order of Lenin—the highest state award in the Soviet Union—has been awarded to Yashin and Neto (soccer); Latynina, Turishcheva, Chukarin, and Shakhlin (gymnastics); Botvinik, Smyslov, Gaprindashvili, and Karpov (chess); Vlasov and Alekseyev (weight lifting); Kuts, Bolotnikov, Borzov, and Saneev (track and field); and many others. In recognition of the successes at the 1972 Munich Olympic Games, athletes, trainers, and officials responsible for the success at the games were rewarded by decree of the Supreme Soviet Presidium of 5 October 1972. Six of them received the Order of Lenin, 20 the Order of the Red Banner, 105 the Badge of Honor, 48 the medal for Working Valor, and 74 the medal for Working Excellence.[36]

After the 1976 Innsbruck Winter Olympic Games 1 athlete (Irina Rodnina) was awarded the Order of Lenin, 10 the Order of the Red Banner, 24 the Badge of Honor, 20 the medal for Working Valor, and 19 the medal for Working Excellence.[37] The list after the 1976 Montreal Olympic Games was considerably longer: 8 Orders of Lenin (including Sergey Pavlov, chairman of the Committee of Physical Culture and Sport), 27 Orders of the Red Banner, 28 Orders of Friendship among Nations, 93 Badges of Honor, 7 Orders of Labor Glory—third degree, 124 medals for Working Valor, and 60 medals for Working Excellence.[38] Sportsmen and trainers were not the only persons awarded. After Innsbruck, one could spot among the names in the list sport officials such as Vitaliy Smirnov, first deputy chairman of the U.S.S.R. Committee of Physical Culture and Sport, and Vyacheslav Zakhavin, first deputy chairman of the RSFSR Committee of Physical Culture and Sport; party officials such as Nikolay Nemeshaev, instructor at a CPSU Central Committee Department; Komsomol officials such as Aleksandr Sered, Komsomol Central Committee Department Head; medical doctors such as Lev Markov, head physician of Moscow Physical Culture Dispensary No. 1; state officials such as Oleg Kryukov, group head at the Ministry of Defense's sport committee; scientists such as Vladimir Orlov, laboratory head at the Moscow Physical Culture Research Institute; masseurs, choreographers, etc.[39]

This phenomenon was repeated after Montreal, this time with the addition of several propaganda officials such as Boris Goncharov and Nikolay Rusak, section head and instructor at the CPSU Central Committee Department of Propaganda; frontrankers of the sports equipment industry, and even drivers of the sports delegation.[40] Award winers were received by L. Zamyatin, CPSU Central Committee secretary, who presented them with their awards.[41] This was only the first round. Sportsmen of the various nationalities within the Soviet Union were received by their respective republic's party secretaries, who presented them with yet more awards. Ukrainian sportsmen were received by republican party secretary V. Shcherbitskiy,[42] the Kazakhs by republican party secretary D. Kunayev,[43] and so forth.

This was still not all. After the all-Union and the republican-level receptions, celebrations continued at the professional level. Since all leading Soviet sportsmen officially hold posts in industrial plants, universities, offices, it was only natural that they should be celebrated by their colleagues. Army sportsmen benefited most. According to *Krasnaya Zvezda* they were received by General D. Sokolov, first deputy minister of defense, who stressed that "army sportsmen have demonstrated outstanding qualities, characteristic of the qualities of the Soviet soldiers, namely, Soviet patriotism, stubborness in struggle, heroism, and great willpower in pursuing victory."[44] By decree of the Ministry of Defense the sportsmen were awarded "valuable gifts and higher military ranks."[45]

Sovetskiy Sport of 10 April 1980 carries the list of sportsmen and officials who received awards after the 1980 Lake Placid Olympics. Once again propaganda officials figured among those awarded: Anatoliy Milchakov, instructor at the CPSU Central Committee Propaganda Department, and Mikhail Tikhomirov, instructor at the CPSU Moscow oblast committee of the Department of Propaganda and Agitation. The omnipresent scientist is also on the list: Vasiliy Martynov, laboratory head at the All-Union Physical Culture Scientific Research Institute, Moscow.

So much for the official way of recognizing and rewarding Soviet athletes. The unofficial way—various forms of financial benefits—is a taboo topic on which no Soviet official will elaborate. Nevertheless, several facts about this subject ceased to be great secrets. All leading Soviet sportsmen are "state professionals" whose financial rewards depend largely on the level of their performance. To maintain the impression of amateurism, leading sportsmen are on the payroll of various plants, institutes, universities, offices, and the army, but their salaries are paid for their sports achievements only. Soviet sportsmen are among the best paid groups in the country, and their regular income is no less than double the average income of an ordinary Soviet citizen.[46]

The opportunity to travel abroad is already a major reward in a country that restricts and controls international travel. Such trips also provide an opportunity of doing some business on the side, selling valuable Soviet goods and smuggling back even more valuable foreign goods. Usually Soviet customs authorities look the other way. The boxer Grigoriy

Rogolskiy, Master of Sport and former Leningrad champion, now living in New York, tells about one of this trips abroad:

> Although I knew we could take along as much caviar and vodka as we wanted, I really began to appreciate being in the Dynamos [the team patronized by the KGB] after we piled into the bus at the Hotel Central on Gorki street and headed for Sheremetovo international airport. Instead of waiting in the usual customs lines, a KGB major accompanying the team just waved our papers at the guards and drove us right through the gates without even getting off the bus. When we boarded the Lufthansa jet, our luggage was still untouched by customs. We were home free. In Cologne they broke the team into *troykas*—groups of three—the first day and instructed us to "see the sights," which meant one thing: unload your caviar and vodka. I had twenty bottles of Stolichnaya and four five-pound tins of black beluga. I sold them to the very Vlasov traitors Comrade "Ivanov" [the KGB official accompanying the delegation] had warned us against. The same day I bought fifteen pairs of jeans, six Seiko watches, and four auto cassette recorders—the last strictly *verboten*, particularly in wholesale quantities. But everybody did the same, stuffing their suitcases while our KGB major pretended not to see. On our return to Sheremetovo a bus picked us up at the plane and whisked us off to our hotel. The trip netted three thousand roubles—enough to live well in Russia for a year.[47]

The same source quotes many other (and even more profitable) examples. In the Soviet Union where there is a carrot there is also a stick. Transgressions tolerated or overlooked when Soviet sportsmen return home as winners are punishable when there is no victory to celebrate: The year 1973 was a bad year for Soviet basketball teams. The national team was defeated by the U.S. team during the Moscow World Student Games and later in the same year lost the European championship to Yugoslavia. The Soviet press attacked the team, *Komsomolskaya Pravda* acidly leading the attack with several low punches: "The national team returned from one of its trips not with a load of victories, but rather with a load of unprecedented violations of customs regulations.... The foul play of some athletes has become the concern of judges other then those who judge basketball competitions."[48] The "unproductivity" of the basketball team turned it into a scapegoat and an example for other atheltes, as if they could ever forget that winning pays off well in the Soviet Union.

World and Olympic championships bring special bonuses. Olympic Gold is valued anywhere from $4,000 to $8,000 depending on the international prestige of the sport.[49] By Soviet regulations every world record is greeted with a prize. This used to be the equivalent of $1,500 per record. However, the tremendous series of world records set by weight lifter V. Alekseyev (whose occupation has been given by the Soviet press as logger, miner, student, engineer, physical education instructor, and chemical factory foreman all at once[50]), caused some devaluation of the prize, which was brought down to $700.[51] So much for Soviet amateurs' rewards. Now for the contribution of modern medicine and science to Soviet sportsmen's victories.

MEDICAL MEANS

The importance of victory prompts Soviet authorities to exploit human potential to its fullest. If ideological motivation building and lucrative financial rewards are intended to strengthen sportsmen's willpower, dedication, and inspiration, medical means are pressed into service in order to make the most of their innate physical ability. As Serafim Letunov, head of the Sports Medicine sector of the National Research Institute of Physical Culture says:

> More than 7,000 scientists in our country are engaged in research on problems connected with the development of sport on a mass scale. The Soviet Union was the first country in the world to set up a state-operated system of medical care tailored for people participating in sports and physical education. We also devote much time to the training of top-class athletes. Today an athlete cannot hope to score victories and set records if he has only a superficial knowledge of medicine, biology, and psychology. Only joint efforts by scientists in many different fields can help him register outstanding performances. Considerable attention is paid to application of technological advance in sport. It is even possible, to some degree, to program a champion, that is, to set an athlete on the road to victory.[52]

About three kilometers from the Kremlin in quiet Kazakova Street no. 18, there is an impressive horseshoe-shaped building, which used to belong to Prince Razumovski. Today it is the All-Union Institute for Physical Culture Scientific Research. Among its 600 employees there are 300 scientists, 150 of them specializing in biological medicine.[53] It is here that all modern medical means are studied and developed to increase the physical ability of Soviet sportsmen. A substantial part of the research focuses on developing new training systems, psychological analysis, etc. Subsequent recommendations are relayed to trainers, producers of sports equipment, and sports officials. Many institute employees attend every major international competition, photographing and filming foreign sportsmen. The material is then analyzed by the institute, the techniques of the foreign sportsmen studied and improved.[54] The institute also observes the development of talented children and helps program them as successful sportsmen.[55] Similar institutes exist in Leningrad and Tiflis.[56]

The subject of drugs for boosting sportsmen's ability is very sensitive.

Officially, doping is forbidden in the Soviet Union, and "the control is constantly becoming stricter,"[57] according to Sergey Popov, head of the All-Union Institute for Physical Culture Scientific Research. Nevertheless, a slip of the tongue from the same source indicates that drugs are being used by Soviet sportsmen: "We constantly inform our sportsmen about which medicines are permitted and which prohibited by the IOC,"[58] Popov says. He did not elaborate on why sportsmen who officially never use drugs at all need to be informed about such things. Unofficially, drugs, mainly anabolic steroids, are believed to be used extensively by Soviet and East European athletes. The main research in this area takes place in Moscow's Sport Dispensary No. 2 located in the buildings of the Lenin Stadium. Its director Vladimir Matov denies that there is any official research in this sensitive area, but to the question of whether there are no cases of doping in the Soviet Union he answers: "There are always black sheep."[59]

Soviet and East European sportsmen have repeatedly been sanctioned by international sports authorities for using prohibited drugs. Bulgarian weight lifters (among them gold medal winner Valentin Khristov) were ordered to return their medals and were disqualified from competing for a long period, after they failed the dope test at the 1976 Montreal Olympics. In 1979 at the European track and field championship, Soviet athletes Nadezhda Tkachenko (pentathalon) and Yevgeniy Mironov (shot put) were disqualified after having failed the steroid test.[60] Several similar cases (among them disqualification of Bulgarian 800-meter dash world record holder Totka Petrova) were widely reported by the world press, along with sound medical proof of the long-lasting negative effects of using certain drugs, such as infertility, impotence, and so forth. Arvids Iserlis, former rowing coach of the Soviet National Olympics team and now living in New York, freely admits to having administered anabolites to his crew (both men and women) to develop their muscles and increase their weight. After relating the side effects of his women rowers (larger arms, bigger hands and so forth), he maintains that the same system has been used on weight lifter V. Alekseyev, whose weight increased from 220 to 344 pounds as a result of using steroids.[61]

As long as gold medals are viewed as evidence of the superiority of a particular social system, sportsmen's health and various unpleasant long-term effects are of lesser consequence. What is astonishing (although it should not be by now) is the hypocrisy of Soviet authorities. Four years before the 1980 Olympic Games they created the Anti-Drug Commission of the XXII Olympic Games, headed by Viktor Rogozkin. The commission would test each winner and the two runners-up for three items: regular drugs (narcotics and stimulants), anabolic steroids, and alcohol.[62]

CHEATING

There is a special category of means of securing victory for Soviet sportsmen which includes fraud, cheating, biased refereeing, and so forth. Soviet authorities have a very flexible, selective, and subjective set of moral values. Since victory, with its political and ideological ramifications, is treasured above all else, truthfulness, respect for the opponent—often a representative of the opposing political system—and justice are easily sacrificed on the altar of patriotism, dedication to the communist cause, and Soviet prestige. This is a special communist morality, considerably different from that accepted in the West, and aimed at justifying the means toward achievement of goals.

The Soviet Union does not hesitate to use fraud on a large scale if it can ensure the coveted victory. Several examples:

During the 1976 Montreal Olympics Soviet fencer Boris Ovcharenko (world champion in modern pentathalon, major in the Soviet army) was caught using an epee fitted with a sophisticated device allowing him to deceive the electronic scoring system by indicating hits for him when there had been none. Since Ovcharenko was caught red handed, there was no way of denying he had cheated or blaming it on anyone else, and he was disqualified. The Soviet mass media had to employ some verbal acrobatics in the attempt to conceal the true nature of Ovcharenko's disqualification: "Unfortunately, Boris Ovcharenko upset everyone and put his team mates on the spot. He was disqualified for a blatant violation of the rules: he fenced today with a sword which did not meet the requirements of the international rules."[63] *Sovetskiy Sport* was even more enigmatic in reporting the incident: "B. Ovcharenko, who during the fencing competition committed a flagrant violation of technical regulations, is certainly to be blamed for the team's poor showing."[64]

The sudden disappearance of the sisters Tamara and Irina Press (both gold medal winners in track and field at the 1964 Toyko Olympic Games) after the introduction of sex tests by the IOC did not surprise many. The two, who disappeared with several other Soviet athletes, such as 200-meter dash champion Marya Itkina and all-around athlete Aleksandra Chudina, had been a real puzzle for a long time. Their obviously masculine features and body-structure were very conspicuous. Said Wilma Rudolf, the famous U.S. sprinter and Olympic champion:

"I remember the Press sisters very well. In Rome we used to be puzzled by their mannish appearance...."[65]

The sports "battlefield" often requires other forms of manipulation. Such is the subjective and unfair way in which Soviet and East European referees judge athletes' performance in international competition. There is no need for Soviet authorities to apply any pressure on referees. Their traveling abroad depends on the good will of Soviet authorities. Were they to be completely unbiased, they could easily find themselves refereeing in Novosibirsk and Yakutsk instead of Paris and Rome. The partiality of Soviet judges is especially conspicuous in gymnastics and figure skating. Nothing can be done in the area of gymnastics, since the president of the International Federation is former Soviet world champion Y. Titov. In 1977 the Romanian team pulled out of the European Gymnastics championship because of the Soviet judges' partiality. In figure skating things took a different turn. In 1976 Soviet judges were banned from officiating in international competitions for a year. The reason stated by the federation was subjective refereeing.[66] Soviet authorities retaliated with an angry declaration, accusing the federation of tendentiousness, violation of the norms of international justice, violating the Olympic spirit, and so forth.[67]

Soviet officials do not hesitate to accuse other countries' referees when Soviet sportsmen fail to achieve what had been expected of them. Nadya Comaneci's triumph was explained as being the result of partial judging: "'Those who watch the gymnastics competitions at the Montreal Olympics should not be put out that none of the Soviet gymnasts got ten points like Nadya Comaneci of Romania,' a TASS correspondent was told by a senior coach of the U.S.S.R. women's gymnastic team, Larisa Latynina (herself a former Olympic champion). 'I feel that the judges were too generous at the present tournament, and this rather depreciates the Olympic points. I hope that the judging will be more strict for the absolute championship and that the Soviet gymnasts will make a brilliant showing.'"[68] Another refereeing incident in Montreal involved an allegation of Tommy Gompf, leader of the U.S. diving team. He claimed that a Soviet referee had proposed a deal, namely, that Soviet referees would show "generosity" toward U.S. divers in exchange for similar favors. Soviet sources immediately rejected the allegation as an "absurd fabrication."[69]

Soviet authorities do not hesitate to apply rude personal pressure if it can guarantee success in international competition. On 8 March 1980 the quarterfinal match for the world chess championship between Viktor Korchnoi, who had previously defected from the Soviet Union, and Tigran Petrosyan was to begin in Velden, Austria. For more than four years the Kremlin refused to allow Korchnoi's family to join him abroad. This had been done both as punishment for the "traitor" and mental pressure aimed at confusing his game. On March 3, by a curious coincidence just five days before the start of the match between Korchnoi and Petrosyan, Igor, Korchnoi's son, was sent to the Siberian gulag as a "particularly dangerous criminal," according to a court decision.[70] Nevertheless, Korchnoi won the match by a score of 5.5 to 3.5. Later he admitted: "While I was winning in Velden, the KGB won its match against my family."[71] So much for victory, its importance and significance, and the various means of facilitating its achievement. Let us now turn to the specific propaganda uses of Soviet sport.

Notes

1. S. Pavlov, "Sportniy Obmen: Pravda I Vymysliy," *Literaturnaya Gazeta* (17 March 1976).
2. V. Koval, *Sport—Posol Mira* (Moscow, 1974). p. 9.
3. L. Bezymenski, "After the Olympics," *New Times* (no. 38, 1972), pp. 6-7.
4. *Soviet Weekly* (10 September 1959).
5. *Nedelya* (2-8 August 1976), pp. 12-13.
6. *Nedelya* (12-16 November 1976), p. 18.
7. *Nedelya* (2-8 August 1976), p. 13.
8. A. Kolodny, "No Walkovers Expected," *Soviet Union* (no. 6, 1972), p. 56.
9. Koval, p. 9.
10. *Nedelya* (2-8 August, 1976), pp. 12-13.
11. K. Zharov, *Volevaya Podgotovka Sportsmenov* (Moscow, 1976), pp. 26-27.
12. Ibid., p. 131.
13. Ibid., p. 132.
14. Ibid.
15. Ibid.
16. Ibid., pp. 133,135.
17. Ibid., p. 137.
18. Ibid., p. 133.
19. *Sovetskiy Sport* (12 February 1980).
20. Zharov, p. 133.
21. V. Snegiriev, "Kurs—Olympiada," *Komsomolskaya Pravda* (2 October 1979).
22. "K Pobedam Vedut Komsorgi," *Komsomolskaya Pravda* (2 April 1980).
23. Zharov, p. 134.
24. *Nedelya* (26 July-1 August 1976), pp. 8-9.
25. *Otechestven Front* (Bulgaria—25 June 1977).
26. Moscow TASS in English, 1711 GMT (16 July 1976), *D.R.* (20 July 1976).
27. Moscow TASS in English, 1901 GMT (17 July 1976), *D.R.* (20 July 1976).
28. I. Rodnina, "Eto Nastoyashtee Schastye," *Izvestiya* (27 March 1980).
29. Ibid.
30. Zharov, p. 30.
31. P. Pinigin, "I Press Myself to the Earth for Strength," *Olympaid* (no. 13, 1977), p. 34.
32. Y. Brokhin, *The Big Red Machine* (New York, 1978), p. 144.
33. "Interview with the Minister," In H. Lathe, *Geheimnisse Des Sowjetsports* (Vienna, 1979), p. 257.
34. Zharov, pp. 25-26.
35. *Trud* (12 August, 1967).

36. *Sovetskiy Sport* (6 October 1972).
37. U.S.S.R. Supreme Soviet decree of 10 May 1976. In A. Dobrov (ed.), *God Olympiyskiy 76* (Moscow 1977), pp. 14-15.
38. U.S.S.R. Supreme Soviet decree of 10 September 1976, *Ibid.*, pp. 74-83.
39. Ibid., pp. 14-15.
40. Ibid., pp. 74-83.
41. Moscow Domestic Service in Russian, 1600 GMT (13 August 1976), *D.R.* (16 August 1976).
42. *Sovetskiy Sport* (3 November 1976).
43. *Pravda* (12 August 1976).
44. *Krasnaya Zvezda* (4 November 1976).
45. Ibid.
46. N. Norman Shneidman, *The Soviet Road to Olympus* (London, 1979), p. 70.
47. Brokhin, p. 109.
48. *Komsomolskaya Pravda* (23 October 1973).
49. Brokhin, p. 186.
50. Ibid., p. 218.
51. Ibid., p. 219.
52. Serafim Letunov, "Programming a Champion?" *Soviet Union* (no. 7, 1972), p. 16.
53. Lathe, pp. 39-40.
54. Ibid., p. 40.
55. Ibid., p. 55.
56. Ibid.
57. Ibid., p. 43.
58. Ibid.
59. Ibid., p. 48.
60. N. Amdur, "7 Women Athletes Banned for Drugs," *New York Times* (26 October 1979).
61. Brokhin, p. 123.
62. "A Ban on Drugs," *Sputnik* (no. 12, December 1979), p. 149.
63. Moscow Domestic Service in Russian, 0730 GMT (20 July 1976), *D.R.* (20 July 1976).
64. *Sovetskiy Sport* (28 July 1976).
65. Brokhin, p. 126.
66. *Kurier* (Austria—3 June 1976).
67. *Sovetskiy Sport* (19 June 1977).
68. Moscow TASS in English, 1021 GMT (21 July 1976), *D.R.* (22 July 1976).
69. Moscow TASS in English, 1756 GMT (23 July 1976), *D.R.* (26 July 1976).
70. L. Unger, "Playing with the Kremlin," *International Herald Tribune* (12 April 1980).
71. Ibid.

4

Sport's Other Functions

Soviet authorities expect the victories of Soviet athletes to enhance Soviet international prestige and demonstrate the advantages of the socialist system. Soviet sport is frequently officially said to have three other aims: physical education of the Soviet people on the basis of Marxism-Leninism; strengthening of peace and understanding among nations; and preparing Soviet citizens to defend their Motherland.[1] This does not exhaust the list of functions of Soviet sport, most of which are charged with heavy political and propaganda overtones.

GENERAL SUPPORT OF SOVIET FOREIGN POLICY LINE

Despite the fact that the theme of the entire Soviet counterpropaganda offensive against the proposed boycott of the Moscow Olympics was "to separate the sport from politics," (see chapter 7), Communist sources have repeatedly underlined the political significance of sport.[2] Statements to that effect appeared in almost all leading East European newspapers in April and May 1980, when the counteroffensive to the boycott reached its climax. Typical of this trend was the article "Physical Education Is Part of the Ideological Struggle," which appeared in *Rude Pravo* (Czechoslavakia). The author, Antonin Himl, chairman of the Czechoslovak Union of Physical Education Central Committee, dwells on the ideological content and value of sport: "We look at things realistically. Sport always was, and

51

is, a political matter—just as other spheres of social superstructure are. The Olympic movement, too, is political; it is the reflection of a class-divided world."[3]

Soviet sources are even more explicit as to the particular direction Soviet sport follows: "Our sport and physical culture organizations have always facilitated practical implementation of the Leninist peace policy, expansion of international cooperation, and strengthening of peaceful coexistence of states with different social systems."[4] Sport and physical culture are called upon to "intensify their ideological-political activity, to broadly propagate the social achievements of socialism, criticize the bourgeois concept of sport, unmask anticommunism and anti-Sovietism,"[5] and so forth. Soviet sportsmen are exhorted to "unmask the modernization of the reaction's ideological diversion of sport... something that will facilitate mutual understanding among nations and social progress."[6]

One should distinguish among three different aspects of Soviet sport's general political activity: the competitions themselves, the "extracurricular" activity of Soviet sportsmen, and the activity of sports functionaries and officials. The official Soviet view is that the competitions themselves further various facets of their foreign policy: "Sports events are 'peaceful battles' which must replace rivalry and hostility in the future world of friendship and cooperation. International sports competitions, by the very fact of their being held, confirm the profound correctness of the policy of international detente, which paves the way to cooperation and exchange in all fields among nations."[7] In addition to their performance on the "peaceful battlefields," Soviet sportsmen frequently pursue "extracurricular" activities which supplement the ideological content of their sports victories: "From the first postwar days of 1945, Soviet sportsmen began to establish friendly international relations with their foreign colleagues. These relations were subjected to one idea—the struggle for peace and democracy, and against imperialism and the new warmongers."[8]

In one of his numerous interviews for the Soviet press, Sergey Pavlov, chairman of the U.S.S.R. Committee on Sport and Physical Culture, elaborates on the participation of Soviet sportsmen in international propaganda campaigns: "I would like to stress that our cooperation with foreign countries is not limited to merely the sports-technical aspects of the matter... Soviet sportsmen are traditional and active participants in such events as the 'holidays' of communist newspapers in Austria, Belgium, and the Federal Republic of Germany... and Soviet 'weeks' and 'days' held in Italy, Portugal, and the Netherlands."[9] The "extracurricular" activity of Soviet sportsmen is organized by the Propaganda Administration of the U.S.S.R. Committee on Sport and Physical Culture. A. Valiakhmetov, head of the administration, states in a *Sovetskiy Sport* article: "When competing abroad sports officials, team members, and trainers must utilize in their conversations with their foreign colleagues cogent arguments concerning the great advantages of our system, reflected by the new U.S.S.R. draft-Constitution."[10]

Soviet sportsmen participating in the 1976 Montreal Olympics meticulously followed Valiakhmetov's instructions. They not only initiated political discussions with foreign sportsmen, but also distributed among them propaganda material concerning Soviet life and achievements."[11] Valiakhmetov emphasizes the effectiveness of Soviet sportsmen's behavior abroad, and considers it an important factor in their popularity. As for the popularity itself, Valiakhmetov maintains that a television poll was conducted in the Federal Republic of Germany in 1972, the participants being asked to name the most popular athletes: 93 percent named Soviet sportsmen in first place.[12]

Soviet sports officials participating in various international forums fulfill similar functions. At the 65th IOC session in Tehran in 1967, the Soviet representative introduced a resolution on peace. Adoption of the resolution was greeted with pleasure by the Soviet Union, and the opportunity to criticize the IOC for refraining from political action was not missed: "(Adoption of the resolution) is a step forward as compared with the position held by the IOC for many years. On the plea of keeping sport out of politics, until very recently it [IOC] refrained from any actions in defense of peace."[13] In 1976 a novel entitled *Olympic Concerns* was published in the Soviet Union. It described the activity of an imaginary Soviet representative in an international sports federation. *Sovetskiy Sport* reviewed the novel positively, stressing that Soviet representatives in international sports federations always struggled for the "democratization" of international sports life and purity in sport[14]—and concludes: "Presenting the Soviet representative as a conductor of his country's policy...a patriot...and a fighter against the advocates of racism—this is how the author constructed the image of the Soviet sports diplomat."[15]

Soviet party and state leaders make use of Soviet and international sports events, as well as meeting with the IOC officials, to voice various aspects of Soviet foreign policy. In his greeting message to participants in the 1973 Moscow World Student Games Brezhnev said:

> Following the behests of the great Lenin, the Soviet state has always sided and continues to side with the forces fighting for freedom and social progress, for lasting peace in the world and understanding among peoples. These days, when significant positive changes are taking place in the international situation, when a switch is taking place from "cold war" to détente and cooperation, more favorable opportunities are opening up for the student youth of all countries to broaden cultural and sport contacts, to further

activate the struggle for the triumph of the ideas of humanism, understanding, and friendship among nations.... May the World Student Games in
Moscow be not only a festival of sport and youth, but worthily serve the
further consolidation of cooperation among young people in the struggle for
peace, progress, and democracy.[16]

The same idea was expressed at a 19 November 1976 meeting between N.
Podgorniy, then chairman of the Supreme Soviet Presidium, and Lord
Killanin, IOC president: "During their talk... it was stressed that sports
exchanges and cooperation in this field, promote and deepen international
relations, mutual understanding among peoples, the easing of international tension, and the preservation and strengthening of peace."[17]

PARTICIPATION IN OPERATIONAL
PROPAGANDA CAMPAIGNS

Despite the fact that sport is an instrument of impregnational propaganda, it has sometimes been involved in specific operational propaganda
campaigns. The pattern usually involves refusal to compete against a
country engaged in a political conflict in which the Soviet Union supports
the other side, or simply boycotting a country when its policy has become a
target of the Soviet propaganda apparatus. Refusal to compete against
such a country draws public attention, exacerbates the issue, intensifies the
operational propaganda campaign, and facilitates implementation of
Soviet foreign policy goals in that particular matter. Refusal by the Soviet
Union to play against a country because of its policy or even its very
existence, first occured in the 1953 World Basketball Championship in
Chile, when the Soviet team refused to play Formosa, pronounced a "U.S.
satellite" by Soviet authorities.[18]

A similar case was Soviet refusal to participate in the 1967 Tokyo World
Student Games. The decision was made "as a way of protesting against
absurd discrimination against students of the Korean Democratic People's
Republic."[19] "Under pressure from Japanese reactionaries, egged on by
South Korea, the organizers of the games were willing to let the North
Korean students take part only under a set of meaningless initials—KSSA.
And this despite the fact that they were a member of FISU—the International Federation of University Sports—which sponsors the games."[20] A
rare case of boycotting vis-à-vis the United States took place in July 1966,
when Soviet athletes refused to participate in the annual U.S.-Soviet
athletic competition scheduled to take palce in Los Angeles on 23-24 July
1966, "as a protest against the U.S. policy in Vietnam."[21] Czechoslovak
and Polish athletes immediately followed suit.[22]

Refusal to play against Chile in the soccer world cup qualifying matches was part of the sharp Soviet propaganda campaign against the military junta that had overthrown Allende. Chile and the Soviet Union were in the same qualification group of four soccer teams, competing for a place in the 1974 Munich Soccer World Cup finals. Only one team from each group qualified for the finals, each country playing twice against each other—at home and away. The Chilean team surprised the Soviet national team and ended the Moscow match in a draw. To regain at least some chance to qualify, the Soviet team had to win the return match in Santiago. Several weeks before the return match Allende was killed and his regime toppled. A major operational propaganda campaign against the new military regime was launched by the Soviet Union, all instruments of the Soviet propaganda machine actively participating in the campaign. The Soviet Soccer Federation joined in demanding that the return match be held not in Santiago but on the territory of a third country. The official explanation: Santiago's stadium "had been turned by the military junta into a concentration camp and the scene of torture and execution of Chilean patriots... and was stained with their blood."[23] An international angle had to be added to lend the Soviet refusal to play some measure of international or legal justification: "Following the fascist coup and overthrow of the legitimate Popular Unity Government, an atmosphere of bloody terror and reprisals reigns in Chile; an unbridled campaign of provocation is being carried out against the socialist countries and all democratic forces; anti-Soviet sentiments are being whipped up, and there have been instances in which Soviet citizens in Chile have been the victims of violence."[24]

A "stadium stained with blood" became a key phrase, echoed in numerous statements and declarations issued by various Soviet front organizations and socialist countries' soccer federations.[25] When Chile suggested that the match be played in another (unstained) stadium, the Soviet Union refused on the grounds of inadequate personal security for the sportsmen, TASS stressing that "under the conditions prevailing in Chile even foreign diplomats are not guaranteed personal security."[26] The International Football (soccer) Association (FIFA) declared that Soviet refusal to play against Chile—in Chile—would eliminate the Soviet team from further participation in the World Cup. FIFA president Sir Stanley Rous immediately became the target of acid attacks accusing him of pursuing personal goals: "One cannot help thinking that his sole purpose is to deprive the U.S.S.R. of the right to play in the World Cup games. Others too might well refuse to play in protest, thereby opening vacancies in the finals for some teams and maybe for England as well."[27]

The Soviet Union was disqualified. No East European team which had qualified for the finals yielded to the Soviet call for a "solidarity boycott." Bulgaria, Poland, and Yugoslavia took part in the finals. After its disqualification "which has shown that FIFA members and President Rous... are men far removed from the pure principles of world sport—cooperation, mutual understanding, and the strengthening of friendly relations,"[28] the Soviet Union decided to punish England which, although it had no part in the whole affair, was the homeland of Sir Stanley Rous: "It is only natural that in the given situation the U.S.S.R. Federation of Automobile Sport issued a statement in which it refused to take part in the London-Moscow rally, devoted to the World Cup Games. It was planned that the rally route would include our country, but now this is, of course, impossible. That was how one unfair decision influenced another most interesting competition, for which Soviet drivers had been enthusiastically preparing."[29]

The "blood stains" were used by the Soviet Union again in 1979, this time against China, in protesting its admission to the IOC (for which the Soviet Union had struggled for years before Chinese policy found itself the target of Soviet propaganda as a result of the Sino-Soviet split): "How can the aggressive, bandit-like war, unleashed by China against socialist Vietnam, serve as an argument for China's admmission to the Olympic movement? The Olympic games are a great world festivity for mankind. How can anybody be permitted to attend this festivity with blood-stained hands? This blood of the Peking aggressors is the greatest obstacle in China's path of the Olympic family."[30]

The Soviet propaganda campaign against having the 1976 Chess Olympics and congress of the International Chess Federation (FIDE) held in Israel was once again based on refusal to play on the territory of a country whose policy was opposed by the Soviet Union and which was involved in a conflict in which the Soviet Union was not a direct participant. Since the Israeli government is legitimately elected and there is no military junta or "bloodstained stadium"—the grounds for refusal were different. The declaration of the Soviet Chess Federation pointed out the "close relations between the Israeli ruling circles and South Africa," and the permission to participate given to Viktor Korchnoy, "who had been disqualifeid by the Soviet Chess Foundation for unworthy behavior."[31] FIDE was accused of mixing politics and sport because of its refusal to change the venue of the games.[32] This time, the federations of East European countries showed support for the Soviet campaign. The Bulgarian chess federation issued a statement criticizing the FIDE decision and basing its refusal to play in Israel on "Israel's aggressive policy... the usurpation of Arab states' territory... refusal to comply with UN resolutions and the generally accepted norms of international law."[33] The Hungarian Chess Federation based its refusal to play in Israel on "the close relaitons between Israel and South Africa."[34]

In 1976 the Soviet Union was disqualified from the Tennis Davis Cup because of its refusal to play against Chile, Rhodesia, and South Africa.[35]

The president of the International Lawn Tennis Federation (ILTF), Dereck Hartwick, who based the disqualification of the Soviet team on the principle of separating sport and politics, was promptly accused of being an "instrument of the most reactionary regimes."[36] At the time the Soviet press amplified the interpellation of an Italian Communist member of parliament, criticizing the decision of the Italian government not to interfere with the decision of the Italian Tennis Federation to play its Davis Cup match against Chile.[37]

"The struggle against racism and apartheid" is a constant theme of Soviet operational propaganda. By the end of 1979 Soviet sport authorities and federations had become deeply involved in that particular campaign. The Soviet Union remembered well that most African countries had boycotted the 1976 Montreal Olympics because of the participation of New Zealand, which had previously allowed a friendly rugby match between a local team and a South African team. Openly stating its concern that "there are reactionary circles who want to inflict a blow on the Olympic movement by staging a similar boycott of the Moscow Olympic Games,"[38] Moscow intensified its campaign against racism.

In October 1979 the Soviet Rugby Federation issued a strong protest against the visit of a South African rugby team to England.[39] As a consequence of the tour the Soviet AVIATOR team from Kiev canceled its visit to Great Britain, a "decision fully supported by the federation."[40] In December 1979 a special delegation of the Soviet Olympic Committee led by its chairman, I. Novikov, deputy chairman of the Council of Ministers, visited several African countries and repeatedly stressed that "no racist will be admitted to Moscow." The delegation pointed out that the Soviet Union had always condemned sports contacts with racist regimes and elaborated on the "excellent conditions awaiting African sportsmen in Moscow."[41]

Soviet sports federations and individual sportsmen frequently issue statements supporting Soviet policy in matters that have absolutely nothing to do with sport, such as the production and deployment of the neutron bomb, the Middle East conflict, the conflicts in Southeast Asia, and so forth—all subjects of typical operational propaganda campaigns and outside the usual impregnational propaganda activity of Soviet sport.

PROMOTING GOOD WILL TOWARD THE SOVIET UNION

The main function of impregnational propaganda is to facilitate Soviet operational propaganda by generating good will toward and further interest in the Soviet Union. Soviet sport, as one of impregnational propaganda's main instruments, has exactly the same goals. Soviet gymnasts' frequent trips abroad are a typical example of such propaganda activity. The 1976 trip to the United States was called by U.S. sports commentators "The Russian wonder in America."[42] *Sovetskiy Sport* in reporting this tour stressed the tremendous enthusiams of the audience wherever the Soviet gymnasts performed, evoked not only by the excellent performance but also by the "cordiality, amiable disposition, and dignity with which Soviet sportsmen represented the Motherland."[43]

Sergey Pavlov in his frequent interviews often stresses the performance of Soviet gymnasts abroad as an effective instrument for generating good will toward the Soviet Union: "I would like to recall our gymnasts' performances in the United States, England, and the FRG. During the performance at the huge Earls Court, the English announcer exclaimed: 'The U.S.S.R. can be proud of such youth and athletes. This is a happy country.'"[44] In the same interview Pavlov described the fact that Olga Korbut had been awarded the Italian prize Ambassador of Peace as highly indicative of Soviet gymnasts' performance abroad.[45]

The official line of Soviet authorities is that "the foreign policy of the CPSU and the Soviet government is reflected in international sports relations, which must play their part in establishing firm foundations of mutual understanding and friendship among nations."[46] In accordance with this line Soviet sportsmen are frequently sent to compete against inferior opponents in developing countries. These are probably the only cases in which the score does not matter, the most important thing being the performance of Soviet sportsmen and the impregnational effect of their skills. In 1976 Igor Platonov and Yuriy Kotkov, two fairly well-known Soviet chess players, visited Pakistan. Later they published their impressions of the trip. The results of the competitions were not mentioned. They dwelled mostly on the friendly and hospitable reception they had been accorded, and stressed that the goal of their visit was to promote friendship by competing and lecturing.[47] Similar "good will tours" are frequently conducted in many African and Asian countries.

As is the case with various operational propaganda campaigns, Soviet sport's propaganda activity pursuing the development of good will toward the Soviet Union is not limited to the realm of sports competition. Sports exhibitions, participation in various solidarity "weeks" and "days," and so forth, contribute their share to Soviet sport's impregnational activity. In 1979 a major exhibition called "Sport in the U.S.S.R." was sent to the United States. In six months the exhibition was shown in San Francisco, Knoxville, Atlanta, Kansas City, and San Antonio, some 137,000 people visiting it.[48] Brezhnev himself greeted visitors: "Acquaintance with Soviet sport history relays a visual impression of how the Soviet Union implements the Olympic charter's ideas of mutual understanding and friendship among nations in the name of peace and mankind's better future."[49] Some of the visitors wrote in the exhibition's book: "A beautiful exhibition! It eloquently speaks of how your country cares for the people's health." "I am amazed by this wonderful exposition! How little we know about your country." "The exhibition will positively influence the development of relations between our countries."[50] Another article describing the same exhibition concluded: "Sports helps us to better understand each other... it is a way toward peace."[51] Similar exhibitions have been sent to many other countries, such as Cameroon[52] and Algeria.[53] The latter exhibition was part of the Algiers-Moscow Friendship Week.[54]

Indirectly, sport often facilitates other impregnational propaganda instruments. Later in this chapeter we shall consider the exposure of foreign sportsmen visiting the Soviet Union to other instruments of Soviet impregnational propaganda. This phenomenon can also be observed abroad. When the U.S. television network NBC negotiated with Soviet authorities for the right to televise the Moscow Olympic Games, Moscow made this conditional upon their accepting in addition shows of Soviet ballet, circus, dancing ensembles, and so forth for televising, "to facilitate the acquaintance of U.S. viewers with Soviet culture."[55]

In the same category belong the various Soviet sports publications in foreign languages such as *Sport in the USSR* (Russian, German, English, French, Spanish, Hungarian), *Olympiade-80* (English, French, German, Russian, Spanish), and *Olympic Panorama* (Russian, German, English, French, Spanish). While dealing mostly with sports news and preparations for the Moscow Olympic Games, they also devote much space to presenting various aspects of Soviet life, working successes of the Soviet people, tourist attractions, and so forth. A typical example is Boris Vanyushin's article "Leningrad Prepares to Receive Its Guests." The author promises that "we are doing everything we can to ensure that the guests who will come to the banks of the Neva River will not only be properly accommodated but also be able to see the city's unique and beautiful sights and the treasures of its famous museums and picture galleries and acquaint themselves with the life of Soviet people, with how they work and relax."[56] "I am certain that Olympic participants and fans will take home the most pleasant memories of Leningrad's hospitality and of the wonderful city on the Neva, the cradle of the October Revolution."[57]

There are also various "sports quizzes" promoted by the numerous Soviet publications in foreign languages, which invariably aim at supplying more information about Soviet life and arousing interest in its various aspects. The Soviet sports exhibition in the United States organized a quiz in every city it visited entitled "What do you know about Soviet sport?" Winners received a free trip to the Moscow Olympics.[58] A similar quiz was organized in 1979 by *Soviet Woman* (a magazine for women published in fourteen foreign languages). It drew 8,242 answers from 64 countries. First prize again was a trip to the Moscow Olympic Games. *Soviet Woman* published the results and some of the participants' letters, which expressed admiration for the Soviet Union. V. Naidu (India) is quoted as saying: "The program of the Moscow Olympics is grandiose. The entire Soviet people strive to decorate Moscow like a bride, to show hospitality to thousands of foreign guests. Judging by the preparations for the Olympics, Soviet people are aspiring to have the Olympic Games a success, so that there will not be the slightest ground for critical remarks. One of the mottos of the 1980 Olympics—"Friendship-Peace"—excellently reflects that which will take place in Moscow in 1980."[59]

DEVELOPING RELATIONS WITH THIRD WORLD COUNTRIES

Soviet sport has a crucial role in strengthening relations between the Soviet Union and the Third World. There is nothing altruistic or innocuous about the assistance rendered by Soviet sport to developing countries. Soviet sources present these relations as "part of the Soviet Union's international duty and general solidarity and support it renders developing countries."[60] The same sources distinguish between various forms of Soviet sports assistance to developing countries. Students from developing countries study physical education in Soviet higher schools, the entire cost of their education being borne by the Soviet government. Some eighty such students from twenty countries, including Tanzania, Jordan, Tunisia, Madagascar, Afghanistan, and Peru were enrolled in the various Soviet Physical Culture Higher Education Institutes in the 1979-80 academic year. Twenty-five trainers from countries such Niger, Afghanistan, Syria, Thailand, and Guinea-Bissau were undergoing further training in the Soviet Union in 1979.[61]

Many Soviet trainers work in developing countries. In 1972 there were 200 working in 28 countries.[62] In the late seventies the number of Soviet trainers working in the Third World sharply increased. In 1979 alone, 40 Soviet trainers were sent to 15 African, Asian, and Latin American states.[63] In 1980 it was revealed that Soviet trainers were at work in 52 African, Asian, and Latin American countries.[64] Among them were former Olympic and world champions and record holders such as Robert Shavalkadze (high jump, working in Congo) and Vasiliy Romanov (boxing, Nigeria). These trainers are much more than sports instructors. The Soviet Union considers them ambassadors of good will—representing the Soviet Union and promoting its image abroad.

Although Greece does not belong to the category of "developing countries," the reaction evoked by the work of Soviet soccer coach Igor Netto, former captain of the Soviet national team, is typical of the results of Soviet trainers' activity in the Third World. This is what Kostas Tsolakis, president of the Panionios club, trained by Netto, said to a Soviet reporter: "We are extremely grateful to the U.S.S.R. Committee on Sport for sending Netto to our club. His work surpassed our expectations. Netto is a wonderful man and trainer. Thanks to him we learned to love your country. I think that people like Netto help you to acquire friends in every country throughout the world."[65]

The Soviet Union sends sports equipment to more than forty developing countries. The cost is met by the Soviet government.[66] Sports delegations from developing countries are frequent visitors to the Soviet Union. Some one hundred such delegations from African, Asian, and Latin American countries visited the Soviet Union in 1979.[67] Very often these visits have no sport value, their nature being purely political. In March 1980, for instance, a delegation of Afghan boxers visited the Soviet Union. The visit was described as a "symbol of Afghanistan's revival and a sign of the strengthening of the sports friendship between the two countries."[68] Admitting that they had not won any competition in the Soviet Union, the delegation leader pointed out that because of the boxers' low level of skills, they would not be taking part in the Moscow Olympic Games.[69]

Even more interesting (for the Soviet Union) are the visits of sports officials and trainers from developing countries. Such delegations are taken on extensive tours within the Soviet Union and often subjected to ideological indoctrination. Following the visit, the members of such delegations are usually coaxed to make statements about the beauty and achievements of the Soviet Union—the statements later being amplified by Soviet magazines and radio broadcasts in foreign languages. For instance, a delegation of the Bangladesh Committee on Sport visited the Soviet Union in June 1977. After touring the country and visiting the sites of various Olympic projects, the delegation members praised Soviet successes in various areas, called the Soviet Union "an astonishing and amazing country," an "unforgettable country and people," and finally declared that they "felt themselves free and unburdened like in their own country."[70]

A delegation of the Lao Olympic Committee visited the Soviet Union in November 1979 and was asked about the importance of Soviet-Lao sports relations. The leader of the delegation, Singkapo Sokhotchunlaman, chairman of the Lao Olympic Committee, said: "Sports relations with the Soviet Union facilitate not only the progress of Lao sport and the preparation of Lao sportsmen for the Moscow Olympic Games, but also make an important contribution to strengthening the friendship and mutual understanding between the peoples of our two countries."[71] Often special sports seminars with obvious political overtones are organized for trainers and officials from developing countries. One such seminar, which lasted for six months, was organized in 1979-80 for young trainers from Benin, Upper Volta, Guinea, Congo, Tunisia, Morocco, Laos, and Cuba.[72] The participants studied Russian in addition to various physical education subjects, and in March 1980 adopted a resolution "scoring the dirty game of American politicians, who are trying to interfere with the Moscow Olympic Games."[73] Visits by developing countries' sports officials to the Soviet Union are by no means rare events. In July 1979 it was reported that "in recent months officials from thirty developing countries visited the U.S.S.R."[74]

Soviet athletes and sports officials reciprocate with frequent visits to developing countries. In 1979 alone 140 Soviet sports delegations visited many African, Asian, and Latin American countries.[75] While scores did not really matter, the competitions themselves were part of broad propaganda campaigns. The Lenin centenary was marked in Nigeria, Sudan, and Egypt by a "sport week." Soviet sportsmen took part in sports competitions and other activities included in the centenary celebrations.[76] "Sports weeks" were institutionalized in a treaty signed with Egypt, the first such event held in 1970.[77] Similar agreements exist with twenty-five developing countries.[78]

There are frequent visits by Soviet sports officials to developing countries, mostly African, where they invariably express the Soviet Union's support for their stand on various political matters such as apartheid, the struggle for independence and freedom, and so forth.[79] Sports relations between the Soviet Union and Third World countries are almost totally devoid of any sports value. They serve as an instrument to develop political relations between the Soviet Union and these countries, or to develop interest in the Soviet Union and a positive attitude toward Soviet life and achievements.

EXPOSING FOREIGN SPORTSMEN TO OTHER PROPAGANDA INSTRUMENTS

The Soviet Union is very eager to host major international sports events. There are two basic reasons: first, victory comes easier on home ground. The crowds, familiar sports grounds and atmosphere, and one's own referees or functionaries contribute to the triumph of Soviet sportsmen. Second, major international sports events are an excellent opportunity for exposing participants to Soviet propaganda. The next chapter will be devoted to the Soviet effort to acquire the right to host the Olympic games. Presently we shall concentrate on the exposure of foreign sportsmen to Soviet propaganda when visiting the Soviet Union.

The 1973 World Student Games which took place in Moscow are an example of the good use Moscow makes of foreign sportsmen's free time: "A diversified program has been prepared for our guests outside the stadiums. Young people of Moscow's industrial enterprises and educational establishments have 'adopted' each of the delegations of sportsmen. Interesting meetings, concerts, and parties are held at the International Club. The foreign athletes go on excursions around the city and in the Moscow area visiting theaters, cinemas, exhibitions, and parks— everything has been done so that our guests should get better acquainted with the Soviet way of life and spend their spare time usefully."[80]

The same pattern is followed when other international competitions are held in the Soviet Union. Once again sportsmen and officials are asked to share their good impression of Soviet life and successes, which are then amplified by the Soviet mass media. Typical of these statements was the one made by an official of the Finnish delegation to the 1976 figure skating competitions: "Your sponsoring such international competitions helps toward understanding and international friendship in the spirit of the Final Act of the Helsinki Meeting."[81]

Similar statements were made by U.S. mountaineers who visited the Soviet Union in 1977.[82] (The special case of American athletes in the service of Soviet propaganda will be discussed in the chapter dealing with the Olympic boycott.) Organizers of the Moscow Olympic Games did not overlook this particular angle in their preparation for the games. While preparations for athletes' "extracurricular" activity will be described in the chapter dealing with general preparations for the Moscow Olympic Games, let it merely be said at this point that the program for acquainting foreign visitors with Soviet culture, literature, ballet, music, cinematography, painting, theater, and other instruments of Soviet impregnational propaganda, as well as the organization of various political discussions, was prepared several years before the games.[83]

STATEMENTS BY LEADING IOC AND OTHER TOP SPORTS FEDERATIONS' OFFICIALS

Statements by leaders of various international sports federations and IOC officials are frequently used by Soviet propaganda. Such statements (praising the Soviet Union and Soviet life and achievements) were most extensively used during the months preceding the Moscow Olympics and will be dealt with in the chapters dealing with preparations for the games and the boycott. Several examples can be given at this point to illustrate this particular aspect of Soviet sports propaganda.

The statements are usually made during or immediately following a visit to the Soviet Union. The most important are immediately amplified by all

Soviet magazines in foreign languages. *Soviet Union* of January 1977 carried a cluster of such statements by the world's top sports officials, such as Avery Brundage (the IOC president), Lord Killanin (then IOC vice-president), Paul Libaud (France, president of the International Volleyball Federation), and A. Paulen (Netherlands, president of the European Athletic Association), all lavishly praising Soviet sports facilities and Moscow's ability to organize major sports events (that was the period of Moscow's concentrated effort to acquire the right to host the Olympic games), as well as expressing admiration of various achievements, stressing that "quite a few countries could learn something from the U.S.S.R."[84]

Almost all foreign dignitaries attending the 1979 VII Spartakiade of Soviet Peoples, intended to serve as a dress rehearsal for the Moscow Olympics, were interviewed by the Soviet mass media. Their statements reflected not only the usual admiration of Soviet sports achievements and organizational ability but also the overtly political overtones of Soviet sport. IOC vice-president Masayi Kiyokawa of Japan said: "One must fight for peace and protect peace. That thought was clearly expressed by all the achievements of the VII Spartakiade of the Soviet Peoples."[85] The same official was quoted by another Soviet magazine as saying: "We all learned to know the Soviet people better and to strengthen our sports friendship. This is important for further developing the friendly relations between our countries."[86]

The same phenomenon occurred after the 43rd Moscow congress of sports journalists, some of whom were interviewed by *Sport in der UdSSR* about their impressions of the progress of preparations for the Moscow Olympics and the contribution of sports journalists to the idea of peace and friendship among nations.[87] On such occasions, prominence is given to statements by representatives of "sensitive" countries. After the March 1980 Podubniy wrestling competition, Muhammad Jama, leader of the Iranian delegation, made the not unexpected statement on the Moscow Olympics as being a means of furthering peace and cooperation—which was duly reported by the Soviet mass media.[88] The practice of using such statements by foreign sports officials follows the classic propaganda pattern of using foreign sources for making one's point, as a means of enhancing credibility and weight.

ANTI-AMERICAN PROPAGANDA THROUGH SPORT

The United States is one of the most important topics and targets of Soviet sports propaganda. This aspect of Soviet propaganda became its most important characteristic during the months leading up to the Moscow Olympic Games, and will be analyzed in detail in the chapter dealing with the Olympic boycott. Nevertheless, the topic itself has existed since sport became one of Soviet impregnational propaganda's most important vehicles. Ideological and political rivalry between the two superpowers extends to the field of sport. For the Soviet Union it is all-important to beat the Americans—in order to prove that they are better, and to demonstrate that American sport is not only inferior to Soviet sport but also corrupt, cruel, and rotten, just like the entire U.S. social system.

The Lake Placid Winter Olympics served as a pretext for an extensive propaganda campaign scoring American life in general and the organization of the games in particular. Viktor Baklanov's article "Meetings in Lake Placid" criticized the border checks, the cold faces of the people, the behavior of policemen and security personnel, the big cars, the driver of the Soviet delegation's bus, the situation of Soviet emigrants living in New York, the U.S. press, children robbing an old woman, U.S. television, commericials, U.S. business, and more. The article also speaks of the great love many American citizens cherish for the Soviet Union and its sportsmen.[89] Similar articles criticized the housing arrangements, the climate, the food—almost everything connected with the Lake Placid Winter Olympics.

The corruption and cruelty of U.S. Sport is another favorite theme. Many articles paint in dark colors various aspects of American sport and relate them to the general characteristics of American society.[90] Sometimes U.S. audiences are addressed by Soviet sports officials, the incidence of such cases increasing after the Olympic boycott was announced. In March 1980 Sergey Pavlov himself received a delegation of U.S. tourists, explained to them various aspects of Soviet life and sport, described the preparations for the Moscow Olympics, expressed the Soviet view about the proposed boycott of the games, and acquainted the U.S. tourists with several famous Soviet sportsmen, who expressed their eagerness to meet their American rivals.[91]

The most important thing is to beat the Americans on the sports fields. The propaganda value of such victories is described by A. Kiknadze. After elaborating on the victories of Soviet athletes at the 1960 Rome Olympic Games, he describes a meeting with Italian Communist Pierro Richia, who expressed his exhilaration at the Soviet victories over the Americans: "We in Italy were used to seeing the United States as the most powerful, the first, the most skillful country in the world. But what did you do to the Americans? You cannot imagine what went on in the heads of the Italians when they saw the Yankees losing one competition after another to the Soviet team. They are not used to being beaten!"[92]

Notes

1. *Sovetskiy Sport* (25 June 1977).
2. S. Popov and A. Srebnitskiy, *Sport in the USSR: Questions and Answers* (Moscow 1979), quoted by *New York Times* (27 January 1980).
3. A. Himl "Physical Education Is Part of the Ideological Struggle," *Rude Pravo* (Czechoslovakia—12 April 1980).
4. *Sovetskiy Sport* (25 June 1977).
5. Ibid.
6. Ibid.
7. Y. Lomko, "An Excellent Contribution to the Building of Friendship among Nations," *Moscow News* (no. 12 March 1974), p. 16
8. *Otechestven Front* (Bulgaria—25 June 1977).
9. "Sports Exchange: Truth and Invention," interview with Sergey Pavlov, *Literaturnaya Gazeta* (17 March 1976).
10. *Otechestven Front* (26 June 1977).
11. Ibid.
12. Ibid.
13. K. Andrianov, "Olympic Committee for Peace," *Soviet Weekly* (22 July 1976), p. 15.
14. B. Bazunov. "Povest O Sportivnom Diplomate," *Sovetskiy Sport* (28 December 1976). The novel appeared in *Yunost monthly* (nos. 10-11, 1976).
15. Ibid.
16. L. Brezhnev, "To Participants and Guests of the World Student Games—Universiade 73," *Moscow News* (no. 33, 1973), p. 3.
17. Moscow TASS in English 1836 GMT(19 November 1976), *D.R.* (22 November 1977).
18. Jean Meynard, *Sport et Politique* (Paris, 1966, p. 183).
19. *Soviet Weekly* (26 August 1967), p. 14.
20. Ibid.
21. AFP (12 July 1966), quoted by *Le Monde* (13 July 1966, 23 March 1980).
22. Ibid.
23. *Soviet News* (6 November 1973), p. 472.
24. Ibid.
25. TASS in English 1407 GMT (6 November 1973), *D.R.* (7 November 1973).
26. TASS in English 1410 GMT (6 November 1973), *D.R.* (7 November 1973).
27. Anatoly Ivanov, "The Farce," *Moscow News* (no. 48, 1973), p. 15.
28. "Once Again about FIFA Decision," *Moscow News* (no. 4, 1974), p. 16.
29. Ibid.
30. *Süddeutsche Zeitung* (28 March 1980), quoting *Sovetskiy Sport* of "about a year ago."
31. *Sovetskiy Sport* (30 November 1976).
32. Ibid.
33. BTA in English 1430 GMT (9 December 1976), *D.R.* (10 December 1976).
34. *Sovetskiy Sport* (7 December 1976).
35. *Sovetskiy Sport* (8 December 1976).
36. Ibid.
37. Ibid.
38. W. Wassiljew, "So wird es auch sein," *Sport in der UdSSR* (no. 1, 1980), p. 11.

39. *Sovetskiy Sport* (28 October 1979).
40. Ibid.
41. *Sovetskiy Sport* (19 December 1979).
42. *Sovetskiy Sport* (31 December 1979).
43. Ibid.
44. *Literaturnaya Gazeta* (17 March 1976).
45. Ibid.
46. *Sovetskiy Sport* (27 June 1973).
47. TASS in English 1615 GMT (19 February 1976), *D.R.* (20 February 1976).
48. *Sovetskiy Sport* (20 December 1979).
49. Ibid.
50. Ibid.
51. V. Tschernyschev, "Der Weg zum Frieden," *Sport in der UdSSR* (no. 9, 1979), p. 14.
52. *Sovetskiy Sport* (23 December 1979).
53. *Sovetskiy Sport* (2 April 1980).
54. Ibid.
55. *Literaturnaya Gazeta* (23 February 1977).
56. B. Kanyushin, "Leningrad Prepares to Receive Its Guests," *Olympiad* (no. 13, 1977), p. 24.
57. Ibid.
58. *Sovetskiy Sport* (20 December 1976).
59. "Our Olympic Quiz—Finish," *Soviet Woman* (no. 2, 1980), pp. 28-29.
60. W. Awilow, "Mit offenem Herzen," *Sport in der UdSSR* (no. 3, 1980), p. 26.
61. Ibid.
62. *Sport V SSSR* (no. 12, 1972), p. 25.
63. Awilow, p. 26.
64. Ibid., p. 27.
65. *Sovetskiy Sport* (26 June 1977).
66. Awilow, p. 27.
67. Ibid.
68. *Sovetskiy Sport* (15 March 1980).
69. Ibid.
70. *Sovetskiy Sport* (24 June 1977).
71. *Sovetskiy Sport* (2 December 1979).
72. *Sovetskiy Sport* (4 March 1980).
73. Ibid.
74. I. Denissov, "Auf dem Kontinent, der der Zukunft zustrebt," *Sport in der UdSSR* (no. 7, 1979), p. 18.
75. Awilow, p. 27.
76. *Sovetskiy Sport* (14 July 1971).
77. *Sovetskiy Sport* (3 August 1971).
78. Awilow, p. 27.
79. Denissov, p. 19.
80. A. Ivanov, "Everything for Our Guests," *Moscow News* (no. 34, 1973), p. 14.
81. *Moscow News* (no. 51, 1976), p. 16.
82. *Sovetskiy Sport* (7 November 1976).
83. *Otechestven Front* (25 March 1977).
84. "Soviet Sport as Seen by Personalities from Abroad," *Soviet Union* (no. 1, 1971), p. 23.

85. *Sport in der UdSSR* (no. 10, 1979), p. 26.
86. *Olympisches Panorama* (no. 12, 1979), p. 13.
87. "Heute über die Zukunft," *Sport in der UdSSR* (no. 8, 1979), pp. 6-7.
88. *Sovetskiy Sport* (27 March 1980).
89. V. Baklanov, "Meetings in Lake Placid," *Nedelya* (no. 10, 3-9 March 1980), pp. 7-8.
90. Y. Gudkov, "Death in the Ring," *New Times* (no. 14, April 1980).
91. *Sovetskiy Sport* (6 March 1980).
92. A. Kiknadze, *Veter S. Olympa* (Moscow, 1978), p. 90.

5

Moscow Wants to Host the Games

The political and propaganda connotations of the Olympic games in general and of hosting them in particular have always been clear to Soviet authorities. In stating the predominantly sports character of the Olympic games[1] Moscow never ignores their political and ideological aspects: "Since the turn of the century the modern Olympics have developed into a large-scale social movement, whose ideals are cherished by the people of the world."[2] Borrowing favorite concepts such as "progressive forces," "reactionaries," and "struggle" from communist ideology, Soviet phraseology encapsulates the entire Olympic history in one sentence with a high ideological charge: "The history of the Olympic movement is a long struggle between progressives, whose aim is that sport should promote the health of the human race and world peace, and reactionaries who want to use the games in their selfish interest."[3]

Despite the "reactionaries," the Soviet Union regards the Olympic games as a movement which "furthers peace, better understanding and friendship among nations";[4] "promotes an atmosphere of trust and good will,"[5] and so forth. The Soviet Union is aware of the tremendous propaganda potential of hosting the games, both as an opportunity to expose thousands of foreign athletes to other instruments of Soviet propaganda and as a means to facilitate the activity of the Soviet propaganda machine, by focusing world attention on Moscow, creating interest in the Soviet Union and promoting good will toward it.

Soviet authorities started toying with the idea of hosting the Olympic games long before their first unsuccessful application in 1970. Although it is impossible to point to a specific date or step as the beginning of the Soviet effort to acquire the right to host the Olympics, it is plausible to assume that the first feelers were put out during the 59th IOC session, which opened in Moscow on 4 June 1962. During the opening session IOC members were addressed by Leonid Brezhnev (at that time only chairman of the Supreme Soviet Presidium, but thus also titular head of state of the Soviet Union). In his speech Brezhnev did not mention the possibility of holding the games in Moscow. But then, there was no need. The speech was so conceived as to lead smoothly to that obvious conclusion. Observing that the international sports movement promotes "friendship, comradeship, humanism, and broad democracy,"[6] Brezhnev described what the Soviet government was doing for man, stressing the large-scale construction of sports facilities and the large number of already existing stadiums, swimming pools, and similar facilities. Then he dwelled on the "peaceful foreign policy conducted by the Soviet government,"[7] and, comparing it with the IOC activity, he pointed out the common goals and aims, concluding that there was great similarity in the activities of the two. Dwelling on the Soviet contribution to the development of the Olympic movement Brezhnev emphasized: "The Soviet public views the holding of this IOC session in the Soviet Union as a recognition of the contribution of our sportsmen and organizations to the international Olympic movement. This is very gratifying."[8]

There is no official indication, let alone evidence, that IOC officials were sounded out by Soviet authorities about Moscow's chances if it submitted an application to stage the Olympic games in the Soviet Union. Nevertheless, the various points Brezhnev emphasized would soon turn into Moscow's main arguments in making its application. The key phrases "Soviet contribution to the development of the Olympic movement" and "recognition of the contribution of Soviet sportsmen and organizations to the international Olympic movement" were to be repeated time and again in many official Soviet statements related to justifying the grounds of Moscow's suitability for hosting the Olympic games. Seven years later it was officially decided to put forward Moscow's application to host the 1976 Olympics. This decision was ostensibly taken by the Moscow city council and immediately seconded by the Soviet National Olympic Committee.[9] The other candidates who had already submitted their applications were Montreal and Los Angeles.

Moscow's first campaign was rather amateurish, especially compared to its second 1971-74 campaign, a masterpiece of propaganda and manipulation skills. In the earlier campaign Moscow had offered to fly all the gold medal winners home free,[10] while Montreal had promised free travel to and from Montreal and free lodging in the Olympic village—"promises it did not fulfill."[11] Montreal frequently and lavishly hosted the IOC members, a technique Moscow condemned[12] and afterward itself developed to perfection. Another argument presented by Moscow in 1970: no other city could offer such a broad culture program. Konstantin Andrianov, chairman of the Soviet Olympic Committee stressed that the time had come for the Olympic Games to be hosted by a socialist country, that they should not just be the privilege of the West.[13] According to him, "there were no political, economic, or sports reasons why Moscow should not be chosen."[14]

This sentence became a favorite of Moscow officials. They used it repeatedly—in the same form or with insignificant modifications—throughout the 1971-74 campaign. Andrianov himself used it: "We are confident of Moscow's ability to provide excellent facilities for the games. There are no political, economic, or technical reasons that could interfere with the natural course of the Olympic games here."[15] Again, in a 1974 article by Alexandr Gresko, member of the Soviet Olympic Committee: "There are neither political, economic, nor sporting problems that could interfere with the Olympics in Moscow. Moscow city authorities and Soviet sports organizations, supported by the Soviet government, guarantee truly favorable conditions for the Olympics in Moscow."[16] This sentence, only one in a series of many near identical statements issued and used by Moscow, testifies to the coordinated and effectively controlled character of Soviet propaganda generally and the Moscow 1980 campaign in particular.

Back to 1970. Thirty-seven votes (majority of the IOC members) were required to determine the venue of the games. In the first round Los Angeles got 17 votes, Montreal 25, and Moscow 28. In the second round Moscow got the same 28 votes, while Montreal gathered 41, thus obtainig the right to host the 1976 Olympic Games.[17] Moscow angrily accused IOC members of collusion, attributing their voting to the special treatment they were given by Montreal, "despite the fact that Montreal had no rich sports tradition, modern facilities, or people who knew how to organize such an event."[18] The two Western cities were accused of planning deceit—in the event either of them lost on the first ballot. TASS went so far as to define Moscow's rejection as a "blow to the Olympic movement and its ideas."[19]

After the initial angry reaction reason prevailed: "Our sports public accepted the failure in Amsterdam calmly. All in all 43 cities have applied for the right to organize the Olympic Games and only 17 have succeeded in gaining it. Mexico city succeeded in gaining it. Mexico city succeeded on its third attempt. Montreal on its fifth. Buenos Aires has applied unsuccessfully 5 times, and Detroit 7 times."[20] Soviet authorities also learned a valuable lesson. Their application to host the 1976 games was issued in November 1969, only six months before the IOC was to select the location. A decision was made to apply as soon as possible for the right to host the 1980 Olympics and develop a broad and intensive campaign aimed at improving Moscow's chances.

On 19 November 1971, three years before the IOC was to select the location of the 1980 games, V. Promyslov, chairman of the Executive Committee of the Moscow Soviet of Working People's Deputies (Moscow's mayor) sent a letter to Avery Brundage, IOC President, which read in part:

> Considering the genuine desire of the population of the capital of our state to become organizer of the Olympic games and prompted by the aspiration to make a worthy contribution to the development of the modern Olympic movement, the Moscow Soviet of Working People's Deputies has the honor of officially inviting the XXII Olympic Games of 1980 to the city of Moscow. Moscow already disposes of a large number of sports facilities for holding the Olympic games, and possesses all the necessary accommodations for numerous participants and guests of the Olympic games, as well as ample experience in organizing big international sports and cultural events. We hope the International Olympic Committee will favorably regard our invitation and decide to hold the XXII Olympic Games in the city of Moscow.[21]

Three days later, Konstantin Andrianov, chairman of the Soviet Olympic Committee, also addressed a letter to Brundage, which read in part:

> The U.S.S.R. Olympic Committee has considered the offer of the Moscow Soviet of Working Deputies to invite the 22nd Olympic Games of 1980 to Moscow and wholeheartedly supports it. The Soviet capital has everything essential for the successful arrangements of the Olympic games. The U.S.S.R. Olympic Committee is willing to hold in Moscow the IOC session before staging the Olympic games. The government of the U.S.S.R., the city authorities, the U.S.S.R. Olympic Committee, all city public and sports organizations will extend to the organizers of the Olympic games all possible assistance and support. The U.S.S.R. Olympic Committee feels confident, Mr. President, that the members of the International Olympic Committee will favorably consider the invitation of the Moscow Soviet of Working People's Deputies and adopt a positive decision.[22]

The wheels had been set in motion. A big campaign aimed at making Moscow the site of the 1980 Olympic Games began. Several arguments were frequently advanced by Soviet sources as to why Moscow should host the 1980 Olympic Games. (Those arguments differed from the ones stated after Moscow acquired the right to host the games, and shall be analyzed further on.)

An authoritative source is Konstantin Andrianov, chairman of the U.S.S.R. Olympic Committee. On the eve of the fateful October 1974 Vienna session of the IOC he published an article in *Soviet Union* (this monthly is published in 19 languages by the Soviet Union). Stating that IOC members usually take account of a country's political stability, economic potential, and sporting record in making their choice of Olympic venue,"[23] as well as that "in the host country there must be no rules or limitations of a political, racial, religious, or any other kind hindering the normal staging of the competition,"[24] he concentrated on these particular aspects and emphasized: (1) The Supreme Soviet "had given assurances that the games would be successfully staged in accordance with the rules and statutes of the IOC";[25] (2) Moscow was endowed with many first-class sports facilities; (3) Moscow was experienced in holding major competitions. He also stressed the frequent visits of IOC members to Moscow, where they "have been given every opportunity to acquaint themselves with the sporting and general cultural amenities which our capital offers."[26]

Other Soviet sources listed the following arguments: (1) Moscow is a major industrial and cultural center linked with practically all countries by air, water, and rail"; (2) Moscow has experience in holding major sports events; (3) the U.S.S.R. Council of Ministers had adopted an ambitious plan for further developing Moscow's facilities; (4) Moscow's hospitality is well known.[27] V. Promyslov, chairman of the Executive Committee of the Moscow Soviet of the Working People's Deputies, adduced the following: (1) "Moscow has direct rail, water, and air links with many countries. Any point on the planet can be contacted by telephone and radio and the direct satellite television system makes possible live transmissions from Moscow. (2) "We have many organizations with executive authority and they would help to prepare and organize the games." (3) Muscovites are keen on sport. (4) Moscow has 61 open-air stadiums, 1,306 gymnasiums, 31 swimming pools, 7 indoor stadiums, and more than 100 football grounds.[28] Identical phraseology agains leaves no doubt about coordination of the campaign.

Alexandr Gresko, member of the U.S.R.R. Olympic Committee, adds the following arguments: (1) "Soviet sport's contribution to the Olympic movement; (2) keeping the tradition of alternating continents; (3) the IOC's agreement to hold the XXII Olympics in Moscow will provide the opportunity for Soviet sports organizations to contribute even more heavily toward propagation of the ideas and principles of the Olympic movement, and toward the further progress of the Olympic spirit in international sport."[29] Sergey Pavlov also concentrated on the political aspects of the arguments and added: (1) Moscow's policy of detente; (2) Soviet foreign policy, which promotes peace and international understanding; (3) The merits of socialist countries in "promoting world sports and the international Olympic movement."[30]

From the very beginning of its 1971-74 campaign Moscow realized that the IOC in general and its president, Avery Brundage, in particular were not inclined to select Moscow. While already in 1970 Avery Brundage and many other IOC members had visited Moscow to attend the 1970 Sparta-kiade and praised both Moscow's ability to host major international competitions and the development of sport in the Soviet Union,[31] Avery Brundage's anticommunist views were no secret. When Brundage resigned in 1972 Moscow's sigh of relief could be clearly heard. While one source simply accused Brundage of "refusing to adjust to the times" and "impos-ing his views on others by making single-handed decisions,"[32] other sour-ces were much more radical: "Changes have taken place within the IOC as well. Avery Brundage, the senile U.S. millionaire, who had headed the committee for the last twenty years has resigned at long last."[33] Killanin was quoted as saying that he "intended to consult the IOC members more... and make the Olympic movement more democratic."[34]

From the outset Moscow's campaign had two directions: publication of an unusual quantity of articles, booklets, pamphlets, and magazines aimed at familiarizing the world public with its ability to host the games; and applying personal influence on IOC members. Much of the printed mate-rial was aimed at pointing "Moscow's favorable influence" over the IOC:

> There was a time when a policy of restricting the spread of sport was pursued in the IOC, when democracy was disregarded and a distorted view of IOC aims prevailed. Today the IOC is increasingly compelled to heed the voice of the world sports public.... Entry of the Soviet Olympic Committee and national Olympic committees of other socialist countries into the interna-tional Olympic movement has had a favorable effect on its subsequent development, for they vigorously advocate equality of all countries, closer friendship and better understanding among athletes, and broader demo-cracy in the International Olympic Committee and international federations.[35]

Such articles usually concluded by saying that if Moscow was awarded the right to host the 1980 Olympic Games this would contribute to the positive trends taking place "in a spirit of friendship, mutual understanding, and promotion of world peace."[36]

The Soviet campaign reached its climax in 1973. Two events were scheduled for 1973, both expected to improve Moscow's chances: the World Student Games (August 1973), intended to demonstrate once again Moscow's ability to cope with hosting a major international sports event; and the X Olympic Congress, which took place in October 1973 in Varna,

Bulgaria. Thirty-two members of the IOC visited Moscow in 1973 "and commented favorably on the city's Olympic possibilities, noting the high standard of its cultural life, the well-developed rail, air, and waterway system, linking it with practically all the countries of the world, and finally, Moscow's traditional hospitality."[37]

During the August 1973 World Student Games some four thousand athletes from seventy states, foreign guests, and journalists went to Moscow,[38] but no visitor was more important than Lord Killanin, who was singled out for special treatment. The deference he was shown in Moscow was unprecedented. He was honored at the opening ceremony, where he spoke,[39] was received by various Soviet leaders, among them Kosygin, chairman of the Council of Ministers, who "assured the IOC president that in making our bid to hold the Olympics in Moscow our object was to give all parties interested in the games the opportunity to acquaint themselves with the achievements of our state and sportsmen,"[40] and he was repeatedly interviewed by various Soviet newspapers and magazines. In those interviews Lord Killanin invariably expressed his satisfaction with everything he saw in Moscow: "The Universiade is not a dress rehearsal prior to an application by Moscow for the 1980 Olympic Games. But it is also quite natural that while in Moscow, as the IOC president I made inquiries about administrative problems, communications, television, telephone, and other such problems. And I must say that everything I learned has been extremely favorable."[41]

The journalist interviewing Lord Killanin did not miss the opportunity to make a "delicate" hint. Question: "I fully appreciate that as president of the IOC you have to be neutral, but I can only say that all Soviet people, journalists, would be happy to play host to the Olympic games and would do so in a manner worthy of the prestige of the Olympic movement." Answer: "Indeed, I have to be neutral on this, but the only city that has applied thus far for the 1980 Olympics is Moscow. Questionnaires have been sent out to all national Olympic committees, and we will know by March 31 whether any other cities are applying for the Olympic Games and the Winter Olympics. Then we will be in a position to make a decision."[42] In the same interview Lord Killanin expressed admiration for the Soviet space program ("I keep a photograph signed by the late Colonel Gagarin") and satisfaction with his meeting with Kosygin ("I spent almost an hour with him, discussing various sporting problems and some of them in relation to the political situation in sports").

The idea to convene the Olympic Congress was a brilliant move on the part of the Soviet Union. Stressing the "ever increasing role that is being played today by the international assemblies and conferences where constructive ideas for cooperation between countries and peoples are worked out,"[43] the Soviet Union and other socialist countries urged the convocation of the congress after a break of forty-three years."[44] Another source put it as "the first gathering of its kind in nearly forty years."[45] The purpose of convening the congress was stated with what looks like deliberate vagueness by the Soviet Union: "We place big hopes in the congress. We expect it to introduce greater democracy into the International Olympic Committee, and to unite the progressive forces against everything archaic and conservative that still lingers on in world sports."[46]

After the congress, which took place in October 1973 in the Bulgarian Black Sea resort city Varna, its results were heralded by the Soviet Union as a "considerable victory for the democratic trends in the international sports movement."[47] One must distinguish between the apparent and intrinsic results of the Varna congress. On the official side: the congress was attended by 62 IOC membrs, officials from 26 international federations, representatives from 92 national Olympic committees, Olympic champions, observers from many sports associations, and journalists.[48] The five-day congress was addressed by 100 speakers (it required three tons of paper to print the translation of their speeches).[49] The three subjects which were the basis of the discussion concentrated on the modern Olympic movement and prospects for its development, relations between IOC and national and international federations, and the program of the Olympic games.

The discussions were summed up in two documents: an appeal to sportsmen and a declaration. "Sportsmen of the whole world," the appeal read, "we call on you to remember that Olympic games are not only for the Olympians (a phrase which later became one of the slogans of the Moscow-80 Committee, and which leaves little doubt as to the identity of the initiator of the appeal), they spread the spirit and principles of friendly games to the youth of the world, thus creating international trust and good will leading to peace in the world."[50] The declaration, unanimously adopted, "embraces all problems which should be patiently and unswervingly dealt with in the future by the joint efforts of the IOC, national Olympic committees, and international federations, the three leading forces of world and Olympic sport."[51] In addition, "the congress revealed the unpopularity of proposals to abolish the traditional Olympic ritual of raising flags and playing the national anthems of the winners' countries. Many speakers emphasized the importance of this ceremony for the patriotic upbringing of sportsmen."[52]

The real purpose of the congress was to improve Moscow's chances of hosting the Olympic games. First of all it was intended to demonstrate the extent of Moscow's influence on a large majority of the Olympic movement members. Varna was an appropriate stage for this demonstration, which hardly failed to impress IOC members. On the more practical side, four additional members were elected to the IOC: Keba M'Baye (Senegal), Ashiwini Kumar (India), Manuel Gonzáles Guerra (Cuba), and Roy Anthony Bridge (Jamaica), thus increasing IOC membership to seventy-eight.[53] Their election considerably improved Moscow's chances. But this was not all. At one of the sittings Lord Killanin announced that he had received a message from the Supreme Soviet Presidium endorsing Moscow's application to stage the 1980 Olympic Games. The letter was dated 24 September 1973 and signed by Presidium vice-president M. Yasnov:

> In connection with the invitation sent to the International Olympic Committee by the Executive Committee of the Moscow City Soviet of Working People's Deputies requesting that the XXII Olympic Games in 1980 be held in the city of Moscow, the Presidium of the Supreme Soviet of the Union of the Soviet Socialist Republics hereby informs you that it completely approves and supports this invitation. All necessary assistance and support will be extended to the authorities of the city of Moscow, the Olympic Committee of the U.S.S.R., and all sports organizations of the Soviet Union to ensure the successful staging of the XXII Olympic Games in keeping with the rules and regulations of the International Olympic Committee.[54]

One cannot help but admire the careful planning and effective execution of the 1971-74 campaign. What was done in 1973 amounts to a brilliantly executed strategic operation. First, there was an incredible quantity of printed material, films, and so forth, propagating Moscow's advantages. Then frequent visits to Moscow by IOC members (each visit including lavish receptions, tours, etc.); organization of the Universiade-73 Games (once again attended by Killanin and many other IOC members) as a visual demonstration of Moscow's organizational ability; the Varna Congress, which convened weeks after the Student Games; election of pro-Soviet members to the IOC; and finally the Supreme Soviet letter—all conceivable means were utilized to "soften up" the IOC before the major attack. The Varna Congress and subsequent 74th IOC session which also took place there were apparently used to individually sound out all attending IOC members. Moscow calculated that its chances were excellent (obtaining at least verbal commitment from enough IOC members), because both the tone of its campaign and its practical moves changed after Varna. It all attested to great confidence and certainty of obtaining the right to host the games.

The most important (and revealing) practical step was creation of the Moscow-80 Preparatory Committee, almost immediately after Varna. The committee was set up in January 1974 on the initiative of the U.S.S.R. Committee on Sport and Physical Culture. Its members were the secretaries of the All-Union Central Committee of Trade Unions; the secretaries of the Komsomol Central Committee; the executives of the Moscow Soviet; deputy ministers of Culture, Civil Aviation, Communications, and Radio Industry; vice-chairmen of the State Committees on Cinematography, Television and Radio; and executives from state and public organizations and agencies involved in preparing and hosting the games.[55] Fifteen of the committee's members held the rank of deputy U.S.S.R. ministers,[56] which speaks eloquently of its importance.

Committee meetings were usually chaired by N.A. Mikhaylov, first secretary of the Komsomol Central Committee.[57] They took place every month and dealt with subjects such as construction of new sports and facilities and the Olympic village (a fact which demonstrated the self-confidence of Soviet sports authorities), transportation facilities for competitors and officials, TV transmission from the Olympic arenas, service for tourists, and preparation of an exhibition, album, and film to be presented at the October 1974 IOC Vienna session.[58] In its tenth-month existence the committee was intensely active. It published a regular bulletin, translated into five languages, which was sent out to all IOC members, international federations, news agencies, and major newspapers throughout the world.[59] It prepared a film, "Welcome to Moscow," which was dubbed in many foreign languages, released several months before the Vienna IOC session, and shown at the session itself.[60] An exhibition, "Moscow Welcomes Olympics-80," was also prepared and put on by the committee.[61]

The committee also frequently invited foreign journalists to Moscow, to acquaint them with preparations. In 1974 a group of twenty-four sports journalists from fifteen countries, headed by F. Taylor, president of the International Sporting Press Association, and B. Naidoo, secretary general of the association, visited the Soviet Union from June 5 to 15 at the invitation of the U.S.S.R. Committee on Physical Culture and Sport. They were acquainted with Moscow's sports facilities, toured the country, met famous Soviet sportsmen, and were received by prominent leaders.[62] Frank Taylor repaid his hosts immediately. In an article entitled "No One Can Doubt That Moscow Is Ready to Stage The Games,"[63] he quotes two delegation members on their impressions: Ian Wooldridge (Great Britain); "From what I have seen I could write a book. For the present I shall content myself by saying it was absolutely fantastic."[64] George Hanson (Canada): "This is a dream come true."[65] Several influential IOC members (in addition to Lord Killanin) were singled out for special treatment. One of them was Willi Daume, chairman of the Organizational Committee for the XX Olympic Games. Sergey Pavlov himself on several occasions had exceptionally kind words for Daume: "In particular, we have had a host of useful advice from Mr. Willi Daume, chairman of the Organizational

Committee for the XX Summer Olympic Games, who was our guest a short time ago."[66]

The same issue of *Moscow News* which carried Pavlov's interview also carried pictures of scale models of the Olympic village, the indoor stadiums and swimming pools, etc. (all of which were indeed subsequently constructed!)—another demonstration of Moscow's confidence after Varna. This confidence permeated all pamphlets, interviews, and booklets published in 1974. It is very difficult to avoid the conclusion that this confidence was based on solid guarantees obtained in Varna. So overt and unmitigated was this confidence that in many interviews Soviet sports officials began to speak of the Moscow Olympics as a fact.

In his *Moscow News* interview Pavlov was asked questions such as: "How do you see the 1980 Olympics? In what way will they differ from previous ones? What does Moscow plan to build for the games? How will Moscow receive the tourists? How will they reach our capital and where will they stay?"[67] Only seldom did Pavlov use the conditional "if." The same issue of *Moscow News* carried short interviews with sixteen presidents and high officials of Soviet sports federations. They were asked two questions: "Do you think that your federation has enough experience to organize competitions for the Olympics?" and "Where are the competitions for the 1980 games to be held?"[68] With total certainty and confidence, no qualifications and in a matter-of-fact manner, they explained where the various competitions of the 1980 Olympics would take place, what facilities were to be used, and so forth—all this months before the IOC was supposed to decide the site of the games.

Still, in the summer of 1974, in a last effort to avoid any unpleasant surprises, the Supreme Soviet sent another letter to the IOC, inviting all eighty IOC members to Moscow as guests of the government in order to provide a first-hand impression of Moscow's ability to host the games.[69] Many came, and were repeatedly interviewed by Soviet journalists. *Moscow News*[70] carried a cluster of reactions titled "They Are in Favor of Moscow." Lord Killanin, Willi Daume, Herman van Karnebeek, Paul Libaud, and others expressed their opinion on Moscow's ability to host international events and its chances of being selected for the 1980 Olympics. Several months before the IOC Vienna session, which was to determine the venue of the games, many IOC leaders had no qualms about publicly committing themselves. Paul Libaud: "There is no doubt about the nomination of Moscow as host to the 1980 Olympics." Herman van Karnebeek: "I'd like to wish Moscow every success in holding all the competitions.... I am full of admiration for your sports facilities and your hospitality." Willi Daume: "There is a well-grounded opinion within the IOC that the U.S.S.R. has contributed greatly toward developing the

Olympic movement. The contribution has been so considerable that your capital has won the right to organize the Olympic games. Moscow has a good chance of becoming the capital selected for the 1980 Olympics. I am quite optimistic on that score."

Finally Lord Killanin himself, who less than a year earlier in another interview[71] had spoken of the "need to be neutral" (as IOC president) and of not yet being in a "position to make a decision," was rather outspoken this time: "Moscow is a quite suitable place for holding the Olympic games. There can be no doubt that it has at its disposal all the necessary facilities for successfully organizing them.... One can say outright that Moscow is a city better equipped with modern sports facilities than most others. If it should become host of the 1980 Olympics it will organize the games extremely well and in complete accord with the IOC statute and rules." Moscow's confidence was well founded. Several days before the October 1974 IOC session in Vienna the members of the Moscow-80 Preparatory Committee met for the last time. They reviewed their activity during the past months, the preparations which had been made so far, and the cultural program prepared for the Olympic Games participants. They approved of the exhibition prepared for the IOC Vienna session and wished success to the Soviet delegation for the session, which was to be headed by Sergey Pavlov and Vladimir Promyslov, chairman of the Executive Committee of the Moscow Soviet of Working People's Deputies.[72] In Vienna, the decision fell in the morning hours of 23 October 1974.

The Soviet propaganda campaign related to the XXII Moscow Olympic Games consisted of four separate campaigns: (1) Moscow's effort to acquire the right to host the games—1971-74; (2) the "preparations" campaign of 1975-80—construction of facilities and housing for the games, preparation of a cultural program, and various other areas; (3) the January-June 1980 "Olympic boycott" campaign; (4) "the games"—the propaganda campaign surrounding the actual games and their immediate aftermath. Three of these campaigns have several common denominators and are interconnected parts of the "Moscow Olympic Games" campaign. The fourth was a sudden, unexpected, erratic, unplanned and —at least in the beginning—defensive campaign.

The three interconnected parts of the "Moscow Olympic Games" campaign were of course "the effort," "the preparations," and "the games." The exception—the "Olympic boycott" campaign. The first three campaigns were conceived and planned by the Soviet propaganda apparatus. Their goals, instruments, potential audience, and themes were clearly defined long before the campaigns started. Their results were anticipated and even programmed. All three were initiated by Moscow and executed with a determination which attested to the self-assurance of Moscow's propaganda apparatus.

The propaganda campaign connected with the Olympic boycott was different. First, it was a countercampaign, which Moscow was compelled to organize swiftly and execute—at first—hectically and erratically. Not only was it unexpected, it was unwanted, abhorrent, and paralyzing, in that it jeopardized the results of the "effort" and "preparations" campaigns and the very existence of the Moscow Olympic Games. It was one of the few propaganda campaigns in which Moscow found itself on the defensive, the initiative having been taken elsewhere. Planning, one of the most important elements of propaganda, was nonexistent in the beginning and very difficult afterward, for Moscow often found itself surprised as circumstances changed daily and developments came tumbling upon each other. The instruments, techniques, and themes were frequently to be changed and efforts dispersed in several directions.

The "effort" campaign was a different story. This was the easiest campaign. Its audience was clearly defined and rather limited: IOC members, leaders of the varous international sports federations, and other top officials in the world of sports. In short, anyone who had anything to do with selecting the Olympic site or who influenced the decision. There was only one goal: to acquire the right to host the XXII Olympic Games. The limited audience and single goal dictated the character of the campaign. Only a few selected instruments were brought into play, but their effectiveness was high. The small and highly specialized audience made it possible to apply a somewhat "personal" touch, untypical of other propaganda campaigns. At some point during the campaign Moscow apparently became assured of success, which permitted the Soviet propaganda apparatus simultaneously to conclude this campaign in a highly confident tone and begin preparation of the next campaign. It was one of the few propaganda campaigns whose clearly defined final goal was eventually achieved. Although it is impossible to isolate and evaluate the share of propaganda in achieving the campaign's final goal—acquiring the right to host the games—from related instruments (personal pressure, manipulation) it can safely be assumed that although propaganda was not the only instrument used, its share in the success was substantial.

Notes

1. "Sport in the World Today," interview with Konstantin Andrianov, president of the Soviet Olympic Committee, *Soviet Union* (no. 7, 1972), p.5.
2. Ibid.
3. Ibid.
4. "Die soziale Verantwortung des Sports," interview with Sergey Pavlov. In V. Steinbach, *Moskau '80: Beitrag zur Olympische Geschichte* (Moscow, 1980).

5. S. Pavlov, "Our Conception of the Olympic Ideas," *Sputnik* (no. 5,1980), p. 42.
6. A. Starodub, *Do Vstrechi V Moskve* (Moscow, 1978), p. 4.
7. Ibid., pp. 43-44.
8. Ibid.
9. Ibid., p. 45.
10. *New York Times* (8 April 1970).
11. Starodub, pp. 45-46.
12. Ibid.
13. *New York Times* (8 April 1970).
14. Ibid.
15. "Sport in the World Today," p. 5.
16. A. Gresko, "Moscow: Candidate for Olympics-80," special supplement to *Moscow News* (no. 21, 1974), p. 45.
17. Starodub, p. 45.
18. Ibid., p. 46.
19. *New York Times* (13 May 1970).
20. Starodub, p. 47.
21. Special supplement to *Moscow News* (no. 40, 1974), p. 1.
22. Ibid.
23. K. Andrianov, "Moscow Prepares to Host the Olympic Games," *Soviet Union* (no. 10, 1974), p. 21.
24. Ibid.
25. Ibid.
26. Ibid.
27. A. Pegov, secretary of the Moscow City Soviet Executive Committee, "Moscow 1980 Olympics," special supplement to *Moscow News* (no. 31, 1972), p. 6.
28. V. Promyslov, "Moscow Invites Olympics-80," *Moscow News* (no. 21, 1974), p. 3.
29. Gresko, p. 2.
30. "Moscow's Olympic Guarantees," interview with Sergey Pavlov, special supplement to *Moscow News* (no. 40, 1974), p. 2.
31. "Soviet Sport as Seen by Personalities from Abroad," *Soviet Union* (no. 1, 1971), p. 23.
32. Starodub, p. 39.
33. A. Starodub and Y. Khromov, "Triumph of Soviet Sport at the 20th Olympic Games," *Moscow News* (no. 37, 1972), p. 14.
34. Ibid.   .
35. "Sport in the World Today," p. 5.
36. Ibid.
37. Interview with Pavlov, Special supplement to *Moscow News* (no. 40, 1974), p. 2.
38. *Moscow News* (no. 34, 1973), p. 15.
39. Ibid.
40. Andrianov, p. 21.
41. "Excellent Facilities for Everyone," interview with Lord Killanin, *Moscow News* (no. 34, 1973), p. 15.
42. Ibid.
43. B. Bazunov, "For the Sake of the Olympics," *Soviet Union* (no. 12, 1973), p. 54.

44. Ibid.
45. "Sport in the World Today," p. 5.
46. Ibid.
47. Gresko, p. 21.
48. Bazunov, p. 54.
49. Ibid.
50. Ibid.
51. Ibid.
52. G. Khachkovanyan, "IOC Congress and Session: A Time of Change," *Moscow News* (no. 41, 1973), p. 15.
53. Bazunov, p. 54.
54. Special supplement to *Moscow News* (no. 40, 1974), p. 1.
55. "Moscow's Olympic Guarantees," p. 1.
56. Gresko, p. 2.
57. *Otechestven Front* (Bulgaria—25 June 1977).
58. Gresko, p. 2.
59. "Moscow's Olympic Guarantees," p. 2.
60. Ibid.
61. Ibid.
62. Ibid.
63. F. Taylor,"No One Can Doubt that Moscow Is Ready to Stage the Games," *Moscow News* (no. 40, 1974), pp. 6-7.
64. Ibid., p. 6.
65. Ibid.
66. "Moscow's Olympic Guarantees," p. 2.
67. Ibid.
68. *Moscow News* (no. 40, 1974), pp. 4-5.
69. *Soviet Union* (no. 5, 1974), p. 5.
70. *Moscow News* (no. 21, 1974), p. 7.
71. "Excellent Facilities," p. 15.
72. "A Meeting of the Moscow-80 Preparatory Committee," special supplement to *Moscow News* (no. 40, 1974), p. 6.

6

The Greatest Ever!

The IOC decision to select Moscow as the venue of the XXII Olympic Games was enthusiastically greeted by the entire Soviet mass media. Soviet journalists and officials hailed the decision as a "recognition not only of Soviet merits, but also of those of all socialist countries, which have made so great a contribution to the development of the Olympic movement,"[1] a result of the U.S.S.R.'s contribution to the international sports movement," and the "existence of suitable sports facilities and specialists."[2] Other sources stressed the unusual number of medals and victories won by Soviet athletes, Moscow's being the "capital of a sport-loving country," "Moscow's cultural traditions," and "Moscow's being a clean and green city"[3] as reasons for awarding Moscow the right to host the 1980 Olympic Games. Most stressed was that the IOC decision was "clear evidence of the effectiveness of the Soviet government's policy of developing international links, broadening cooperation, relaxing tension, and promoting peace."[4] For Moscow, holding the games in a socialist state was to usher in a new and glorious era in the history of the Olympic movement:

> The fact that Moscow has been entitled to stage the 1980 Olympic Games is the result of the purposeful, consistent, and peaceful policy pursued by the Soviet Union, a bulwark of peace, democracy, and social progress, and an expression of the respect for the great Soviet achievements in physical education and sport. The fact that the next Olympic games are to be held for

the first time in a socialist state, which does not merely proclaim the Olympic ideals but also implements them and whose Constitution contains a clause on the development of physical culture and sport, constitutes a qualitatively new phase in the Olympic movement and a prominent landmark in the history of the Olympic games.[5]

As for the character of the Moscow Olympics:

> We don't only consider the Olympic games the biggest international sports meet which happens to be held every four years. We also value the games because they give people from practically all over the world a splendid opportunity to get together, mingle, make contacts, and help strengthen relations among people of different political views, different ways of life, and different beliefs. And all that greatly contributes to strengthening peace, to developing international understanding and friendship. We want the Moscow Olympics to be a vivid and colorful festival of young people from all countries. We hope it will give new impulse to the Olympic movement. We hope that the 1980 Olympics will not only be remembered as part of Olympic history, but will remain forever in the hearts of millions of people around the world. The Soviet people's desire for friendship and cooperation among nations echoes the spirit of the Olympic rules. We appreciate that the Olympic games help strengthen peace. It is in this that we see their supreme goal.[6]

By interpreting the IOC decision as a recognition of the Soviet Union's peaceful foreign policy and its contribution to the democratization of the Olympic movement, considering it recognition of the contribution of all socialist countries to the development of the Olympic movement, and declaring the fact of the games being held for the first time on socialist territory as a qualitatively new stage in the Olympic movement, Moscow was defining the main themes of its "preparations" propaganda campaign. Above all there was the awareness that holding the games on the territory of the first socialist state was a unique event of far-reaching political and ideological significance, which had to be turned into the ultimate symbol of world acceptance. The event had to be used to demonstrate the advantages of the Soviet political and socioeconomic system, enhance the Soviet Union's international prestige, consolidate its international status as a leading superpower, and develop a worldwide propaganda campaign in connection with preparations for the games to show the Soviet Union's superiority in every area. In short, the 1980 XXII Moscow Olympic Games had to be the greatest ever!

Under IOC rules the Olympic campaign (commercial contracts, publicity) should only begin once the previous Olympic games have ended.[7] But Moscow was not prepared to wait until August 1976. In May 1975 the organizing committee Olympiade-80 was created.[8] The composition of the committee (as chairman I. Novikov, deputy premier; A. Safonov, deputy minister of health; S. Nikitin, chairman of the State Administration for Foreign Tourism; K. Simonov, CPSU Central Committee Transportation and Communications department head; V. Kukharskiy, deputy minister of culture; L. Tolkunov, Novosti's director general; I. Rudoi, CPSU Central Committee Propaganda Department instructor; and other high officials)[9] left no doubt about the importance attached to it by the Soviet government. It also indicated the direction of the forthcoming preparations for the games: construction, data processing, planning of cultural events, medical services, transportation and communications, tourism, and of course propaganda.

Officially, Olympiade-80's task was to supervise preparations for the games, coordinate the activity of the various ministries and organizations, and maintain contact with the IOC and the national federations and committees on all matters related to the games.[10] The committee created a presidium, which was to oversee day-to-day administration, and an executive committee.[11] An apparat was also created. In the beginning it had 30 members, by the end of 1975 it had 100, and in 1976 more than 200 members.[12] In 1979 the apparat numbered 400 members. It was divided into 19 commissions, which in 1978 alone held 154 meetings and dealt with 265 issues.[13] The Olympiade-80 committee convened once a month and reported to the Council of Ministers and sometimes to Brezhnev personally.[14] Olympiade-80 was not the only organ in charge of supervising preparations for the games. The Moscow City Soviet established a city commission on preparations for the Olympic games. Its meetings were chaired by Viktor Grishin, first secretary of the CPSU Moscow City Committee and CPSU Politburo member, one of the most powerful men in the Soviet Union.[15] The other Olympic cities—Leningrad, Kiev, Minsk, and Tallin established similar commissions. Their representatives were members of the Olympiade-80 committee, so that complete coordination was ensured.

Preparation of the propaganda campaign was one of the most important aspects of the Olympiade-80 activities. Close relations were promptly established with two of Soviet propaganda's main agencies: Novosti, "which has many publications in foreign languages,"[16] and the Union of the Soviet Societies for Friendship with Foreign Countries, which "has its own channels and means of propaganda."[17] Another related decision of Olympiade-80 was to utilize not only existing means of propaganda (press, radio, cinematography, exhibitions), but to establish its own instruments. In the summer of 1975 the committee started publishing the monthly *Olympiade-80* and *Olympic Panorama*, which appeared four times a year. Both magazines were published in Russian, German, French, English, and

Spanish and were distributed free to newspaper editorial boards, television and radio stations, IOC, national and international sports organizations, tourist agencies, friendship societies—"to inform the world public on the progress of preparations."[18] Both publications were of very high quality— glossy paper, color pictures, extravagant layout—*Olympic Panorama* being printed in Japan. Despite the fact that they were distributed free, they were of much better quality than that of regular Soviet magazines in foreign languages. Those publications along with other instruments of the 1974-80 campaign will be discussed later in this chapter.

In one of the numerous books published during the "preparations" campaign and dealing with the Olympic games, their history, and preparations for the Moscow Olympics—*Geroi Olympiyskikh Bataly* (Heroes of the Olympic battles)—the author, Valeriy Steinbach, says of the 1936 Berlin Olympics that in order to surpass all previous games Nazi Germany's Ministries of Foreign Affairs and Propaganda were put in charge of preparations for the games, and a special effort was made to attract as many foreign tourists as possible.[19] In this area (and several others related to impregnational propaganda) the Soviet Union surpassed Nazi Germany. Not only did the Olympiade-80 committee include a deputy premier, several deputy ministers, high party and state officials, and leading propagandists, but in various stages of the "preparations" campaign and throughout the "boycott" campaign, the entire party and state leadership had to share the propaganda burden.

INSTRUMENTS

The list of propaganda vehicles utilized during the "preparations" campaign is long. While some were "classic," utilized by all countries in all propaganda compaigns, some were uncommon and created for that specific propaganda campaign. Some may disagree with the list presented here (it even includes a soft drink as an instrument of propaganda), but *anything* can be used as a propaganda instrument, as long as it stirs certain thoughts in the direction foreseen by the propaganda source.

Radio

Radio is listed first, not because it was the most important instrument of the "preparations" campaign, but because it is the basic instrument of international propaganda. The Soviet propaganda apparatus did not have to make any special preparations to utilize Soviet broadcasts in foreign languages throughout the "preparations" campaign. The Soviet Union has no peer in its foreign languages broadcasting. The number of foreign languages in which Moscow broadcasts changes from time to time, therefore a fixed number can only be correct for the date of its publication. A BBC report on Soviet foreign language broadcasts (no. 162/1979) published in October 1979 lists more than 500 hours a day of Soviet broadcasts in more than 100 languages. This gives a fair idea of the scope of Soviet radio propaganda in foreign languages. All Moscow had to do was introduce more programs related to the Olympic games in general and preparations for the Moscow Olympics in particular. These programs were entitled "Olympic Corner," "Olympic News," "Olympic Moscow," and so forth. Radio Moscow and Radio Peace and Progress conducted Olympic quizzes—also done by Soviet magazines in foreign languages—related to Olympic history, Soviet history and geography, etc. Since "questions and answers" are an integral part of almost every Soviet foreign language broadcast (providing, among other things, data on listeners' preferences, interests, background) listeners' questions were also utilized to provide additional information about the Olympic preparations.

Special preparations were made for shortwave radio operators. *Olympiade-80* reported that Soviet shortwave radio operators, who maintain links with 150 countries,[20] would carry special broadcasts from each Soviet city in which Olympic competitions were to take place. Every foreign shortwave radio operator who was merely to *hear* these broadcasts (and send a postcard to Soviet authorities), was to receive "a special diploma and could call himself a participant in the Olympic games."[21] According to this source, the "shortwave campaign" was expected to contribute to peace and the triumph of Olympic ideas. "A shortwave operator once said: If on the planet there were only shortwave radio operators, the road to peace would be as broad as the planet itself. This is perhaps a bit bold, but still, Soviet shortwave radio operators are doing everything in their power so that the Olympic ideals triumph in their sports area."[22]

Press

One must distinguish between the extensive net of Soviet magazines and newspapers in foreign languages that already existed, and those especially created during the "preparations" campaign. The quantity of Soviet publications in foreign languages and the number of languages in which they are published are awesome. Weeklies and monthlies such as *Soviet Union* (nineteen languages), *Soviet Woman* (fourteen languages), *Sputnik* (seven languages), *Moscow News* (seven languages), *Sport in the USSR* (six languages), *New Times* (six languages), *XXth Century and Peace* (five languages), and many others, introduced special sections or columns dealing with preparations for the Olympic games. Numerous sports officials, Olympiade-80 members, and party and state officials were repeatedly interviewed, the interviews dealing not only with the preparations but also with the contribution of the Moscow Olympic Games to peace and friendship, Soviet successes in various areas, and related subjects. Some magazines such as *Soviet Woman* and *Soviet Union* conducted quizzes and contests (to be discussed later as a separate instrument of propaganda) aimed at developing further interest in Soviet life and the Moscow Olympics.

Publications of the numerous friendship societies throughout the world such as *Sowijet Union Heute* (published by the press bureau of the Soviet Embassy in Vienna) also introduced special sections dealing with the Olympic games and columns of "questions and answers" related to preparations for the Olympics, "Olympic miscellania and curiosities," and so forth. [23]

All this was obviously considered insufficient, because special "Olympic" publications were introduced, the two most formidable being *Olympic Panorama* and *Olympiade-80*. The latter appeared every month in five languages and carried information on the progress of preparations, Olympic history, extensive tourist information, data on Soviet cities and historic sites, and conducted frequent quizzes and contests. *Olympic Panorama* appeared every four months, each issue being devoted to a special topic (progress of construction, the 1979 Spartakiade, tourism), in addition to current information on Olympic preparations. Both magazines were high-quality editions distributed free of charge to radio and TV stations, newspaper editorial boards, friendship societies, and so forth.[24]

Just as Soviet publications in foreign languages were used for Olympic propaganda, the "Olympic" publications were used for general impregnational propaganda not always related to the Moscow Olympics. They frequently carried information on Soviet life, industrial and cultural achievements, Soviet history, and similar topics. Soviet sources repeatedly expressed the hope that the "Olympic" publications would help foreign mass media to "better inform their readers, listeners, and audience about preparations for the Moscow Olympics."[25] To facilitate implementation of this task a special effort was made to establish contacts with foreign journalists. Moscow expected 3,000 journalists, 400 photographers, and 800 radio and TV commentators for the games.[26] Contact with many of them was established during the 1974-80 "preparations" campaign. This was done in several ways: by holding press conferences in the Soviet Union and abroad, and by inviting hundreds of foreign journalists to the Soviet Union at the expense of the Olympiade-80 committee. In 1978 alone the Olympiade-80 committee held twenty press conferences for foreign journalists in Moscow, New York, Paris, Athens, Prague, Algiers, and other cities, at which information on the progress of preparations was imparted.[27] In July 1979 it was reported that "fifty big international press conferences have been held."[28]

Entire groups of foreign journalists from many countries were brought to Moscow and acquainted both with the Olympic preparations and Soviet life. In the fall of 1979 a group of more than 20 West German journalists came to the Soviet Union and toured the various Olympic sites. Subsequently several of them (Wolfgang Gernar, *Merkur*, Munich; Klaus Peter Andorka, *Sonntag Aktuell*, Stuttgart, and others) were interviewed by *Olympiade-80*. All expressed great enthusiasm, paid compliments to the organizing committee, and stated their conviction that the "Moscow Olympic Games would make a worthy contribution to strenghtening peace and friendship among nations."[30] They were not the only ones. In 1978 more than 400 foreign journalists visited the Soviet Union at the invitation of the Olympiade-80 organizing committee.[31]

The 43rd congress of the International Association of Sports Journalists (AIPS), which took place in Moscow, was an appropriate opportunity to reach even more journalists. The congress took place under the Moscow Olympics motto "For Peace and Friendship," and was attended by sport journalists from 49 countries. They were addressed by several Soviet sports and state officials and made the inevitable tour of the Olympic sites.[32] Subsequently the journalists expressed admiration for the progress of Olympic preparations, construction of Olympic sites, Soviet life, and even Moscow's air.[33] *Sport in the USSR* devoted two pages to the AIPS congress. Several foreign journalists were asked three questions: (1) How do you evaluate the achievements of the 43rd AIPS congress? (2) What can you say about preparations for the Moscow Olympic Games? (3) What is your opinion of the role and responsibility of sports journalists in propagating the ideas of peace and friendship among nations?[34]

The journalists interviewed (from Italy, the United States, India, Venezuela, among others) lavishly praised the progress of Olympic preparations and offered their thoughts on the role of sports journalists in furthering peace and friendship. The Moscow Olympic Games were always mentioned in this context. AIPS president Enrico Crespi (Italy) was reported as saying: "The motto of the 43rd AIPS congress was 'For Peace and Friendship.' To put it in few words—our task is to rally millions of people around this slogan."[35] Another prominent figure—Juan Antonio Saramanch of Spain—who was interviewed by *Olympiade-80* not only defined the Moscow Olympic Games as "the greatest ever" (a favorite theme of the "preparations" campaign to be discussed later), but also spoke of the Moscow Olympics as "the first twenty-first-century games."[36] A final word about foreign journalists as instruments of Soviet propaganda: Soviet magazines in foreign languages frequently expressed amazement at foreign journalists' "ignorance of Soviet life," emphasizing that their visits to the Soviet Union were also used to enlight them on "various aspects of Soviet society and life."[37]

Books

This is another instrument of propaganda which did not require special preparations. Mezhdunarodnaya Kniga, the huge Soviet conglomerate in charge of publishing and distributing Soviet books, photo albums, and records abroad has more than 1,000 outlets in 133 countries.[38] Thus marketing books related to the Moscow Olympic Games was no major problem. A large number of high-quality photo albums and books (of unusually superior technical quality for the Soviet Union) related to the Olympic games were published in foreign languages between 1974 and 1980. Many (*Moscow: Olympic City, Olympic Moscow*) hailed not only preparations for the Olympic games but also the beauty of Moscow, achievements of the Soviet people, various aspects of Soviet history, and so forth. Typical of this genre was *Olympiastadt Moskau*. The book consists of photographs depicting achievements of Soviet sportsmen, the Olympic construction sites, and scenes of Moscow, as well as facts about the Soviet capital and life in the Soviet Union. In addition to sports information, the book informs readers that Moscow is a great scientific center,[39] an exemplary communist city,[40] 100,000 new apartments and 20 schools are built annually in Moscow,[41] small European states such as Monaco, Andorra, Liechtenstein, San Marino, and the Vatican can all be accommodated together within Moscow's boundaries,[42] 3,000 TV sets are produced daily in Moscow,[43] the city's industrial plants export their production to 70 countries,[44] 15-20 apartments per 1,000 citizens are built annually—"more than any other capital in the world,"[45] the city's water is of superior quality,[46] the city has more green areas per inhabitant than any other European capital,[47] the city has a great amount of medical doctors and ambulances [48] (obviously considered reassuring information for foreign tourists), the city publishes 34 sports magazines and newspapers with a general circulation of 7 million copies[49]—*Soviet Sport* with a daily circulation of 3.9 million copies being the most popular sports newspaper in the world. No other city in the world has won so many Olympic medals (146 gold, 153 silver, and 135 bronze),[50] and so forth. The book also expresses the hope that the forthcoming Olympic games "will provide Moscow with the opportunity of showing its progress and achievements in social development, science, spiritual life, and sport."[51] Similar books were published in many foreign languages.

To boost sales, sports books were exhibited at Moscow's two international book fairs, in 1977 and 1979. After the 1977 fair "twenty foreign firms expressed interest, after visiting the Olympic Committee's stall, in publishing and distributing in their territory journals, booklets, and other printed material produced by the Moscow Olympics Organizing Committee."[52] During the 1979 fair Fizkultura i Sport, the major Soviet sports publishing house, signed fifty contracts for translating Soviet sports books, mostly on Olympic themes, into foreign languages.[53]

Television

Television has not yet been developed as an effective instrument of international propaganda. Despite its great potential as a vehicle of propaganda, television still remains mostly an instrument of domestic propaganda. Direct telecasting to foreign lands is virtually impossible without permission from the country to which the telecast is beamed. Soviet television played a small role during the "preparations" campaign. Nevertheless, Moscow tied the rights of telecasting the Olympic games to the condition that the station purchasing the rights also agreed to show films on Soviet life and culture. This provision was included in the agreement Olympiade-80 signed with NBC.[54] It was pointed out that "this will facilitate the acquaintance of the American people with Soviet culture" and "strengthen relations between the two peoples."[55]

Special preparations were made to ensure effective use of the medium during the games. They included expansion and modernization of the Ostankino television and radio complex,[56] special training of cameramen and technicians,[57] and so forth. In 1979 it was estimated that 2 billion people, "500 million more than in 1976," were going to watch the Moscow Olympics on television.[58]

Films

Shortly after it was established the Olympiade-80 Committee began to produce documentry, historic, and popular scientific films "aimed at propagating the Moscow Olympic Games."[59] These films were reported to have been "willingly shown by foreign TV and film companies."[60] While sport and Olympic preparations were ostensibly the main theme of these films, many of them touched on various aspects of Soviet life. "Moscow—Olympic City," one of the films produced by the Olympiade-80 Committee, extolled Moscow's achievements in every area, while "A Sportland," another Olympiade-80 production, glorified the efforts of the Soviet government to develop sport and physical culture in the Soviet Union.[61] Many similar films were produced between 1974 and 1980, in addition to film reports combining information on preparations for the Olympics and on various Soviet achievements. They were freely distributed by the Olympiade-80 propaganda department. Special steps were taken to encourage filmmakers to produce films on the forthcoming Moscow Olympic Games. Already at the X Moscow Film Festival of 1977 Olympiade-80 established a special prize for "the best film furthering ideas and friendship among nations" and dealing with sports.[62] The first such prize was awarded at the XI Moscow Film Festival in 1979. The recipient was Italian film director R. Marcellini, who received his award for "his activity of long standing in disseminating the ideals of the Olympic movement and propagating the successes of Soviet sport."[63]

Special preparations began for producing the official film on the Moscow Olympic Games. The film "Oh Sport, You Are Peace!" was supposed not only to show the competitions, but also "to demonstrate the close connection between sport and the twentieth-century explosion of science and technology, the development of the people's social awareness, and their constant striving for peace and friendship."[64] The film's director, Yuriy Ozerov, pointed out that "names, seconds, meters and points will not form the main content of the film. Sport as an ambassador of peace will be its main hero."[65]

Tourism

While this instrument became operational only during the games, a few things must be said both about its impregnational propaganda value and preparations for its use during the games. The Soviet Union regards international tourism as a means of "exchanging information and implementing détente."[66] Authorities make a special effort to "thoroughly acquaint foreign tourists with the achievements of the developed socialist society and the successes of the Soviet people in economy, science, technology, culture, and sport."[67] International tourism is also viewed in the Soviet Union as an effective means of combating anti-Soviet propaganda: "It is difficult to overestimate the importance of international tourism. It serves as an instrument for strengthening trust and developing mutual acquaintance among citizens of different countries. In some countries people have been indoctrinated from childhood in an anti-Soviet spirit, they come to us with apprehension and prejudice, but leave as great friends of our country and the Soviet people."[68]

To ensure thorough exposure of foreign tourists to impregnational propaganda illustrating the advantages of Soviet society and the achievements of the Soviet people (as well as to guarantee better control), Soviet authorities discouraged individual or independent tourism, and arranged only collective tours which included viewing some Olympic competitions and a lot of special sites.[69] The latter included museums, exhibitions, monuments, "which could give the tourist a complete impression of the U.S.S.R."[70] Other sources were even more explicit and revealed that the "other sites" would be mostly exhibitions of scientific and technological achievements, museums and places connected with the October Revolution and other "bright dates of Soviet history," monuments and memorials related to World War II, meetings with Soviet writers and artists, and so forth.[71] Special preparations were made to acquaint foreign tourists with a "subject which has always aroused their interest"—Lenin's life. Plans were made to take as many foreign tourists as possible to various places connected with Lenin's life, visit Lenin's museums, see exhibitions devoted to Lenin, read documents related to his life, and even hear his voice on old records.[72]

There was some uncertainty about the number of foreign tourists expected to visit the Soviet Union during the games. Soviet sources estimated their number at "about 200,000," although sometimes the number varied and was given as 350,000,[73] 250,000,[74] and "over 160,000."[75] At least one source went as low as "between 110,000 and 115,000 visitors."[76] As in all other aspects of the games, it was invariably concluded that "no other Olympic city had so many visitors."[77] All preparations for tourists were coordinated by the Olympiade-80 commission in charge of tourism, headed by S. Nikitin, chief of the Main Administration for Foreign Tourism. Close contacts were maintained with the Olympiade-80 propaganda commission, which assisted in distributing hundreds of tourist pamphlets, prospects, brochures describing the Olympic tours, the Olympic construction, construction of hotels and restaurants, the friendship and hospitality of the Soviet people. This was only one of the Olympic preparation areas in which the Olympiade-80 propaganda commission played a decisive role.

Quizzes and Contests

Quizzes and contests are a tried and true instrument of reaching and activating propaganda audiences, assessing their size, popularizing certain issues, and drawing attention to related issues. Several such quizzes and contests were conducted during the "preparations" campaign and during the games. One of the major ones was organized by *Soviet Woman*. The questions, dealing with Olympic history, were published in October 1978 and January 1979 issues. They drew 8,242 answers from 64 countries.[78] Many letters went far beyond the questions in the quiz. In the words of the editorial board: "It is pleasant to note that in many letters there were not only answers to the questions in our quiz, but also words of appreciation to our editorial offices for organizing it, thoughts about the forthcoming festival of world sport in Moscow, and expressions of kind, sincere feelings toward the Soviet people."[79] *Soviet Woman* published excerpts from many readers' letters praising the quiz as a "means of learning about the country of the great Lenin," stressing that their participation in the quiz was a "sign of their best feelings toward the U.S.S.R.," extolling the program of the Moscow Olympics, and so forth.[80]

A similar enterprise was the International Children's Drawing Contest dedicated to the Moscow Olympic Games and sponsored by the Olympiade-80 Committee and the Union of Soviet Societies for Friendship and Cultural Relations with Foreign Countries.[81] Some 350,000 entries from 73 countries were received and the best 1,500 drawings were selected for a special exhibition to take place during the games.[82] Similar quizzes and contests were organized by Soviet radio for its foreign listeners, and other magazines in foreign languages. Very often, answering the questions required extensive information about the progress of the Olympic preparations, Soviet history, and other aspects of Soviet life. Thus the quizzes facilitated the activity of other instruments of Soviet impregnational propaganda.

Friendship Societies

Friendship Societies and similar front organizations are an exclusive, loyal, and effective means of Soviet propaganda. They sponsor events promoting friendship with and knowledge about the Soviet Union, such as "friendship weeks" and "months," exhibitions, rallies, and demonstrations. They publish material related to Soviet life, policy, and successes, and do everything possible to promote Soviet interests in every area. It was only natural that their activity intensified during the "preparations" campaign. The Austrian-U.S.S.R. Friendship Society sponsored organized tours to the Soviet Union during the Olympic games, stressing that these especially low-priced tours were open only to "workers, employees, and students."[83] Members of the Finland-U.S.S.R. Friendship Society came to Moscow to attend a seminar on "captialism and its influence on the situation of the working people," and subsequently praised preparations for the games and the successful selection of Moscow as the Olympic site.[84]

Brigitte Benkler-Dassler, heiress to the Adidas sports equipment empire and an activist in the F.R.G.-U.S.S.R. Friendship Society, published several articles describing preparations for the Moscow Olympic Games, praised Soviet successes in various areas, and made a special effort to facilitate the propaganda activity of the Olympiade-80 Committee. Describing her "special pride" in meeting Brezhnev personally, she expressed the hope that "with her work for the benefit of the Moscow Olympic Games she would make a modest contribution to the general cause of strengthening détente and securing lasting and stable peace."[85]

Delegations of various Friendship Societies visited the Soviet Union during the "preparations" period. One of them was the U.S.-U.S.S.R. Friendship Society led by Kathy Rotchild. The delegation toured Olympic construction sites and met "responsible Olympiade-80 members."[86] Many events related to the Moscow Olympic Games, such as exhibitions and visits of Soviet sports officials, were also sponsored by Friendship Societies. Such events will be discussed later as separate instruments of Soviet propaganda related to the Olympic games.

Exhibitions

Exhibitions of Soviet achievments in sport and the progress of Olympic preparations became an important propaganda instrument during the "preparations" period. In the chapter dealing with the general propaganda functions of Soviet sport we described the "Sport in the U.S.S.R." exhibition, shown in several U.S. cities. A large part of this exhibition was devoted to the Olympic preparations and Moscow's successes in various areas.[87] The major exhibition, devoted to preparations for the Moscow Olympic Games, was the "Moscow—Olympic City" photo exhibit. Sometimes presented under the name "Moscow—Olympic Capital," it showed the "progress of the Olympic construction, the beauty of Moscow, the development of mass sport in the Soviet Union, and the triumphs of Soviet athletes."[88]

The exhibition was shown throughout the world. In 1979 it was announced that it had already been shown in 47 countries and 10 more were expected to show it before the end of the year.[89] Again in 1979, the exhibition was viewed by 2.5 million people.[90] It was also reported that until the opening of the games 61 similar exhibitions would be shown in 50 additional countries.[91] The exhibition was utilized for additional propaganda activities. When shown in Dusseldorf, it was accompanied by a Soviet delegation of state and Olympiade-80 officials, who provided more information on the progress of preparations.[92] In many countries press conferences were held during the exhibition, as well as meetings with famous Soviet sportsmen, Olympiade-80 officials, and so forth. The visitor would have the opportunity to utilize his visit to the exhibition in order "to receive information about how contacts in the areas of sport and culture contribute to achieving peace and better understanding, and strengthening friendship among nations."[93]

Posters

Posters are a favorite instrument of Soviet propaganda. They are usually big and predominantly red, depicting smiling workers—masses led by Brezhnev marching under Lenin's silhouette (presumably symbolizing the sun) toward their bright future. Usually they are rudely drawn, poorly printed, and seldom fail to invite ridicule. The Olympiade-80 Committee was aware of the low propaganda effectiveness of Soviet posters, and in 1978 announced an international competition for the official poster of the Mowcow Olympic Games.[94] The competition was sponsored by the Olympiade-80 Committee, the U.S.S.R. Committee on Sport and Physical Culture, the Central Committee of U.S.S.R. Trade Unions, the Komsomol Central Committee, the Ministry of Culture, and other bodies. The very list of official sponsors testifies to the importance attached to posters as propaganda vehicles. The members of the jury were Nikolay Romanov, chairman of the Union of Soviet Artists; V. Popov, first deputy chairman of Olympiade-80; cosmonaut A. Leonov, and others, plus a group of foreign painters and graphic artists.[95] Among them were old hands of Soviet propaganda such as U.S. painter Anton Refregier,[96] who has often participated in Soviet propaganda campaigns in the past.

The jury received about 5,000 works from 45 countries.[97] The vast participation was interpreted by Moscow as an "expression of the great interest and sympathy of the progressive public and all people of good will toward the U.S.S.R., the XXII Olympic Games, and Moscow, the capital of the first socialist state, which opened its gates in so friendly a way to sportsmen everywhere. It is also a recognition of the great Soviet contribution to developing sport and physical culture, and the daily care on the part of the CPSU and the Soviet government for man, his spiritual and moral world, health, beauty, well-being, and happiness."[98] The main themes of posters submitted were the struggle for peace and disarmament, friendship and cooperation, sport and its contribution to peace and progress.[99] The poster that won first prize shows Brezhnev (big smile and six medals) waving against the background of the Soviet flag, the Moscow Olympics official emblem, and Brezhnev's words of wisdom in Russian: "The Olympic Games...reflect mankind's striving for peace and progress." The poster, drawn by M. Manuylov and N. Popov (U.S.S.R.), was immediately printed in all Soviet publications in foreign languages, together with other prize-winning posters.

Soviet Delegations Abroad

The importance of Soviet delegations visiting foreign countries as an instrument of Soviet propaganda was analyzed in the chapter dealing with sport's general propaganda functions. What characterized the use of this particular instrument during the "preparations" campaign was the easily predictable intensification of its usage and its total subjection to preparations for the Moscow Olympic Games. Between 1977 and 1980 Olympiade-80 members visited almost every country in the world, some of them (predominantly in Africa) repeatedly. The visits were geared to several goals: to report the progress of preparations for the Moscow Olympics, conclude cooperation agreements and commercial contracts, seek information about the host country's preparations for the Moscow Olympics, and encourage large-scale participation. In 1977 a V. Koval-led delegation visited Cuba, Mexico, Colombia, Venezuela, Panama, and Costa Rica. In all the countries the delegation held press conferences on the preparations for the Moscow Olympics, heard information about the host countries' preparations for the Olympic games—the "host countries expressing their support for the forthcoming games"—and signed several commercial contracts.[100] In 1979 a I. Rudoi-led delegation visited Syria, the Arab Republic of Egypt, Yemen, and Jordan. In addition to the usual activities, the delegation signed communiques expressing support for these countries' policies, as well as sports exchange protocols.[101] During their visits the Soviet Union delegations repeatedly stressed that the Moscow Olympic Games "will facilitate the development of the international sports movement and the strengthening of peace, international cooperation, and understanding among nations."[102]

The frequent visits to African countries constituted a special case. Throughout the "preparations" campaign Moscow repeatedly expressed concern that "reactionary forces will try to inflict a blow on the Olympic movement by staging a situation similar to the 1976 Montreal Games, which were boycotted by African states in protest against the participation of New Zealand which had previously competed against racists."[103] The main goal of delegations to Africa was to forestall such a boycott. Their members usually met with African countries' leaders, explained the U.S.S.R.'s constant struggle for the isolation of apartheid countries in the international sports arena,"[104] and "the U.S.S.R.'s intention to struggle against racism and apartheid"[105] and "expel Rhodesia and South Africa from the world sports community."[106] In each country they visited, Soviet delegations were eager to obtain assurances of participation in the games, as a guarantee of averting a possible boycott prompted by considerations of the struggle against racism.

Delegations to Moscow: Foreigners in the Service of Soviet Propaganda

The number of Soviet delegations to foreign countries was surpassed only by the number of foreign delegations and various international figures, who visited Moscow during the "preparations" campaign period. It would be impossible to list all the foreign delegations, IOC officials, sports journalists, and other foreign visitors such as Prince Philip, the Grand Duke Jean of Luxembourg, and others, who visited Moscow at the invitation (and expense) of the Olympiade-80 Committee. Suffice to cite one figure: During "several months in 1979 Moscow was visited by foreign guests from more than 30 countries, who came at the invitation of the Olympiade-80 Committee."[107]

The visits usually followed the same pattern: the delegations were bombarded with material related to the preparations, taken to see construction sites, met sports and state officials, and were asked to express their opinions about the progress of preparations and Soviet life in general. The visitor's status and importance determined the rank of the Soviet officials they met. Prince Philip[108] and the Grand Duke Jean of Luxembourg[109] were received by I. Novikov, deputy premier and Olympiade-80 chairman, Lord Killanin, IOC President, by N. Podgoniy, (then) Supreme Soviet Presidium chairman,[110] while less prominent visitors were usually entertained by Olympiade-80 officials.[111]

These visits were repeatedly reported and publicized by the Soviet press in foreign languages, and especially the Olympiade-80 Committee's publications, which also analyzed guests' statements in admiration of everything they had seen in the Soviet Union and preparations for the Olympic games. A 1979 delegation from Mozambique was reported to have said: "We saw the construction of the Olympic village...the enormous dimensions are most impressive. We do not need any tables or numbers to be convinced that everything will be ready on time. We saw the people on the construction sites, and that was enough."[112]

UNESCO director general M'Bow, who visited the Soviet Union in early 1980: "I saw the impressive construction with my own eyes....In no other country have I seen such comfortable sports gymnasiums and palaces....I am convinced that the 1980 Olympic Games will serve peace and strengthen friendship among people."[113] Donald Miller, member of the U.S. Olympic Committee delegation which visited the Soviet Union in 1979: "You have impressed us very much....I have never seen a better Olympic village."[114] Similar views were expressed by I. Szabo, vice president of the Canadian Olympic Committee,[115] C. Collard, president of the French Olympic Commitee,[116] and many others.

It was not only sports officials and journalists whose statements were utilized by Soviet propaganda. Lord Noel-Baker, chairman of the UNESCO Council on Sport and Physical Culture, was quoted as having said: "The Olympic movement and the struggle for world disarmament and peace are connected.... The Moscow Olympiade will be a symbol of the Soviet people's love for peace, their friendliness, and hospitality."[117] He also expressed admiration for the Soviet government's care in developing sport in the Soviet Union, the high skills of athletes, and the organizational ability of Soviet authorities."[118]

The most outspoken were the "old hands" of the Soviet propaganda apparatus, such as "the U.S. fighter for peace, singer, and actor" Dean Reed: "I deem it very important that thousands and thousands of people will come to Moscow, the capital of the first socialist state in the world, and will acquaint themselves with the Soviet way of life. Numerous tourists from the capitalist countries will see for the first time the real socialism. I am absolutely sure that this visit will open their eyes about many things.... I am convinced that the guests of the Moscow Olympic Games will leave the U.S.S.R. with reversed notions about socialism and better understanding of détente and peaceful coexistence."[119] Reed's statement was a typical example of both the way foreigners were utilized and the "propaganda effect" anticipated by organizers of the Moscow Olympic Games.

The Cultural Program

When they were held in ancient Greece, Olympic sports competitions were accompanied by parallel cultural events, making the Olympic games a real festival of sport and culture. The early modern Olympic Games ignored or neglected the ancient custom of combining the games with cultural events. Not until 1912, at the Stockholm Olympic Games, were special cultural events organized as part of the Olympic program. There even was an artistic contest devoted to the games, in which architects, painters, sculptors, musicians, and writers presented their works on Olympic themes. It was at this contest that Pierre de Coubertin won a gold medal for his famous "Ode to Sport."[120] For a time such contests became a integral part of the games, but for some reason after the 1948 London Olympic Games they disappeared from the Olympic scene.[121] Cultural events continued to be organized parallel to the games, serving as a showcase of the host country's cultural heritage. Despite the fact that they were taken out of the Olympic program their importance developed, and the first item on the IOC questionnaire sent to prospective host cities (until 1976) was "What cultural and artistic program can you offer?"[122]

The impregnational value of arts and culture is nothing new to the Soviet Union. From the moment the first socialist state came into being, its artistic and cultural life has been completely subjected to the needs and goals of the CPSU and plays an important indoctrinational and impregnational role. The Olympic games provided Moscow with the opportunity of fully utilizing the propaganda potential of various cultural events. Several years before the games various Communist sources had shown enthusiasm at the unusual opportunity which presented itself to the Soviet propaganda apparatus:

> Moscow—the bubbling center of the world cultural, political, social, scientific, and cosmic ideas! Moscow! The summit of world literature, world theater, world music, and world cinema! Moscow—the capital of the most

Olympic country in the world! Finally after only four years the Olympic games will take place in an atmosphere as close as possible to the classic ones. Was it not in ancient Greece that sports festivals took place along with cultural festivals? At last the Olympic games will be saved from the menacing siege of all sorts of threats created by capitalism, and will reside in the friendly atmosphere of socialism.[123]

Repeatedly stressing the conviction that "cultural ties facilitate the strengthening of peace and friendship among nations,"[124] and invariably claiming this to be the main goal of the Moscow Olympic Games, the Olympiade-80 Committee began immediately after it was established to plan the cultural program of the Moscow Olympics. V. Kukharskiy, deputy minister of culture, was appointed chairman of the Olympiade-80 Commission on Cultural Programs and Cultural Services.[125] It was determined that while the official cultural program of the games would begin on 28 June 1980 (the day the Olympic village opened its gates) and continue until 8 August 1980,[126] a broader cultural program connected with the games would continue for sixteen months—from 1 July 1979 to October 1980.[127] The general idea, which no one took the trouble to conceal, was to expose the hordes of foreign athletes and especially tourists to as many instruments of impregnational propaganda as possible, using to the limit their stay in the Soviet Union for what was usually defined as "acquainting them with the rich traditions of Soviet cultural life and achievements."

The organizers planned to mobilize 250 groups of amateur and professional performers for appearances during the games.[128] Some 80 of the most famous Soviet films were to be shown in the Olympic cities of Moscow, Leningrad, Kiev, Tallin, and Minsk, among them "Battleship Potemkin," "Ivan the Terrible," and "Chapaev."[129] The shows were to run continuously from 9 A.M. to 10 P.M. Some 600 theater shows and 1,500 concerts were planned for tourists, "so that they can feel the spiritual wealth of the U.S.S.R. understand the special place culture has in Soviet life, and realize the great contribution of the Soviet peoples to the treasure of world culture."[130]

The free time of foreign sportsmen was also subjected to meticulous planning. A special committee in charge of free time activities at the Olympic village was established, chaired by Zanaida Fedorenko.[131] The Ministry of Culture adopted a special plan on an exhibition to be shown at the Olympic village.[132] All planned cultural events were free of charge.[133] Special meetings of foreign sportsmen and tourists with leading Soviet writers, painters, filmmakers, and cultural figures were also planned.[134] Various "culture days" devoted to the various Soviet republics were prepared.[135] "Friendship meetings" and various quizzes and contests were planned for the visiting sportsmen.[136] Social events and exhibitions devoted to Lenin's life were scheduled by the "free time" committee.[137] The

Soviet Union's scientific and technological achievements and the merits of sport in strengthening peace were also scheduled to be the subject of an exhibition at the Olympic village.[138] Foreign athletes were to be taken to sites of famous World War II battles, October Revolution events, and Lenin's life.[139]

Soviet cultural figures began preparations of their own. Since works of art related to sport and the Olympic games were demanded, the various Artistic Unions created a special commission to deal with the subject. They organized meetings of Soviet writers, painters, and artists with workers on the Olympic construction sites, athletes, and trainers, in order to improve their creativity by boosting their inspiration.[140]

In the months preceding the games the cultural events related to the Olympics began to dominate the Soviet cultural scene. In the fall of 1979 the RSFSR branch of the U.S.S.R. Union of Artists organized an exhibition of paintings devoted to the Olympic games.[141] The exhibition was also to be shown during the games. An ice review devoted to the Olympic games opened in January 1980, and was scheduled to run throughout the games.[142] A ballet review on the same subject opened in January 1980.[143] On 25 December 1979 the Supreme Soviet convened to review preparations for the Moscow Olympic Games. It expressed satisfaction with their progress and the hope that "the plan to acquaint visiting athletes and tourists with the life, work, and culture of the Soviet peoples will be fully and successfully implemented, and will achieve its goal."[144]

MISCELLANEOUS

The list of propaganda instruments is endless. The instruments listed so far were just a part of the complex and interwoven net of propaganda vehicles used by Moscow during its "preparations" propaganda campaign. In this concluding part several secondary instruments will be listed. They did not merit a special section, because some were used infrequently, while other were propaganda curiosities rather than full-fledged instruments.

Russian Language Studies

The study of Russian is an important instrument of Soviet propaganda. The studies (which presuppose an interest in the Soviet Union on the part of the student) expose students to other instruments of Soviet impregnational propaganda and provide Soviet authorities with the opportunity of teaching Russian using texts which constitute clear propaganda. The study of Russian, to which a section in almost all Soviet foreign-language magazines is devoted, was also subjected to the "preparations" campaign needs. *Sport in the U.S.S.R.* introduced a new column, "Have a Chat with

Misha" (the official mascot of the Moscow Olympic Games), which included words related to sports competitions and short stories about the triumphs of Soviet athletes. Bilingual books on the forthcoming Olympic games were published, so that readers could simultaneously improve their Russian and learn about the progress of Olympic preparations. One such book was *Moscow Awaits the Olympiad,* published in basic Russian with German summaries on each page. It described preparations, quoting foreign athletes and sports officials on Soviet organizational capabilities, the importance of sport as an instrument of peace, friendship, and cooperation, the triumphs of Soviet athletes, and so forth. Twenty-two similar books in eight languages were published in 1979, in addition to Russian cassettes with the voices of famous Soviet sportsmen.[145]

Soft Drink

It may seem strange to describe a soft drink as an instrument of propaganda, but when the drink in question is called Druzhba (friendship) and the factory which has introduced it in honor of the Moscow Olympic Games is awarded a special diploma by the Olympiade-80 Committee for its friendly idea,[146] it is safe to assume that quenching thirst was not the main idea behind producing the drink.

Misha

The official mascot of the Moscow Olympic Games was a cheerful bear cub, "Misha." It was selected by the Olympiade-80 Committee out of 40,000 proposals and suggestions, the bear being the work of Moscow artist Viktor Chizhikov.[147] The mascot was described as "the embodiment of kindness and strength, hospitality and sportsmanship, nerve and calm. Chizhikov's cub reveals an independent character and confidence in its strength—qualities essential in each competitor."[148] This is a bit much, especially when one remembers that the compliments are being paid to a stuffed (or painted) grinning bear cub. Misha became prominent (especially during the boycott countercampaign)—the subject of countless cartoons. The mascot was even taken up into space to the Salyut 6 laboratory by cosmonaut Kovalyonok—it is still there. The event was extensively reported with pictures and articles by all Soviet magazines in foreign languages.[149]

Music

Music also played a role in the "preparations" campaign. Melodiya, the Soviet record company, intensified production of Soviet songs, expected to be taken home as souvenirs by foreign tourists to visit Moscow during the games, "to remind them of their beautiful holiday in the U.S.S.R."[150]

The Olympiade-80 Committee, together with the Ministry of Culture and the Committee on Radio and Television, announced a contest to find songs and marches devoted to the Olympic games. The jury, headed by Tikhon Khrennikov, heard hundreds of works with titles such as "Olympic Victor," "Long Live Friendship," "Friendship Always Wins in Sport," and "Moscow Gives the Start." The best works were repeatedly played during the games.[151]

Social Events Abroad

During the "preparations" period the Olympiade-80 Committee organized many social events in foreign countries (usually under the auspices of Friendship Societies) aimed at publicizing the games. When the inevitable agreement on showing the "Moscow—Olympic City" exhibition in the FRG was signed, Moscow inserted the stipulation that the staging of the exhibition would be accompanied by "sports balls" devoted to the forthcoming Olympic games.[152] In December 1979 a "week of Soviet sport" took place in Italy. The week, sponsored by the Italian-U.S.S.R. Friendship Society, included the exhibition "Moscow—Capital of the 1980 Olympic Games," appearances by leading Soviet sportsmen in several Italian cities, and symposiums on various sports themes in which Soviet sportsmen and officials took part.[153] Needless to say, all the events were devoted to the Moscow Olympic Games.

Olympic Flag on Elbrus

In early 1980 all foreign-language Soviet magazines reported (with glossy pictures) that a Soviet expedition had climbed Mount Elbrus and placed the Olympic flag on the top of the mountain. Dozens of articles were devoted to this achievement, many describing and analyzing at length the importance of placing the Moscow Olympic Games' flag on top of Europe's highest peak.[154]

Contacts with Foreign Diplomats
Accredited in Moscow

A special aspect of the Olympiade-80 activities was regular contacts with foreign diplomats accredited in Moscow. Foreign diplomats were involved in two ways in the propaganda campaign. First, I. Novikov, Olympiade-80 chairman, maintained regular press conferences for the staff of foreign diplomatic missions in Moscow, at which detailed information about the progress of Olympic preparations was reported. Those press conferences, which included films and other visual material, as well as question and answer sessions, were subsequently reported and analyzed by the Soviet mass media.[155] The second way involved trips to various Olympic sites, after which the diplomats were asked to express their impressions. After one such trip to Tallin in 1980, George Aoki, Japanese ambassador to the Soviet Union, expressed his admiration for Soviet sacrifices in World War II in Estonia, his long-standing desire to work in the Soviet Union, and his positive attitude toward the Russian language and culture. He also praised the progress of the Olympic construction.[156] Other diplomats expressed similar sentiments.

Sometimes the two techniques were combined. In December 1979 a press conference for diplomats was attended by "28 diplomats from 18 Asiatic countries," and was immediately followed by a trip to various Moscow Olympic construction sites. The propaganda value of the foreign diplomats was not in the press conferences they attended or the trips they made, but in the unusual amplification of these events as well as the diplomats' statements, which added weight to similar statements made by Soviet officials.

The list of instruments utilized by the Olympiade-80 Committee could be continued ad infinitum. Olympic postcards and stamps, "Olympic cooperation" agreements with other countries (*Sovetskiy Sport* of 29 November 1979 reports such an agreement with France), intensification of sports relations with developing countries (Bulgaria's *Narodna Armiya* of 22 December 1979 reports a significant increase in the number of Soviet trainers preparing foreign athletes for the Olympic games), and many other instruments of Soviet Olympic propaganda could be added to this list. Especially interesting, for instance, were the Olympic calendars, published in 1979 and 1980. One very luxurious calendar for 1980 printed in four languages in Japan of the Olympiade-80 Committee and edited by several photographers and artists included beautiful photos of the Olympic sites and words of wisdom on the importance of the Olympic games. Among them a special place was devoted to Brezhnev's words: "The Olympic Games are an all-important event in international sports; they attract close attention from millions of people across the world and reflect mankind's unconquerable aspirations to peace and progress. The fact that sportsmen of all continents have gathered under the Olympic flag is added evidence of the wish of all nations to live in an atmosphere of friendship, mutual understanding, and active cooperation."[157] Although incomplete, the list of propaganda instruments mentioned so far gives an adequate picture of the depth and intensity of the "preparations" campaign.

Every propaganda campaign is made up of four basic elements: (1) a special political development, which necessitates the organization of a propaganda campaign; (2) the instruments utilized by the propaganda apparatus; (3) the major themes around which the campaign revolves; (4) the specific propaganda techniques utilized in the campaign. The Moscow

Olympic Games propaganda campaign was a case of four interwoven campaigns: the struggle for the right to host the games; the "preparations" campaign; the Olympic boycott countercampaign; and the games and their immediate aftermath. Despite the fact that the "boycott" campaign was very different, all four campaigns were prompted by the need to make full use of the games to achieve various political goals—to prove the superiority of the Soviet political system, demonstrate the achievements of the Soviet people, assert the legitimacy of the Soviet regime, and evoke interest in the Soviet social system. All four campaigns used the same instruments, most of them standard instruments of the Soviet propaganda machine, little adaptation being needed to activate them in the Olympic campaigns.

The major differences between the four campaigns (in addition to the specific characteristics of the boycott campaign) were their duration, themes, and techniques. The "hosting rights" campaign revolved around three basic themes: Moscow's right to host the games (based on the credit earned for the development of the Olympic movement and making it more democratic, the international successes of Soviet athletes, etc.), Moscow's ability to organize major events and the guarantees of the Soviet party and government that the games would take place according to IOC regulations. The campign lasted three years—from September 1971 to October 1974.

The "preparations" campaign was the longest and most extensive. It began in October 1974, immediately after the IOC Vienna session, when the hosting rights were acquired, intensified in August 1976 after the Montreal Olympic Games, and lost some momentum in January 1980, when the "boycott" countercampigan became the first priority of the Soviet propaganda apparatus. The "preparations" campaign was characterized by its myriad of instruments, relatively limited number of themes, and an aura of complacency derived from the sweet taste of anticipated triumph.

THEMES

The "preparations" campaign had three major themes: (1) progress of the construction of Olympic facilites and other preparations for the Moscow Olympics; (2) the Moscow Olympics as the greatest sports event ever to take place; (3) the special contribution of the Moscow Olympics to peace, friendship, détente, and international cooperation.

Progress of Preparations

This was the central theme of the "preparations" campaign. For more than five years it occupied most of Soviet foreign publications space. Countless articles, commentaries, press conferences, interviews, and statements by Soviet and foreign officials, journalists, and visitors, as well as information bulletins issued by the Olympiade-80 Committee were devoted to describing the progress of preparations. They repeated ad nauseam various kinds of data about the construction work, number of athletes and guests expected, and so on, sparing absolutely no detail.

Progress of the construction of the Olympic village and facilities was a permanent theme of the Soviet mass media. It was continuously stressed that the Olympic village, consisting of eighteen 16-story buildings, would become regular residential apartments after the games—"something which has never been done before."[158] It was stressed that in the past mistakes in the construction of sports facilities (longer lanes in swimming pools, and so forth) had caused great damage. "No similar situation will mar the Moscow Olympics."[159] The great enthusiasm of workers was also continuously emphasized: "The Moscow builders are in an elated mood as they look forward to the Olympics. And they are not simply waiting for the games, but with their own hands are doing everything necessary to prepare them in the best possible way. Everybody is aware of the importance and responsibility of their assignment.... The pledges assumed in honor of the 60th anniversary of the Great October Socialist Revolution have been fufilled."[160] It was often pointed out that the CPSU Central Committee, the Soviet government, and the Moscow City Party Committee were closely supervising the progress of construction.[161]

Preparation for foreign tourists was the second major aspect of the "progress of preparations" theme. This topic was explored in unusual (even for the "preparations" campaign) detail, every single aspect of the arrangements for foreign tourists becoming the subject of hundreds of articles, photos, commentaries, and interviews. Among the favorite details frequently reported were: the cultural program prepared for tourists; construction of restaurants and cafes ("400 restaurants and cafes are under construction"[162]); the number of taxicabs to serve the guests and the fact that their drivers were studying foreign languages;[163] sophisticated vending machines with which Moscow's cafes were to be equipped;[164] 6,700 cooks and 400 confectioners to be trained for the games;[165] Moscow's 5,195 shops and "close to 15,000 kiosks and vending machines" awaiting the foreign tourists;[166] 2,000 salespersons studying foreign languages;[167] data on the accommodation of foreign tourists, sleeping beds in rows of 20 and 25");[168] data on health services ("some 360 doctors and 90 doctors' assistants will provide medical services for the tourists, 540 medical workers are studying foreign languages");[169] 40 boats sailing on Moscow's river awaiting the tourists (the crews learning foreign languages, of course);[170] Moscow's preparations to deal with transportation during the games;[171] 3,500 guides and translators to help visitors,[172] and many, many similar details.

At this stage one could legitimately ask: Why is the number of restaurants or the fact of Soviet cab drivers learning foreign languages considered propaganda? First, information was continuously recited by the Soviet mass media. Magazines such as *Olympiade-80* and *Olympic Panorama* dealt with almost nothing else but similar constant, insistent repetition, aimed at convincing readers that preparations (some of which were trivial) were part of the Soviet people's general successes, turned "tourist information" into a major theme of the Soviet "preparations" propaganda campaign. Second, the permanent litany of trivial data was intended to add weight to the next major theme of the "preparations" campaign—"The Greatest Games Ever," entirely devoted to proving that the Moscow Olympic Games were supposed to be the greatest sports event ever, whose importance and significance by far exceeded its sports character.

The financial cost of the Moscow Olympic Games was the third major aspect of the "progress of preparations" theme. Despite the major construction (99 Olympic sites, 76 of them in Moscow[178]) and the substantial amount of money spent on propaganda, Moscow maintained that the XXII Olympic Games were the cheapest ever. The sum invariably quoted by Soviet sources was 230 million rubles (about U.S. $340 million.)[179] "Compared to the 2 billion West German marks—the cost of the 1972 Munich Olympics—and the 1.75 billion marks spent on the Montreal Olympics, this sum looks modest indeed."[180] Other, non-Soviet sources, estimated the amount as 25 times higher. The West German *Der Spiegel* maintains that instead of the 700 million DM reported by Moscow, 18 billion DM (about U.S. $10 billion!) were actually spent.[181] No evidence was adduced to support this estimate.

Soviet sources maintain that the cost of construction was reduced or partly offset by the fact that 15,000 Moscow citizens were to move into the Olympic village after the games.[182] It was also pointed out that despite the many commercial contracts concluded by Moscow "in offering Moscow as the site of the 1980 Olympic Games the Soviet state did not seek any economic profits."[183] As with all other aspects of the "preparations" campaign the "cost" theme was not only constantly repeated, but also subjected to strict uniformity—no Soviet source added or subtracted one dollar from the amount officially published as the cost of the Moscow Olympic Games.

The Moscow Olympics as the Greatest Event in History

The organizers of the Moscow Olympic Games did not plan a mere sports event. They planned a "festival of friendship," a "holiday of peace," a "demonstration of cooperation," and most of all—an event intended as sublime proof of Moscow's superpower status, ultimate evidence of its unprecedented achievements and visual incarnation of its foreign policy goals. To achieve all this the games had to be the greatest ever! Years before the games were scheduled to take place, the Soviet propaganda machine started citing evidence to prove that the XXII Olympic Games would surpass anything known until then. Every aspect of the preparations and the future games were defined, described in superlatives, and analyzed as "the best," "more than ever," "the greatest," "the most."

"No country has ever had such a large number of foreign guests"[184] (this was insistently maintained despite the fact that Moscow had no clear idea of how many tourists were to be expected, especially after Jimmy Carter's boycott campaign began to bite). Elsewhere in this chapter we have already pointed to discrepancies in the official number provided by Soviet sources (as low as 110,000 and as high as 350,000). "Never before have so many tickets been sold."[185] The number usually cited by Soviet sources was 5.8 million tickets—"one and a half times more than in past Olympic Games."[186] "More television cameras are going to record the games than in any other Olympics Games."[187] Two hundred and fifty cameras was the number usually cited by Soviet sources.[188] It was reported that Moscow would televise 18-20 simultaneous programs to foreign lands, while in Munich there had been 12 and in Montreal 9.[189] Two billion people, "more than ever,"[190] were expected to see the games on televsion. According to Soviet sources, this number was 25 percent higher than that for Montreal.[191] Moscow could not know in advance (even before the boycott was proposed) how many sportsmen would participate in the games. The number reported varied from one source to another, sometimes given as 12,000[192] and sometimes as "more than 10,000 athletes from 130 countries."[193] Whatever the number, the conclusion was unequivocal: never before had so many sportsmen participated in the Olympic games.

The Olympic village was defined as "the biggest and most comfortable,"[194] accommodating two persons in each room, "while in Montreal there were up to 14-15 athletes in a single room."[195] Donald Miller, secretary general of the U.S. Olympic Committee, was reported as saying that "he has never seen a better Olympic village."[196] I. Szabo, vice-president of the Canadian Olympic Committee, said, according to *Olympiade-80*: "In Montreal we could not provide such conditions."[197] Sports facilities were also supposed to be the best. Even M'Bow, UNESCO director general, attested to that: "I have seen in no other country more comfortable sports gymnasiums and palaces."[198] Working conditions and facilities for foreign journalists were defined as "unprecedented," and "better than ever."[199] Even the Olympic torch used in Leningrad was "more beautiful" and "900 grams lighter and 55 cm longer than the previous model."[200] The picture presented by the Soviet propaganda machine promised the biggest, best, most beautiful, and most comfortable Olympiad ever—the greatest sports event ever held.

The Moscow Olympics as a Contribution to Peace, Friendship, Cooperation, and Détente

Pierre de Coubertin saw the modern Olympic games as an event furthering peace and friendship. Nowhere in his writings is it said that the Olympic games should promote the foreign policy goals of a given country, let alone be used to denigrate the policies of other countries. A few words need be said about the Soviet use of concepts. The Soviet Union uses political institutions and concepts taken from the Western political lexicon. While such concepts are generally used in the West to convey meaning and explain political processes, Moscow uses them to disguise its intentions and conceal the true character of its political system by creating the illusion of legitimacy and integrity where there is none.

Let us ignore the Supreme Soviet, that legislative organ that meets twice a year for a day and a half, the so-called free elections in which there is no alternative candidate, and even the concept of socialist "democracy" as interpreted by the Soviet Union, and concentrate for a moment on the idea of "peace." The Soviet Union is constantly "struggling for peace" throughout the world, even where and when there is no military conflict involved. The reason is simple: while the Soviet Union is referring to the same concept used in the West, it endows it with a completely different meaning and connotations. "Peace" for the Soviet Union means the nonexistence of capitalist regimes. As long as there are nonsocialist regimes, the Soviet Union will continue to "struggle for peace"—utilize propaganda, subversion, and other means to extinguish them. By the same token "détente" is understood by the Soviet Union to be the West's approval of this process. Since Marxism does not recognize apolitical areas, every aspect of human life has political significance and matters in both the construction of communist society and the "struggle for peace."

From the outset it was obvious that the Moscow Olympic Games could not stay out of the realm of politics. Their political and propaganda value was too great to be ignored or not exploited for the furtherance of Moscow's foreign policy goals. It was only natural that immediately after acquiring the right to host the Olympic games, Moscow officially declared that sport per se would not be their most important aspect: "We want the Moscow Olympics to be a vivid and colourful festival of young people from all countries. We hope it will give a new impetus to the Olympic movement. We hope that the 1980 Olympics will not only be remembered as part of Olympic history, but will remain forever in the hearts of millions of people around the world. The Soviet people's desire for friendship and cooperation among nations echoes the spirit of Olympic rules. We appreciate that the Olympic games help strengthening peace. It is in this that we see their supreme goal."[201]

In 1979 Sergey Pavlov, chairman of the U.S.S.R. Committee on Sport and Physical Culture, declared that the entire preparations for the 1980 Moscow Olympic Games were subordinated to the "idea that the Olympic games are a factor for bringing peoples together and strengthening their understanding and cooperation...a magnificent festival of peace and mankind's friendship."[202] This principle was hammered out for five years by all Soviet propaganda's guns. Time and again foreign guests and officials were used by Moscow to reflect this stand and express general admiration for Soviet foreign policy and peace efforts. No article related to the Olympic games nor any interview with Olympiade-80 members failed to repeatedly draw readers' attention to this special characteristic of the Moscow Olympics.

Brezhnev himself on several occasions in his speeches made reference to the role of the Olympic games in strengthening peace and promoting international cooperation and friendship. This theme was part of his greeting to participants in the 1979 Spartakiade.[203] An excerpt from that greeting message became the slogan adorning the official poster of the 1980 Olympic Games, while slightly modified versions were incorporated in many books, brochures, calendars, and bulletins devoted to the games and quoted by everyone who wanted to show competence in basic Marxist-Leninist sources.

Although the key words were usually *peace, detente, friendship,* and *cooperation,* often more precise (and topical) concepts were involved. In January 1980 V. Popov, Olympiade-80 deputy chairman, expected the Moscow Olympic Games to "contribute to the purification of the world political atmosphere."[204] Lord Noel-Baker expressed the belief that the games would bring people closer together and "will thwart the arms race."[205] In their frequent trips to Africa, Olympiade-80 members never failed to emphasize the importance of the games as an instrument in the struggle against racism, neocolonialism, and apartheid.[206] Since it was always more respectable (and credible) to quote foreign dignitaries on the subject of the Moscow Olympic Games and their contribution to peace, détente, etc., a question related to the subject was invariably included in interviews with Lord Killanin, who was frequently asked to comment on Soviet sport's contribution to peace, understanding, and friendship, as well as to the development of the Olympic movement.[207]

The theme of the Moscow Olympics' contribution to peace, detente, and international cooperation acquired special importance in January 1980, when the Olympic boycott was initiated by President Carter. From then on the question of participation in or boycotting the games was presented by

Moscow simply as a question of support for peace or for war. The entire "boycott" campaign will be discussed at length in the next chapter.

We have examined three themes of the Soviet "preparations" campaign. While being the main themes, they were by no means the only ones. Subjects such as the advantages of the Soviet way of life, the achievements of Soviet society, relations with Africa, and Soviet assistance to developing countries were also frequently involved in the "preparations" campaign, and have been mentioned in passing in this chapter. Since they are subjected to a regular treatment by the Soviet propaganda machine, they have not been dealt with as specific themes of the "preparations" campaign.

TECHNIQUES

There are two basic kinds of propaganda campaigns: against a particular thing or person—usually militant or agressive and always insistent—and campaigns in support of a particular thing or person—sometimes subtle or low-key, sometimes intemperately fulsome in glorification and also always insistent. These two kinds differ in several aspects. Militant campaigns invariably pinpoint the enemy, while glorifying campaigns seldom involve any specific adversaries; militant campaigns are usually subjected to continuous changes in the international political situation, and thus to frequent shifts and adaptations of stress, tone, and direction, and the introduction and elimination of various instruments and themes of propaganda. Glorifying campaigsn are not subjected to the pressure of frequently changing international circumstances. Their instruments, themes, and techniques are semipermanent, "new tricks"being only seldom required. Aggressive campaigns are usually shorter, their effectiveness (and vigor) deteriorating with the disappearance of the specific political issue that prompted them. Glorifying campaigns are longer, the political need that creates them usually being a permanent feature of the international situation. The tone of aggressive campaigns is immeasurably sharper, with epithets, name calling, and radical accusations among their basic arsenal of techniques. Glorifying campaigns are restrained, more "respectable," and low-key. Techniques employed in aggressive campaigns are more numerous and inventive than those in glorifying campaigns.

The "Olympic boycott" propaganda countercampaign was a typical aggressive campaign. The "preparations" campaign on the other hand, was a relatively placid and complacent campaign, not aimed *against* anybody in particular. While such campaigns activate as many instruments as the aggressive ones, the objective being to engulf the vastest possible audience, its temperate character does not require a broad range of techniques. The main technique of the "preparations" campaign was repetition. This is a classic propaganda technique based on the premise that constant repetition of certain views or information will firmly implant them in the minds of the propaganda audience.

Since there was a limited number of themes and a large variety of instruments in the "preparations" campaign, the technique of repetition was readily used. Not only were the same principles, slogans, data, and details reported and discussed ad infinitum by the various instruments of Soviet propaganda, but often the same interview or article was reprinted by many different magazines. Information on the progress of preparations or interviews with Olympiade-80 members usually appeared first in the Soviet daily press and radio broadcasts. Then they were immediately summarized and wired by Tass, reprinted by *Sputnik* (the Soviet equivalent of the *Reader's Digest*), *Olympiade-80* and *Olympic Panorama, Sport in the USSR*, and other magazines in foreign languages. This constant repetition significantly amplified the "preparations" campaign.

Another technique was reliance on authority. Being aware of its limited (to say the least) credibility, Moscow often prefers foreign officials, sports functionaries, UN officials, foreign journalists, and IOC officials to be the source of its message. Many such examples were listed when the instruments and themes of the "preparations" campaign were discussed. While repetition was aimed at implanting the propaganda message and amplifying its intensity, the authority technique was aimed at lending Moscow a badly needed measure of credibility. The technique of involving state leaders and organs in the campaign was aimed at demonstrating the importance attributed to the issue and presenting it as a matter of high state importance. The extensively reported meetings of Killanin with Brezhnev, Podgorniy, and Kosygin, the regular involvement of the Council of Ministers, fifty ministries and state organizations,[208] and the Supreme Soviet[209] in the preparations—and widely publicizing their involvement—attests to the importance attributed to the Olympic games by Soviet authorities and their willingness to make this attitude public.

Uniformity is a characteristic technique of every Soviet propaganda campaign. Despite major discrepancies and contradictions regarding the number of expected participants and other matters, the entire Soviet mass media spoke with one voice. Not only were there no significant contradictions (let alone any dissent), but any degree of originality was denied. No Soviet newspaper or magazine dealt with any aspect that was not covered by all other instruments of Soviet propaganda. As with the technique of repetition, the uniformity technique focused the audience's attention on the issues desired by Moscow, increasing the credibility of the propaganda campaign.

The technique of exaggeration was also frequently employed. Its usage was demonstrated when the "The Greatest Ever" theme was dealt with. It is a dangerous technique, seldom used in glorifying campaigns, because it can easily undermine and destroy the credibility of the entire campaign. In this particular case the Soviet propaganda machine was carried away by its effort to prove that the Moscow Olympic Games would really be the greatest ever. Otherwise it is difficult to comprehend statements such as that attributed to UNESCO director general M'Bow maintaining that he had "nowhere seen such sports facilities." Since the Lenin stadium, big as it is, was built twenty-five years ago (and was only renovated for the Olympic games), and other facilities, big and modern as they are, did not represent any revolutionary novelty, similar facilities existing in many other countries, the words of M'Bow, who is not exactly an authority on sports facilities, can be regarded as exaggeration.

These were the main techniques employed in the "preparations" campaign. Their predominately moderate character illustrates the complacent nature of the campaign and the self-assurance of the Soviet propaganda machine. It is difficult to evaluate the effectiveness of the "preparations" campaign. While in the case of the "hosting rights" campaign the goal was unquestionably achieved, and the contribution of propaganda to this end was at least evident if not decisive, the case of the "preparations" campaign is different. This campaign had no clearly defined goals to be attained, aside from the general goals of Soviet impregnational propaganda—developing good will toward the Soviet Union and further interest in the Soviet way of life and the successes of the Soviet people. While it is possible that the "preparations" campaign increased the number of tourists who came to Moscow for the Olympic games, this can not reliably be measured or proven. It is impossible even to estimate the part this campaign played in facilitating the achievement of the general goals of impregnational propaganda.

THE 1979 SPARTAKIADE

The 1979 VII Spartakiade Games of the Soviet Peoples were naturally used for propaganda. Since they epitomized the instruments, themes, and techniques of the entire "preparations" campaign, it does not merit discussion as a separate case of propaganda. Still, a few words about this event are appropriate. The Spartakiade took place from 21 July to 4 August 1979, one year before the Moscow Olympics. This was no coincidence. The Spartakiade was intended to be a dress rehearsal of the Olympics and a first test of many Olympic facilities. This was not always freely admitted by Soviet sports officials. While some, such as A. Kolesov, deputy chairman of the U.S.S.R. Committee on Sport and Physical Culture and chief referee of the Spartakiade,[210] and A. Starodub, head of Olympiade-80 press and information department,[211] openly and repeatedly defined the 1979 Spartakiade as dress rehearsal for the Olympic games, I. Novikov, chairman of the Olympiade-80 Committee,[212] and N. Kiselev, chairman of the Soviet Federation of Sports Journalists,[213] maintained that the Spartakiade was not a dress rehearsal for the Olympics and that the two were in no way compatible. The reason for the contradiction was the organizers' fear that any problems during the Spartakiade would inevitably reflect on the forthcoming Olympics, or at least hurt the "preparations" campaign. After the Spartakiade there was no hesitation—all official sources called it a successful dress rehearsal for the Moscow Olympics.[214]

The 1979 Spartakiade *was* intended to be a dress rehearsal. It was therefore open to foreign athletes. Soviet sources maintained that there was nothing unusual in inviting foreign athletes to the Spartakiade and that 600 foreign athletes had already participated in the first 1928 Spartakiade.[215] This is only partially true, since no foreign athletes participated in the Spartakiade since. There is some incongruence in utilizing the Spartakiade for Olympic purposes. The Spartakiade was originally conceived as an expression of "proletarian sport" against the "bourgeois" Olympiad.[216] That is why the first Spartakiade took place simultaneously with the 1928 Amsterdam Olympic Games. Since inception the Spartakiade had a propaganda and class character, both of which are alien to the Olympic spirit.

The organizers were not certain about the number of foreign sportsmen supposed to take part in the 1979 Spartakiade.[217] Official statements spoke of "2,000 athletes from over 100 countries"[218] and "2,306 athletes from 84 countries."[219] Soviet sports authorities were very interested in the participation of athletes from developing countries. Otherwise it is impossible to understand why Olympiade-80 financed the trip to Moscow and back for athletes of 32 developing countries.[220] Brezhnev himself greeted the participants, not failing to mention that "the Spartakiade was a clear proof of the achievements of the Soviet party and government in developing physical culture, and of their constant care for the health of the Soviet people."[221] He also stressed the role of sport in "bringing people together and helping people better know and understand one another."[222]

The Soviet mass media declared the Spartakiade a complete success, "something also confirmed by foreign participants."[223] The 907 journalists from 46 states[224] who covered the Spartakiade reported numerous cases of poor organization, defects, lack of proper information, and uncomfortable facilities—brushed aside as "Western propaganda" by the Soviet and East European press. (A particularly trenchant article by Petur Krumov was published in Bulgaria's Communist party daily *Rabotnichesko Delo* of 8 October 1979. It vehemently refuted reports on incidents and accidents during the Spartakiade that had been published by *Time* magazine. Some of its points were ridiculous. Krumov countered the *Time* report of a serious lack of interpreters in Moscow by saying: "Only people who have decided to stay away from the official language of the games—the language of friendship, comradeship, and respect—can need interpreters.")

Foreign-language Soviet magazines carried scores of statements by foreign athletes, officials, and journalists, praising every conceivable aspect of the games. Masayi Kiyokawa (Japan, IOC executive member) extolled the organization of the Spartakiade and inferred that the Moscow Olympic Games would be equally successful. He also offered the thought that the Spartakiade contributed to strengthening Soviet-Japanese friendship.[225] Bo Bengston (Sweden, president of the European National Olympic Committee Association) described the organization of the Spartakiade and conditions for athletes as "better than anything else he has seen."[226]

Sport in the USSR interviewed several IOC officials, among them Willi Daume (FRG) and (again) Masayi Kiyokawa, Edward Brown, U.S. athletic team coach, and Raymond Roussat, secretary general of the French-U.S.S.R. Friendship Society.[227] They were asked three questions: How do you evaluate the results of the Spartakiade? How do you evaluate the preparations for the Moscow Olympic Games? How can sports contacts among the world's youth be improved? Their answers were predictable (otherwise they would not have been printed), expressing admiration of the Spartakiade's results, Olympic preparations, and sport's contribution to strengthening peace and friendship.

Soviet Union carried a similar cluster of statements reprinted from various foreign newspapers, praising the Spartakiade as a "great and readily evident festival of friendship" (*Kansan Uutiset*, Finland) and a "confirmation of the Soviet Union's leading role in world sport" (*Aftenpost*, Norway), predicting that on the basis of their impressions of the Spartikiade, the Moscow Olympic Games would be an unprecedented success.[228] Many other Soviet magazines in foreign languages carried similar statements. The Spartakiade blended perfectly into Soviet propaganda's "preparations" campaign, and provided a foretaste of the forthcoming "games" campaign.

Notes

1. "Moscow Looks Forward to the 1980 Olympics," interview with V. Promyslov, *Soviet Union* (no. 1, 1975), p. 4.
2. D. Prokhorov, *IOC and the International Sports Federations* (Russian—Moscow, 1978), p. 9.
3. A. Srebnitskiy, *Dobro pozhalovat Olympiada!*(Moscow, 1978), pp. 12-13.
4. "Moscow Looks," p. 4.

5. Suren Arutyunyan, "Komsomol: The Word and Deed," *Olympiade-80* (no. 13, 1977), p. 4.
6. V. Smirnov, "Moscow Prepares for the Olympics," *Moscow News* (no. 50, 1976), pp. 3,9.
7. Ibid., p. 9.
8. A. Starodub, *Do vstrechi v Moskve* (Moscow, 1978), p. 60.
9. *Radio Liberty Research Bulletin* (no. 286, 25 September 1975), pp. 9-10.
10. Starodub, pp. 60-61.
11. Ibid., p. 61.
12. Ibid., p. 63.
13. "Kommissionen der Organisationskomitees: Initiative plus Aktivitat," *Olympiade-80* (no. 29, 1979), p. 2.
14. Srebnitskiy, p. 4.
15. *Sovetskiy Sport* (4 March 1980).
16. Starodub, p. 154.
17. Ibid.
18. Ibid., p. 152.
19. V. Steinbach, *Gero'i Olympiyskikh bataliy* (Moscow, 1979), p. 79.
20. "On Short Waves," *Olympiade-80* (no. 28, 1979), p. 18.
21. Ibid.
22. Ibid.
23. *Sowijet Union Heute* (no. 3, March 1980), pp. 63-64.
24. Starodub, p. 152.
25. Ibid., p. 153.
26. A. Starodub, "Was, wo, wann?" *Olympisches Panorama* (no. 9, 1979), p. 8.
27. A. Yermakov, "Edle Mission der Presse," *Olympisches Panorama* (no. 9, 1979), p. 3.
28. A. Starodub, "1001 Fragen und Antworten," *Sport in der UdSSR* (no. 7, 1979), p. 7.
29. Omitted.
30. "Erfolgzuversicht," *Olympiade-80* (no. 37, 1979), p. 40.
31. Yermakov, p. 3.
32. "AIPS Congress in Moscow," *Olympiade-80* (no. 33, 1979), pp. 27-30.
33. Ibid.
34. "Interviews with Foreign Journalists," *Sport in the USSR* (no. 8, 1979), p. 7.
35. Ibid.
36. "Eine schwere und edle Mission," interview with Juan Antonion Samaranch, *Olympiade-80* (no. 33, 1979), p. 33.
37. Starodub, "1001 Fragen," p. 7.
38. *Olympisches Panorama* (no. 9, 1979), p. 7.
39. B. Bazunov and S. Popov (eds.), *Olympiastadt Moskau* (Moscow, 1979), p. 11.
40. Ibid.
41. Ibid., p. 7.
42. Ibid., p. 40.
43. Ibid.
44. Ibid.
45. Ibid.
46. Ibid., p. 41.
47. Ibid., p. 41.

48. Ibid., pp. 41-42.
49. Ibid., p. 68.
50. Ibid., p. 101.
51. Ibid., p. 130.
52. *Olympiade-80* (no. 13, 1979), p. 47.
53. V. Steinbach, "The Olympics in Print," *Sport in the USSR* (no. 12, 1979), p. 30.
54. *Literaturnaya Gazeta* (23 February 1977).
55. Ibid.
56. Smirnov, p. 3.
57. "Die ganze Welt am Bildschrim dabei," *Sport in der UdSSR* (no. 6, 1979), p. 37.
58. A. Rusakov, "*Two Thousand Sparks*," *Nedeliya* (5-11 November 1979), p. 11.
59. Starodub, *Do vstrechi*, p. 154.
60. Ibid.
61. S. Palmova and A. Gladkikh, "Sport in Grossaufnahme," *Olympisches Panorama* (no. 9, 1979), p. 76.
62. *Sovetskiy Sport* (7 July 1977).
63. "Tag für Tag," *Olympiade-80* (no. 37, 1979), p. 47.
64. Y. Kushnirskiy, "Sport—Ambassador of Peace," *Literaturnaya Gazeta* (6 February 1980).
65. Ibid.
66. Viktor Boytchenko, "Tourismus in Dienste des Friedens," *Olympiade-80* (no. 39, 1980), p. 2.
67. Arutyunyan, p. 5.
68. *Izvestiya* (25 January 1980).
69. V. Lidin, "On the Eve of the Great Housewarming," *Sport in the USSR* (no. 12, 1979), p. 28.
70. *Izvestiya* (25 January 1980).
71. S. Bulgakov, "Herzlich Willkommen!" *Olympiade-80* (no. 39, 1980), p. 6.
72. *Izvestiya* (25 January 1980).
73. Igor Kirilin, "Olympic Guests in the Center of Attention," *Sputnik* (no. 7, 1978), p. 154.
74. Lidin, p. 28.
75. N. Latyshev, "Gut vorbereitet auf Tourism," *Olympiade-80* (no. 27, 1979), p. 4.
76. "AIPS Congress in Moscow," *Olympiade-80* (no. 33, 1979), p. 30.
77. Lidin, p. 28.
78. "Olympic Quiz Finish," *Soviet Woman* (no. 2, 1980), p. 26.
79. Ibid.
80. Ibid.
81. "Olympic News," *Soviet Union* (no. 3, 1980), p. 53.
82. Ibid.
83. *Sowijet Union Heute* (no. 3, 1980), p. 41.
84. *Komsomolskaya Pravda* (9 January 1980).
85. *Komsomolskaya Pravda* (15 January 1980).
86. *Olympiade-80* (no. 28, 1979), p. 47.
87. V. Chernyaev, "Der Weg zum Frieden," *Sport in der UdSSR* (no. 9, 1979), p. 14.
88. *Olympiade-80* (no. 29, 1979), p. 47.

89. *Sport in der UdSSR* (no. 11, 1979), p. 6.
90. "Die Olympische Haupstadt stellt sich vor," *Sport in der UdSSR* (no. 2, 1980), p. 9.
91. Ibid.
92. *Olympiade-80* (no. 28, 1979) p. 47.
93. *Olympiade-80* (no. 37, 1979) p. 48.
94. "Posters—Olympiade-80," *Sputnik* (Russian—no. 1, 1980), p. 58.
95. A. Shumakov, "Der Wettstreit ist beended, die Arbeit geht weiter," *Olympiade-80* (no. 33, 1979), p. 13.
96. "Posters," p. 60.
97. "Das Plakat spricht jeden an," *Sport in der UdSSR* (no. 8, 1979), p. 16.
98. Shumakov, p. 14.
99. Ibid.
100. *Olympiade-80* (no. 13, 1977), p. 46.
101. Ivanovskiy, "In Vorfeld der Spiele," *Olympiade-80* (no. 29, 1979), pp. 28-29.
102. *Olympiade-80* (no. 30, 1979), p. 47.
103. V. Vasiliev, "So wird es auch sein," *Sport in der UdSSR* (no. 1, 1980), p. 11.
104. I. Rudoi, "Dialog in der Sprache der Freundschaft," *Sport in der UdSSR* (no. 2, 1980), p. 23.
105. Ibid.
106. I. Denissov, "Auf dem Kontinent, der Zukunft zustrebt," *Sport in der UdSSR* (no. 7, 1979), p. 19.
107. Ibid.
108. *Olympiade-80* (no. 30, 1979), p. 47.
109. *Olympiade-80* (no. 33, 1979), p. 47.
110. Moscow Tass in English, 1836 GMT (19 November 1976), *D.R.* (22 November 1976).
111. *Olympiade-80* (no. 18, 1977), p. 46.
112. "Moçambique: Sport wird immer grösser Geschrieben," *Olympisches Panorama* (no. 8, 1979), p. 45.
113. "In Dienste des Friedens," *Olympisches Panorama* (no. 13, 1980), p. 43.
114. "Robert Kane: wir wollen ihre Erfharungen auswerten," *Olympiade-80* (no. 27, 1979), p. 28.
115. "Olympiastaffel Montreal-Moskau," *Olympiade-80* (no. 26, 1979), pp. 34-36.
116. "Claude Collard: Coubertins Nachlass ist in guten Handen,"*Olympiade-80* (no. 39, 1980), p. 38.
117. E. Cheporov, "Philip John Noel-Baker über die Olympiastadt Moskau," *Sport in der UdSSR* (no. 6, 1979), p. 7.
118. Philip J. Noel-Baker, "Olympiade-80 and Detente," *Dnes i utre* (Bulgaria—no. 14, 1979), p. 3.
119. Dean Reed, "Viel Erfolg," interview, *Olympiade-80* (no. 29, 1979), p. 33.
120. Starodub, *Do vstrechi*, p. 83.
121. Ibid.
122. Ibid., p. 86.
123. *Literaturen Front* (Bulgaria—15 July 1976).
124. *Izvestiya* (25 January 1980).
125. *Radio Liberty Research Bulletin* (no. 286, 25 September 1979), p. 10.
126. *Rabotnichesko Delo* (Bulgaria—23 December 1979).
127. *Otechestven Front* (Bulgaria—25 March 1977).

128. *Soviet Union* (no. 3, 1980), p. 53.
129. Z. Fedorenko, "Die Musen starten als erste," *Olympiade-80* (no. 33, 1979), p. 39.
130. *Izvestiya* (11 January 1980).
131. *Olympiade-80* (no. 33, 1979), p. 39.
132. *Sport in der UdSSR* (no. 9, 1979), p. 6.
133. *Rabotnichesko Delo* (23 December 1979).
134. *Otechestven Front* (25 March 1977).
135. Fedorenko, p. 38.
136. S. Bulgakov, "Herzlich Willkomen!" *Olympiade-80* (no. 39, 1980), p. 16.
137. Fedorenko. p. 39.
138. Bulgakov, p. 6.
139. Ibid.
140. *Rabotnichesko Delo* (23 December 1979).
141. *Olympiade-80* (no. 30, 1979), p. 32.
142. "Fire and Ice," *Sputnik* (no. 3, 1980), pp. 110-15.
143. Der Spiegel (F.R.G.—no. 19, 1980), p. 157.
144. Bulgakov, p. 6.
145. "Die Gäste sprechen Russisch," *Sport in der UdSSR* (no. 9, 1979), p. 10.
146. *Sport in der UdSSR* (no. 6, 1979), p. 36.
147. "Misha the Mascot," *Sputnik* (no. 7, 1978), pp. 149-50.
148. Ibid., p. 150.
149. P. Skobelkin, "Meister Petz im Kosmos," *Olympisches Panorama* (no. 8, 1978), pp. 3,5.
150. K. Borisov, "Was stimmt Melodija 80' während der Spiele an?" *Sport in der UdSSR* (no. 5, 1979), p. 11.
151. S. Volodina, "Music für die Olympiade," *Sport in der UdSSR* (no. 9, 1979), p. 47.
152. *Olympiade-80* (no. 13, 1977), p. 47.
153. *Olympisches Panorama* (no. 13, 1980), p. 42.
154. Juri Makunin, "Elbrus Knows Now about the Olympics," *Sport in the USSR* (no. 2, 1980), p. 36.
155. *Olympiade-80* (no. 29, 1979), p. 47.
156. "Wind in den Segeln," *Olympiade-80* (no. 39, 1980), p. 45.
157. *Olympiade-80* (no. 36, 1980), p. 45.
158. "Moscow Olympics in Focus," interview with I. Novikov and S. Pavlov, *Sputnik* (no. 8, 1977), p. 117.
159. Ibid., p. 115.
160. Lev Rossoshik, "The Olympic Spirit on an Olympic Site," *Olympiade-80* (no. 13, 1977), p. 9.
161. V. Promyslov, "Moskau rustet sich zur Olympiade," *Olympiade-80* (no. 30, 1979), p. 7.
162. "Olympiade 1980 in Fragen und Antworten," *Sowijet Union Heute* (no. 3, 1980), p. 63.
163. Ibid.
164. "Maschinen die alle brauchen," *Olympiade-80* (no. 26, 1979), p. 11.
165. "Olympic Guest: In the Center of Attention," interview with Igor Kirilin, chief of the Olympic Games Service Board, *Sputnik* (no. 7, 1978), p. 155.
166. Ibid.
167. Ibid.
168. Ibid.

169. Ibid., p. 156.
170. "Kapitäne der Moskauer 'Weissen Flotte'" *Sport in der UdSSR* (no. 8, 1979), p. 11.
171. V. Mitroshin, "Stadtverkehr bei der Olympiade," *Olympisches Panorama* (no. 8, 1978), pp. 18-19.
172. V. Boitchenko, "Intourist rüstet zu den Olympischen Spielen," *Olympiade-80* (no. 18, 1978), p. 26.
173-177 Omitted.
178. *Izvestiya* (11 January 1980).
179. "What Will the Moscow Olympics Cost?" *Sputnik* (no. 6, 1979), p. 152.
180. Ibid.
181. *Der Spiegel* (no. 19, 5 May 1980), p. 152
182. "What Will," p. 153.
183. Ibid., p. 154.
184. "On the Eve of the Great Housewarming," p. 28; "AIPS Congress in Moscow," *Olympiade-80* (no. 33, 1979), p. 30.
185. "Olympiade 1980 in Fragen und Antworten," p. 63.
186. Ibid.
187. "Die ganze Welt am Bildschirm dabei," p. 37.
188. Ibid.
189. Ibid.
190. Ibid.
191. *Nedeliya* (no. 45, 5-11 November 1979), p. 11.
192. "Moscow: Olympics in Focus," p. 113.
193. *Izvestiya* (11 January 1980).
194. *Nedeliya* (no. 43, 22-28 October 1979), p. 14.
195. Ibid.
196. "R. Kane: wir wollen ihre Erfharungen auswerten," *Olympiade-80* (no. 27, 1979), p. 28.
197. "Olympiastaffel Montreal-Moskau," *Olympiade-80* (no. 26, 1979), p. 35.
198. "In Dienste des Friedens," p. 43.
199. "Der Marathonlauf der Hauptpressenzentrums," *Sport in der UdSSR* (no. 2, 1980), p. 10.
200. "Olympiade Moskau '80," *Sowijet Union Heute* (no. 5, 1980), p. 52.
201. Smirnov, p. 9.
202. *Rabotnichesko Delo* (24 December 1979).
203. *Olympiade-80* (no. 35, 1979), p. 2.
204. *Izvestiya* (11 January 1980).
205. Cheporov, p. 9.
206. I. Rudoi, "Dialog in der Sprache der Freundschaft," *Sport in der UdSSR* (no. 2, 1980), pp. 22-23.
207. "IOC President in Moscow," interview with Lord Killanin, *Olympiade-80* (no. 29, 179), p. 7.
208. *Rabotnichesko Delo* (24 December 1979).
209. *Pravda* (26 December 1979).
210. *Pravda* (26 June 1978); *Komsomolskaya Pravda* (6 February 1979).
211. Starodub, "Do vstrechi, p. 110.
212. UPI, 18 July 1979, *Radio Liberty Research Bulletin* (no. 221, 20 July 1979), p. 3.
213. Ibid.
214. S. Pavlov, "La Veille de l'Olympiade-80," *La Femme Soviétique* (no. 12,

1979), p. 28.

215. "Leb wohl, Spartakiade!" interview with A. Kolesov, *Olympiade-80* (no. 35, 1979), p. 3.
216. G. Rogulski, "Was erwarten wir von der Spartakiade-1979?" *Olympiade-80* (no. 31, 1979), p. 4.
217. *Sovetskiy Sport* (5 July 1979).
218. S. Blisnyuk, "Die Feder der Presse," *Sport in der UdSSR* (no. 11, 1979), p. 22.
219. "Leb wohl, p. 3.
220. *Sovetskiy Sport* (28 June 1979).
221. L. Brezhnev, "To the Participants and Guest of the VII Summer Spartakiade of the U.S.S.R. Peoples," *Olympiade-80* (no. 35, 1979), p. 2.
222. Ibid.
223. "Leb wohl, p. 3.
224. Blisnyuk, p. 22.
225. *Olympisches Panorama* (no. 12, 1979), pp. 12-13.
226. Ibid.
227. *Sport in der UdSSR* (no. 10, 1979), pp. 26,27.
228. *Soviet Union* (no. 10, 1979), p. 55.

7

The Boycott Counteroffensive

By the end of December 1979 Moscow had all the reason in the world to be satisfied with both the progress of Olympic preparations and the scale and volume of the propaganda campaign, which served as sound track for the preparations. It seemed that the forthcoming Olympic games would be a programmed political success, faithfully serving their main purpose of providing an opportunity to show the achievements of the Soviet system and —in a way—selling the Soviet Union and its ideals to the world.

On 27 December 1979 units of the Soviet army crossed the border with Afghanistan, overthrew the government of Hafizollah Amin, and installed a new one under Babrak Karmal. In explaining the military action the Soviet mass media repeatedly presented the whole operation as an act of friendship and good neighborliness on the part of the Soviet Union, which had responded to repeated requests by the Afghan government, based on Article 4 of the Soviet-Afghan friendship treaty and Article 51 of the UN Charter.[1] It was also repeatedly stressed that the action had been necessary because Afghanistan had become the object of various provocations and intrigues by the forces of imperialism and reaction. Moscow accused "U.S. imperialism" of organizing actions aimed against the Afghan people.[2]

The Soviet Union also maintained that "the limited Soviet contingent will be fully withdrawn from Afghanistan" when the cause which necessitated such action no longer exists."[3] The invasion of Afghanistan set in motion a train of events Moscow had dreaded for years.

On 4 January 1980 President Carter read a major address to the American people, in which he stated that the United States might not take part in the Moscow Olympic Games if the Soviet Union continued its "aggressive action." President Carter stressed that the United States would prefer not to withdraw from the Moscow Olympics, but that continued Soviet aggression would endanger both the participation of athletes and travel to Moscow by Americans wanting to see the games.[4] Although according to Western media reports the boycott idea (following events in Afghanistan) first emerged on 1 January at a NATO meeting, Carter's speech of 4 January was the first official statement broaching the subject of a boycott. A more explicit stand was expressed by Secretary of State Vance in a 16 January television interview. Cyrus Vance unambiguously pointed out that if Soviet troops had not withdrawn from Afghanistan within a month, the United States would boycott the Moscow Olympic Games.[5]

On 20 January President Carter sent a letter to Robert Kane, president of the U.S. Olympic Committee:

> We must make clear to the Soviet Union that it cannot trample on an independent nation and at the same time do business as usual with the rest of the world.... I therefore urge the U.S. Olympic Committee, in cooperation with other national Olympic Committees, to advise the International Olympic Committee that if Soviet troops do not fully withdraw from Afghanistan within the next month, Moscow will become an unsuitable site for a festival meant to celebrate peace and good will. Should the Soviet Union fail to withdraw its troops within the time prescribed above, I urge the U.S. Olympic Committee to propose that the games either be transferred to another site such as Montreal or to multiple sites, or be canceled for this year.[6]

On 28 January the Senate Foreign Affairs Committee unanimously approved a resolution calling for the United States to boycott the summer Olympic games if they were held in Moscow. One week earlier the House of Representatives had adopted a similar resolution by a vote of 386 to 12, and on 29 January the Senate approved the resolution of the Foreign Affairs Committee by a vote of 88 to 4.[7] On 20 February the White House issued a statement: "A month has now expired and Soviet troops have not even begun to withdraw from Afghanistan. The president has therefore advised the United States Olympic Committee that his decision remains unchanged and that we should not send a team to Moscow."[8] On 13 March the Department of Commerce issued a statement asking U.S. commercial firms to stop the export to Moscow of products related to the Olympic games.[9]

On 21 March President Carter spoke to the Athletes' Advisory Committee to the U.S. Olympic Committee and again emphasized that the United

States would not participate in the Moscow Olympic Games.[10] One week later, declaring the Soviet invasion of Afghanistan "an unusual, extraordinary threat to the national security, foreign policy, and economy of the United States," Carter ordered a halt to Moscow-bound exports.[11] The position that participation in the Moscow Olympic Games would contradict U.S. national interests was clearly expressed once again in an 8 April telegram from President Carter to Robert Kane, only days before the U.S. Olympic Committee was to officially decide whether the United States should participate in the Moscow Olympic Games.[12] Finally, on 14 April the U.S. National Olympic Committee adopted a resolution stating that the United States would not participate in the Moscow Olympic Games.[13] The White House issued a subsequent statement to the effect that the decision was final.[14] This was a brief survey of the main stages and official statements and steps that constituted the U.S. government's boycott campaign against the Moscow Olympic Games, prompted by the Soviet invasion of Afghanistan. Additional steps and statements as well as the attitude of other countries on the matter will be discussed as we analyze the Soviet "boycott" counterpropaganda campaign.

Self-confidence was never a Russian characteristic. The countless invasions of Russia by its neighbors, the continuous hardship suffered by its people and internal unrest, as well as some deep-seated Slavic traits, combined to produce a general attitude of suspicion of the intentions of others and paranoid mistrust of human nature. Those qualities were inherited by the communist regime and effortlessly incorporated into the Soviet political system. Along with the joyful anticipation of the forthcoming Olympic triumph was always a nagging worry or even recurrent nightmare that somehow "they" might manage to spoil the spectacle. The identity of the "spoilers" was somewhat vague—Moscow took no chances and accused every conceivable political adversary of unholy intentions toward the 1980 Olympic Games. While it was "reactionary forces," which were usually accused of preparing "a blow to the Olympic movement staging again a situation similar to the 1976 boycott,"[15] sometimes "Zionists, racists, all sorts of emigrant groups and ordinary anti-Soviets as well as some political figures of conservative conviction"[16] were accused of planning to compromise the Moscow Olympic Games.

Despite the protest of Soviet dissidents against the games being held in Moscow (the protests of Andrey Sakharov and Vladimir Bukovskiy being reported by the *International Herald Tribune* of 30 August 1979), Moscow's main concern was with a possible African boycott, similar to that of the 1976 Montreal Olympic Games. No effort was spared to prevent this from happening. Frequent visits of Soviet sports delegations and highly placed sports administrators, construction of sports arenas and and training of local sportsmen, payment of trips to attend the 1979 Spartakiade of the Peoples of the U.S.S.R., and the fuss about financial subsidies to enable the developing countries to participate in the Moscow Olympic Games were all aimed at creating a climate that would deter any idea of a boycott and, in all eventuality, win votes in international sports and Olympic bodies. No opportunity was missed to condemn the regimes of South Africa and Rhodesia, and boycott international competitions in which those two countries took part.

The possibility that its foreign policy or some characteristics of its political system could trigger a boycott of the XXII Olymic Games did not occur to Moscow. How many countries boycotted the 1936 Olympic Games in Nazi Germani? Who refused to play against the Soviet Union in the 1956 Melbourne Olympic Games, just one month after the Soviet invasion of Hungary? Did anybody boycott Soviet sportsmen after the 1968 invasion of Czechoslovakia? Did A. Brundage not prevail after the 1972 massacre of Israeli athletes in Munich with the view that the "games must go on?" And finally, did the African boycott of the 1976 Montreal Olympic Games (29 states withdrew) really hurt the games that much? And if worst were to come to worst—were there not the blocs of the socialist and nonaligned countries to univocally condemn any anti-Soviet move and offer unconditional support for Moscow's position?

It is hard to believe that the Soviet invasion of Afghanistan was a spontaneous move. It is also reasonable to assume that the Kremlin considered the possible ways in which the West would respond. In retrospect it seems that the possibility of an Olympic boycott was either overlooked or lightheartedly dismissed. This explains Moscow's paralyzing shock during the first days after President Carter's speech of 4 January, in which the possibility of boycotting the Moscow Olympic Games was clearly spelled out. For about a week there was absolutely no overt reaction on the part of Soviet authorities. Then on 10 January *Komsomolskaya Pravda* carried a very brief news report stating that the Supreme Council for Sport in Africa would not join the campaign launched by the NATO countries for a boycott of the 1980 Olympics on the "pretext of events in Afghanistan."[17]

On the following day, 11 January, Vladimir Popov, first deputy chairman of the Olympiade-80 Organizing Committee, published a major article in *Izvestiya* entitled "The Olympic Days Draw Closer." The article was a roundup of the preparations for the Olympic games. Towards the end of the article Popov mentioned in passing: "Some politicians today are utilizing the present world situation to shape up some 'boycott ideas' related to the Moscow Olympic Games. Reports of the telegraph agencies state that the organizers of this new attempt at political speculations...will sink in the muddy waters of the waves they themselves created."[18]

Ordinary Soviet citizens have no access to reports of foreign telegraph agencies. The vast majority had never heard of the "ideas of boycott," and the lack of any explanation was obviously perplexing. The next paragraph of Popov's article mentioning the possibility of an African boycott was even more puzzling: "A number of sports organizations in Western countries have tried and are continuing to try to drive a wedge between the Olympics and the developing countries, in particular the African sports movement. Sports contacts are being organized with the racists in the Republic of South Africa, as for example the appearance of rugby players from that country in England, which aroused general indignation. The object is clear: to arouse the rightful indignation of African countries and provoke them into refusing to participate in the Moscow Olympics, as happened in an analogous situation with the Montreal Games."[19]

Two more days elapsed and there still was no official response, or even a commentary devoted to the Olympic boycott. On 13 January S. Bliznyuk, head of *Sovetskiy Sport's* "International Life" section, published an article entitled "Old Lyrics to New Music."[20] The subtitle was telltale: "Provocative Maneuvers of the Enemies of the Olympics Are Doomed to Fail." The article did not carry any official statement of response to the boycott idea. No information was provided. It comprised mostly material "refuting" reports that had been broadcast by the Voice of America and the BBC, and that had evidently been heard by the newspaper's readers.

This intitial reaction attested to Moscow's confusion and shock. One could almost hear the Kremlin gasping—"It is not happening!" Suddenly Soviet authorities saw one of their worst nightmares materializing—the Olympic games shrinking to the measure of a regular Spartakiade! Would it turn out that all those unprecedented sums had been spent to impress Bulgarian weightlifters and Zambian boxers? What about the expected 300,000 foreign tourists (and their much needed hard currency?) Would NBC televise the games even if no U.S. athletes took part? Would anybody now consider the Moscow Olympic Games "the Greatest Ever?" Moscow's propaganda apparatus was not programmed to deal with an unexpected boycott offensive. Yet it was evident that an urgent countercampaign was to be organized and conducted with the use of all instruments of Soviet propaganda. Several more days elapsed and there still was no official reaction from Moscow. *Sovetskiy Sport* introduced a new column—"The World Prepares for the Moscow Olympics"—which later became one of the major platforms for citing support for the games and protests against the boycott. Apart from this, there was no reaction.

The first sign that a major propaganda campaign was being prepared and that the highest party organs were involved was a 16-17 January "working meeting" held at the CPSU Central Committee, with the participation of representatives of the Communist parties of Bulgaria, Hungary,

Vietnam, the G.D.R., Cuba, Poland, Romania, The C.S.S.R., and Mongolia. No details were reported. The press merely stated: "Those attending the meeting exchanged views on the progress of the preparation for the XXII Olympic Games, examined questions of information, and visited a number of Olympic facilities in Moscow."[21] A week later, when the Soviet propaganda countercampaign was in full swing, a similar meeting took place in Moscow. Tass reported it in the following manner:

> A routine meeting of the mixed commission of the Olympiade-80 Organizing Committee took place on 22-23 January. Leaders of sports organizations of Bulgaria, Hungary, Vietnam, the G.D.R., Cuba, the P.D.R.K., laos, Mongolia, Poland, Romania, the U.S.S.R., and the C.S.S.R. took part. They exchanged opinions on preparations for the Olympic games in Moscow and visited Olympic sites. The leaders of the socialist countries' sports organizations were received by M. Zimyanin, CPSU Central Committee secretary. Questions of mutual interest were touched on in the talks, which took place in a warm and comradely atmosphere. Taking part in the talks were I. Novikov, deputy chairman of the U.S.S.R. Council of Ministers, and chairman of the Olympic Games Organizing Committee, and E. Tyazhelnikov, head of the CPSU Central Committee Propaganda Department.[22]

While the meeting was described as a "routine affair, participation of the CPSU Central Committee Propaganda Department head indicated the focal point for participants.

The first operational decisions on the "boycott" countercampaign were taken during the 16-17 January meeting. The first signs of a campaign, albeit hastily organized but nevertheless widespread and intense, appeared on 20 January. A day earlier Tass had reported from Damascus the signing of a Soviet-Syrian sports cooperation protocol. This report still did not mention the devil by name: "We know that the imperialists are now concocting various plots against Olympiade-80. They want to do everything possible to slander such a noble cause as sport, and smear relations between the U.S.S.R and other countries. We are confident that all those intrigues are doomed to fail.[23]

This was the last such report. On the same page of *Sovetskiy Sport* there was a long and unusually sharp article by S. Bliznyuk entitled "Peace and Olympism Are Inseparable." The article set the tone of the entire campaign, indicated its main themes, marshalled some of the campaign's main instruments, and introduced new techniques which were not used in the earlier Olympic propaganda campaign. The article consisted of three separate elements. A preamble, news reports on protests against the proposed boycott in several countries, and an extensive commentary. The preamble repeated and developed the article's title and for the first time made use of two techniques not used in previous campaigns—polarization (strictly separating the good and evil forces involved in the conflict, indicating that there was no middle course, and clearly defining the two existing positions) and pinpointing the enemy (there were no clearly defined enemies in the two previous Olympic campaigns).

> We understand clearly why all real friends of sports and Olympism decisively oppose the provocative maneuvers of supporters of cold war in the United States, England, and some other imperialist states, who are striving to utilize sport as an instrument of their policy and hinder the forthcoming meeting of world youth on the arenas of the Moscow Olympic Games.... The foreign policy of the U.S.S.R. which is clear to the peoples of the world, corresponds with their basic interests... and serves as a reliable support of all forces struggling for peace and detente. Supporting the course of preserving the unity of the Olympic movement, striving to prevent interference of politicians in sport, and participating in the Moscow's holiday of youth—despite threats, slanderous tricks, and political pressure—this is the attitude of the sports world and the public of the countries participating in the Olympic movement toward the Olympiade in the first country of socialism."[24]

Further on Bliznyuk reported a statement by Lord Killanin, IOC president, made in a BBC radio interview, to the effect that the XXII Olympic Games would take place in Moscow as planned. Support on the part of the French Communist party, several French newspapers, and Mexican and F.R.G. Olympic Committee members was also cited by Bliznyuk. The article went on to elaborate those examples of support. Carter's administration and the president himself were accused of "political fiasco" and using the "Olympic card" as the last resort. British Prime Minister Margaret Thatcher was also accused of using the Olympic games for political goals. Bliznyuk also quoted B. Fell, president of the Lake Placid Winter Olympic Games Organization Committee, who had expressed concern that the boycott of the Moscow Olympic Games would affect the 1984 Los Angeles Olympics.

The U.S. government was accused of "arm-twisting tactics," pressure, blackmail, and demagogy, "all of which encounter powerful opposition on the part of public opinion and the Olympians of various countries." The U.S. administration was also accused of lying, citing nonexistent support. While according to Bliznyuk, Saudi Arabia had declared that it would not participate in Moscow already in October 1979, this had been cited by Washington as support for the boycott. "Such tactics, as we all know, have always characterized the authors of the cold war. Now they have been borrowed by the present opponents of friendship and détente."[25] This sentence was to become one of the main themes of the "boycott" counter-campaign. Proponents of the boycott were overtly declared opponents of peace and détente, thus lending the issue of boycotting the games (or participating) the much larger dimension of supporting or opposing peace and détente.

During the same day (20 January), Bliznyuk's article was given unusual prominence in Soviet radio' broadcasts in foreign languages. The article was also summarized by Tass and disseminated by its international service.[26] A subsequent short item disseminated by Moscow world service in English focused attention on President Carter, and for the first time accused him personally of "undermining the policy of détente and reviving the cold war."[27] This item also related for the first time the issue of the boycott of Afghanistan: "President Carter has recommended that the U.S. National Olympic Committee boycott the Olympic games in Moscow. He said it in a broadcast on American television on Sunday. The president said that the suggested measure must compel the Soviet Union to withdraw its troops from Afghanistan. As is known a limited contingent of Soviet troops is stationed in Afghanistan, at its government's request and in compliance with the friendship treaty."[28] During the first day of the campaign Moscow still entertained some illusions: "The president's recommendation for a boycott is not mandatory for the U.S. National Olympic Committee."[29]

Earlier that day Tass reported Senator Edward Kennedy's opposition to the proposed boycott (citing Kennedy's speech in Des Moines, Iowa) and mentioned the first action on the part of a foreign front organization: "The influential public organization of the United States, Women Strike for Peace, has come out with a strong criticism of the American administration's line to unilaterally curb Soviet-American relations."[30] Several things had become clear by the end of the day. A new propaganda campaign had opened with all guns firing. The "preparations" campaign was completely overshadowed. New themes and instruments were conceived, new techniques introduced. The entire propaganda apparatus was mobilized for one single goal: to save the Moscow Olympics by foiling the proposed boycott.

THEMES

Nature of the Boycott

From the outset the Soviet Union refused to accept the fact that the boycott was a reaction to the invasion of Afghanistan. The major efforts of the propaganda countercampaign, especially during its first days, were aimed at presenting the "true nature of the boycott." The notion that the boycott was a more or less spontaneous move was rejected by Moscow. Already on 21 January Tass informed the world that the proposed boycott was "in accord with the demands of those circles which already long ago, several years ago to be more precise, opposed the holding of the 1980 Olympic Games in a socialist country."[31]

On the same day Vadim Zagladin, first deputy head of the CPSU Central Committee International Department, was interviewed by French television. This was the first official Soviet reaction to the proposed boycott. Zagladin stated that President Carter had used the Afghan situation as a "pretext to do what he wanted to do before" and that it had been a "premeditated act."[32] In a *Sovetskiy Sport* commentary of 6 February, disseminated by Tass, it was again claimed that the proposed boycott was a part of the U.S. effort to prevent the Olympic games from taking place in Moscow, an effort seen by *Sovetskiy Sport* as going back to the 1969 IOC Amsterdam session, which chose Montreal as the venue of the the 1976 Olympic Games. By "intimidating IOC members, reactionary circles were trying even then at least to postpone the Olympics coming to the country of socialism."[33]

Another source traces the planning of the boycott back to only 1978: "Carter's call for a boycott of the 1980 Olympics did not originate today or even yesterday. He set his sights on this target back in 1978. Suffice it to recall that Washington threatened to 'wreck the Moscow Olympics' at the time of the trial of the American spy Shcharanskiy. A year later, at the time of the provocative ballyhoo fanned by Carter over the 'Soviet presence' in Cuba, there were also threats to wreck the Olympic games in Moscow. Now, fueling the cold war atmosphere, the White House has switched from threats to actions."[34] The fact that it was "preplanned," "preconceived," "coordinated," was only one aspect of the boycott as presented by Moscow. A far more important (and dangerous) characteristic as seen by Moscow was its being politically directed against concepts such as "peace," "detente," and "international cooperation," which constitute the ideological and semantic basis of Soviet foreign policy. This was also established in one of the first reactions of the proposed boycott, the 21 January commentary of Vladimir Goncharov, disseminated by Tass: "The president's demand is clearly political and its aim is to disrupt détente and undermine peaceful cooperation of the peoples."[35]

On 31 January, the Soviet Olympic Committee issued an official declaration against the boycott: "It is absolutely obvious that the point at issue is a preplanned and coordinated hostile act directed against mutual understanding and friendship among nations, against peace and progress... serving [the reactionary forces'] ...policy of blackmail and hegemonism."[36] There were other statements and declarations in the same vein, such as that of Vladimir Kotelnikov, vice president of the U.S.S.R. Academy of Sciences, who concluded that "objectively, the U.S. line, aimed at wrecking the 1980 Olympics in Moscow, contradicts the ideas of peace, international cooperation, and détente."[37] After establishing that the boycott was a "premeditated" and "planned" act, aimed against "peace," "détente," "friendship," and international cooperation," thus clarifying its "true character," Moscow then logically applied itself to the next question.

Why Was the Boycott Proposed?

While Moscow had no difficulty dealing with the nature of the boycott, its difficulty in explaining why the boycott had ever been proposed in the first place was all too evident. Soviet sources were unanimous in saying that the boycott had "nothing to do with Afghanistan." (This statement will be examined later on as a separate theme of Soviet propaganda.) While Moscow sometimes feigned astonishment and declared that "we simply fail to understand the reasons for such a decision,"[38] it usually explained that the boycott was an attempt to exert pressure on the Soviet Union... undermine the policy of easing tension and reviving the cold war."[39] The same sentence was repeated by V. Goncharov in his 21 January Tass commentary already cited, and in hundreds of articles and commentaries dealing with the boycott.

Often, much more specific reasons for the boycott were given. A favorite was the explanation that Carter had initiated the boycott to "salvage his failing popularity... by playing on people's emotions inside the United States."[40] The same explanation alternately used "selfish ends"[41] of the U.S. president, "Carter's personal ambitions,"[42] and his "instrument of internal politics"[43] to describe the "real" reasons behind the boycott. Sometimes the explanation bordered on psychoanalysis. Moscow television stated: "The boycott is caused by personal ambition, personal irritation, and mercenary calculations."[44] The usual conclusion was that Carter simply wanted to be reelected. While Carter remained the center of explanations for the real reasons for the boycott as seen by Moscow, occasionally international issues loomed large. Sometimes it was stated that "Carter was using the boycott to deal a blow to the Helsinki accords and undermine the forthcoming Madrid conference on security and cooperation in Europe."[45] Another theory: the boycott had been conceived by "Carter and his team" to "create a split, disunity, and tension in the world."[46] This and several other standard statements on the boycott were repeated verbatim in an article by A. Kholodniy in *Soviet Union.*

Sometimes England was also accused of conceiving the boycott idea to achieve domestic goals: "The unhealthy racket over the Olympic games has yet another noteworthy feature. U.S. and British ruling circles are evidently trying to use it in order to distract the attention of ordinary citizens from the difficult situation which has developed in their countries' economy. It would be better to pay attention to the situation of the urgent internal tasks and not engage in a provocative fuss which does not reduce the army of unemployment or bring down the level of inflation."[47]

Radio Moscow, in its broadcasts to the F.R.G., had another explanation for the real reasons for the boycott, this time connected with the relations between the United States and its West European allies: "The true motives of the characters in this disgraceful farce are not what they claim to be: the United States does not want the West Germans to stay away from the Olympic games because it seriously thinks that this could in any way influence Soviet policy. To President Carter and his advisers this is a sort of Gessler's hat, a symbolic though effective act of submission by the allies which is doubly important in view of the adventurous plans in the Middle East."[48]

Yet another explanation was that the White House conceived the "Olympic blackmail" to prevent the Soviet Union from gaining international prestige and turning the games into a huge success. This was described as an attempt "to cover the sun with one finger."[49] This explanation was repeated by several Radio Moscow broadcasts.[50] The meticulous avoidance of the Afghanistan issue (usually lightly dismissed as irrelevant) and the wide range of domestic and international reasons for the boycott— as presented by Moscow—demonstrated Moscow's reluctance (or inability) to face the real issue and its confusion during the first stages of the proposed boycott.

Possible Results of the Boycott

This theme was developed in two separate stages. During the first stage (up to 25 May, the deadline for declaring participation in the Moscow Olympics), the negative consequences of the boycott were stressed. During the second stage (up to the end of June) the leitmotif was "nothing serious has happened." Since the decision to participate in or boycott the Moscow Olympic Games was presented as a decision to support or oppose détente, international cooperation, and peace,[51] the possible results of the Olympic boycott were usually described in political terms. The first reaction was to interpret the proposed boycott not only as a measure aimed against the Soviet Union, but as one "undermining the Olympic movement as a whole."[52] Another commentary of the same day already spoke of "disrupting détente and undermining the peaceful cooperation of the people" as the main result of the boycott.[53]

This refrain was immediately picked up and repeated ad infinitum by all vehicles of Soviet propaganda, including all Communist newspapers throughout the world. The Japanese Communist newspaper *Akahata* of 23 January combined the two already introduced trends and warned that the proposed boycott would "introduce serious difficulties in the Olympic movement and aggravate tension in international relations."[54] At the same time the first vague threats against the 1984 Los Angeles Olympic Games were introduced. At this point the first contradictions also appeared. They illustrated the disorganization and confusion that prevailed in Moscow during the first days after the boycott was proposed, as well as a lack of coordination, something very uncharacteristic of Soviet propaganda campaigns. On 23 January Tass quoted the Brazilian newspaper *Jornal do Brasil* (date not given) as saying: "The attempts at boycotting the Olympics can boomerang on the United States and its associates."[55] To this Tass added: "The newspaper recalls that the next Olympic games are to be held in Los Angeles."[56]

The same evening West German ZDF television telecasted an interview with Albert Grigoryants, *Izvestiya* correspondent in Bonn. Asked about the possible results of the boycott, Grigoryants said: "I must say that whenever in ancient Greece a polis, a state, refused to take part in the Olympic games, it was suspected of planning something evil, say making preparations for war. Believe us, we want détente to be continued and sport, so to speak, belongs to the cooperation of the people, it is something all people have in common, and we will continue to take part in sports competitions. But I cannot say today that we will certainly take part in the Olympic games in Los Angeles, should the Americans implement their boycott."[57] Almost at the same time Vladimir Popov, first deputy chairman of the Olympiade-80 Organizing Committee, was telling David Frost on a British ITV sports special that the Soviet Union would not boycott the Los Angeles Olympic Games.[58]

Almost all other possible results of the boycott, as seen by Moscow, were related to one of the two established trends (undermining the Olympic movement and a blow to peace and détente.) Sometimes Moscow was more specific as to what could happen if the boycott were to take place. The effects most frequently mentioned were: "A split in the Olympic movement,"[59] "the clock will be turned back, and we will be taken back to the difficult years of brinkmanship,"[60] "the boycott will create an atmosphere of another cold war,"[61] the boycott will "violate international agreements and accords, including provisions on human rights and on the development of human contacts."[62] One category of possible results was related to U.S. athletes, who were presented as "victims of deceit"[63] and "losers in all respects, who will be made to swallow the bitter pill of total defeat, not by their rivals in sports competitions but by their own politicians."[64] In another commentary Moscow warned the Washington administration that it "will lose all support" as a result of its boycott.[65] On another occasion possible electoral consequences were clearly indicated: "The voters will also give their assessment of the unbalanced and scornful attitude of the White House bordering on unceremoniousness with regard to the Olympic movement and its fate."[66]

Moscow related the possible results of the boycott not only to the United States but also to other participants, most notably the F.R.G. Emphasizing that the decision of the F.R.G. National Olympic Committee to boycott the Moscow Olympic Games was made under heavy pressure from Washington and represented a "dictate,"[67] Moscow pointed out some possible consequences for the F.R.G.: "If the United States administration can sway a decision of the West German Olympic Committee, it may have enough power of persuasion, or something else, to make the country toe its line in other matters too. And, indeed, this has already happened in such vital areas as East-West relations and in particular European security."[68]

Speculations about the future of the Olympic movement, the undisguised threats of possible consequences for peace and détente, warnings against a relapse into cold war, and pity for U.S. athletes, all became of secondary importance after the chips fell on 25 May. Up to this stage, the "results" theme of the boycott countercampaign was aimed at deterring states from taking part in the boycott. After it became clear that the boycott would have at least a partial success and that about two-fifths of the Olympic movement's members would boycott the Moscow Olympic Games, the "results" theme underwent a radical transformation and reappeared under a new slogan.

Nothing Terrible Has Happened—the Boycott Has Failed

This was the dominant theme after 25 May, when the national Olympic Committees made their final decision regarding participation in the Moscow Olympic Games. Nevertheless, some traces could be detected even earlier. One of the early motifs was: "The games will take place in Moscow on time as planned." This was stressed in every single interview with Olympiade-80 members. Vladimir Popov emphasized it on 29 January on Radio Moscow,[69] V. Smirnov said it in his 12 March ZDF TV interview[70]—to mention only two of hundreds of identical statements.

Another early trend was to minimize the importance of support for the boycott that had been expressed by several countries. Usually this support was presented as homage paid by servants to their master:

> The Israeli Embassy in Washington said on Thursday that Israeli Prime Minister Begin supports the boycott of the Olympic games in Moscow, sought by the U.S. administration, and has turned to the Israeli Olympic Committee with a call to support his stand. This is no big gain for Washington, which is striving to use the world Olympic games as small change in its political gambling. It is precisely the regimes that have compromised themselves in the international arena that are in a hurry to back Washington's

position. Tel Aviv's aggressive policy in the Middle East, the flouting by Israeli occupiers of the rights of the Arab people of Palestine, have the unlimited support of the United States and now in gratitude Israeli leaders are readily joining Washington's act of vengeance to bring into sports the methods and tactics of political gangsterism. The U.S.-Israeli anti-Olympic team has been joined by the governments of Oman and Saudi Arabia, whose regimes and finances are know to have completely merged with U.S. capital. The wish to boycott the Olympic games has been declared by representatives of the al-Sadat regime, one notorious for singing in unison for some time with Tel Aviv and Washington. These are perhaps all the "allies" in this dirty and inglorious White House venture.[71]

When it became apparent that the boycott would be at least partially successful, Moscow began to speculate about the number of countries expected to participate in the Olympic games. This was another area of contradictions which again suggested Moscow's confusion. On 22 March *Komsomolskaya Pravda* reported that "104 countries have already accepted the invitation to participate in the 1980 Olympics."[72] I. Novikov, Olympiade-80 chairman, reported on 28 March that "105 national Olympic Committees have informed the Organizing Committee that they definitely intend to participate in the games, which is evidence of widespread international interest in the Moscow Olympics."[73]

On 3 April Tass stated: "The decision of the national Olympic Committees of more than a hundred countries to send their athletes to the Soviet Union to take part in the Olympics shows that the world's sports community is aware of the consequences that a boycott of the Olympics may generate, and regard calls for the boycott as an encroachment of the rights of sportsmen."[74] Again Tass on 16 April mentioned that "it would be wrong to suppose that the boycott will do any harm to the Moscow Olympics.... At this time we have confirmation of intention to participate in the Olympics from 105 national Olympic Committees. Only seven national Olympic Committees have let us know that they will not be able to participate in the Olympic games. This shows to some extent how the Olympic world is reacting to the attempts, the efforts undertaken by the U.S. administration."[75]

On the same day *Komsomolskaya Pravda*, quoting Smirnov's 15 April interview, put the number at "106 participating countries."[76] In a more extensive report of the same interview *Sovetskiy Sport* of 16 April termed the boycott "suicidal." Smirnov was quoted describing the "depression" of U.S. companies "who will suffer severe losses as a result of the administration's acts," as well as the damage to U.S. athletes. Smirnov also admitted for the first time that it was possible that some U.S. tourists would not come to Moscow as a result of the boycott, stressing however, that the tickets which had been sold would not be refunded.[77] In an earlier report

Krasnaya Zvezda stated that NBC would sustain a loss of 87 million dollars.[78]

Up to 25 May the only damage that Moscow admitted the boycott would cause was supposed to be felt by U.S. companies (mainly Coca-Cola) and of course by the athletes who would not be coming to Moscow. Sometimes this was done in a sarcastic and mocking way (sarcasm being a technique frequently used throughout the boycott countercampaign): "Of course we can do without the minor things which we do not have, and which we will replace with our own. We do not necessarily have to drink Coca-Cola. We have good kvass, and besides, our Borzhomi water is fairly good, and we do have enough drinks to quench thirsts without breaking the athletic diet, as they say."[79]

Another example: "it ... would be naive to think that we cannot have the Olympic games without Coca-Cola."[80] The matter was presented somewhat differently to foreign audiences: "And if no Coca-Cola, to which many foreign athletes are accustomed, is on sale, that will be the fault of those who have decided to punish them for taking place in the Olympics."[81] When it became obvious that several sports "superpowers," such as the United States, the F.R.G., Canada, and Japan, would boycott the Moscow Olympic Games, the Soviet propaganda apparatus had to explain why even this would not hurt the games: "Of course, it is regrettable that the athletes of the United States, the F.R.G., and Canada will not come to the Soviet capital, but their absence will not diminish the sports significance of the games. It suffices to mention that the Americans lost their leadership in world sport long ago, and in Montreal they were third according to the number of medals won. And the Canadian sportsmen, despite the fact that they were performing on home ground, were not able to climb on the winners' pedestal even once."[82]

As late as May 1980 Smirnov still maintained that "only six countries, including the United States, have declared that they are boycotting the games. A number of countries will not attend for other reasons."[83] Some difficulties developed after 25 May, when the exact number of countries who had officially declared their participation was published. On the one hand Moscow had to drop the number of participating countries from 105, 106, 107, and so forth, to 80.[84] On the other, it had to be explained that even the reduced number of participants would not hurt the games:

> Twenty-nine Olympic Committees refused to take part in the games. The overwhelming majority of them did so not for political considerations as opponents of the Olympic games try to present matters. Of them only 19 offically informed the Organizing Committee of their refusal to participate, and it is known that in view of demands by sportsmen and the public at large, some of them intend to revise their decision. Twenty-eight Olympic Commit-

tees have not yet decided on their attitude to the games.... In the opinion of the sports public and many statesmen the idea of boycotting the games has failed. The announced list of participants is evidence of extensive support for the Olympic games in Moscow by sportsmen in many countries of the world."[85]

In another commentary Tass tried to present the boycotting countries as a coalition of fascists, racists, and dictators: "The countries which have decided to boycott the Olympics form quite a strange company. They include the fascist Chile, the dictatorship of Haiti, Honduras, Paraguay, South Korea—currently in the grip of large-scale popular demonstrations against the reactionary clique—China, Israel, and Pakistan. It is only regrettable that Washington succeeded in dragging into the 'anti-Olympic team' such countries as Canada and Japan, whose sportsmen were dying to attend the Olympic games."[86] It is astonishing that despite the fact that Moscow officially admitted that "19 countries have offically informed the Olympiade-80 Committee that they will boycott the Games," on 1 June Radio Moscow was still claiming: "The allegation by Western propagandamongers that dozens of countries have decided to join the boycott of the Moscow Olympics is incorrect. This is absolutely wrong. Only six countries, including the United States, have announced that they are boycotting the games. Other countries are not coming for other reasons and do not allude to the boycott."[87]

This particular broadcast (the "round table" weekly review) was beamed to the Soviet public and not to foreign audiences. Even a week after the final deadline for declaring participation in the games, Moscow was still afraid to tell the Soviet public the real dimensions of the boycott. The only area in which some damage was admitted to was international tourism. Vladimir Promyslov, mayor of Moscow, and other Soviet officials admitted in the first week of June that only about 70,000 foreign tourist were expected during the Olympic games. "Fewer is better," Promyslov told Western reporters, "they will get better service."[88] Amazingly one month later, Spartak Beglov, Novosti's political observer, writing for the Bulgarian *Rabotnichesko Delo* of 18 July, was still maintaining that "some 250,000 foreign tourists will attend the Olympic games."

Afghanistan

Since the Soviet invasion of Afghanistan was the direct reason for the Olympic boycott, the Afghanistan issue immediately became a natural theme of the Soviet "boycott" countercampaign. It was intended exclusively for foreign audiences, the Soviet daily press and radio broadcasts for domestic audiences scarcely mentioned Afghanistan when treating the subject of the Olympic boycott. As early as 20 January Moscow admitted that the boycott was aimed at "compelling the Soviet Union to withdraw its troops from Afghanistan."[89] On the following day, this version was changed and the motto "Afghanistan has nothing to do with the boycott" adopted. It remained predominant until the opening of the games. In an already quoted 21 January interview with Zagladin for French television, he said that President Carter had used the Afghanistan situation as a "pretext to do what he had wanted to do before," and that the boycott proposal had been a "premeditated act."[90] Simultaneously, the Soviet invasion was justified in terms of commitment to Afghanistan and abiding by agreements: "It [the boycott] is blackmail. The Soviet Union has a commitment to Afghanistan, had an agreement, and under no condition would it cede to that kind of pressure.... You do not talk to any country— especially the Soviet Union—in that way."[91]

In many broadcasts aimed at English-speaking countries, Moscow not only denied that there was any connection between the boycott and Afghanistan (following the established pattern of presenting the boycott as premeditated act), but also suggested a link between the future of Carter's administration and the American people learning the "truth" about Afghanistan: "As the truth about Afghanistan gradually reaches the American people—and ultimately it must—the present administration will lose the support it supposedly has in calling for an Olympic boycott. As a matter of fact it may lose all support."[92]

The principle that sport and politics should be separated, a notion previously rejected as naive by the Soviet Union, was applied by I. Novikov to the Afghan issue: "As chairman of the XXII Olympics Organizing Committee I must tell you that we are profoundly convinced that preparations for and staging of the Olympic games should not be linked with events in Afghanistan or with any other political events. We must be guided by the principles and rules of the Olympic charter, while the modern world's political problems should be solved by political means and on a political level."[93] The leader of the Afghan Olympic Committee added his own effort to Moscow's and sent President Carter a letter protesting the boycott and stating that it contradicted the spirit and principles of the Olympic movement. The letter was disseminated by Tass throughout the world.[94]

Foreign communist leaders and newspapers, who took an extensive part in the campaign, repeatedly endorsed Moscow's stand on Afghanistan. Their statements were immediately amplified by Tass. Such was the case with a speech by Georges Marchais, secretary general of the French Communist party, who was reported by Tass to have said: "There is one fundamental question to answer concerning events in Afghanistan which one should have the courage to do: Does a country that has established a progressive regime have the right to conclude an agreement on mutual security with a friendly country, allowing it to rebuff outside intervention? ....Current developments... make me return to the question of the Olympic games. From this rostrum I want to voice my indignation at the inadmissible conduct of U.S. President Carter."[95]

Sometimes Moscow went as far as accusing the United States of actually conducting a war in Afghanistan: "Echoing the statements of Washington administration officials, certain circles in the F.R.G. are trying to put forward the events in Afghanistan as an excuse for their anti-Olympic actions. However, it is well known that responsibility for these events is totally and completely borne by those circles in the United States and their agents who began and are still waging an 'undeclared war' against the sovereign Democratic Republic of Afghanistan, trying to overthrow the established revolutionary regime in that country.... The essence of the matter is not the events in Afghanistan; it is well known that these events themselves are being used by Washington as a pretext for stepping up tension, including the justification of anti-Olympic acts."[96] On the subject of the Olympic boycott the Afghanistan connection was the only theme exclusively reserved for foreign audiences. There was no hint of any link between the Afghanistan invasion and the Olympic boycott for domestic consumption.

The Boycott and the Law

The legal aspects of the Olympic boycott were dealt with by the Soviet propaganda apparatus in three different categories: international law, human rights in the United States, and alleged U.S. plans to subvert the Olympic games by using CIA and FBI agents.

International Law

On 1 and 2 April 1980 Tass disseminated a commentary signed by Oleg Sadikov, Doctor of Jurisprudence and RSFSR-accredited figure of science, which dealt with the international legal aspects of the Olympic boycott. According to Sadikov the boycott contradicted the Olympic charter on two points. First, the games were the IOC's games and not the host country's, therefore a boycott against the host country violated the Olympic charter, because the IOC is independent in its decisions and moves. Second, the IOC confers the rights to host the games on a city and not a country. Therefore whatever the policy of the host country may be, it has nothing to do with an Olympic boycott.[97]

The additional points raised by Sadikov: the boycott violated the Helsinki agreement and the UN charter, both demanding and encouraging the strengthening and expansion of human contacts and cooperation in all areas.[98] This point had already been made at the very beginning of the boycott countercampaign: "With its stand on the Moscow Olympics, the American administration has again placed its country in the position of a nation that violates international agreements and accords, including provisions on human rights and on the development of human contacts. That will inevitably also be the position of the governments of those countries that took part in the all-European conference and who intend to follow the American lead."[99]

According to Sadikov, the boycott also violated the UNESCO charter, which stresses the necessity of using physical culture and sport for bringing nations together and promoting mutual understanding and respect.[100] Furthermore, Sadikov claimed, the boycott contradicted U.S. law and specifically the U.S. Congress Act on Amateur Sport of 8 November 1978, which states that the U.S. Olympic Committee is the only authoritative body that may decide on participation in the Olympic Games.[101]

Another claim in the same category (international law) was made on 28 January 1980, when Tass maintained that "the United States is continuing its rude interference in international sporting relations and in the internal affairs of various countries, including the affairs of the North Atlantic bloc allies, attempting to foist upon them a decision pleasing to Washington."[102]

The same commentary labeled countries which had expressed support for the boycott as "reactionary": "The idea of a boycott of the 1980 Olympics has been supported by only a few of Washington's allies in the aggressive blocs, and also the governments of Oman, Saudi Arabia (a few days earlier Tass had maintained that Saudi Arabia's nonparticipation had nothing to do with the boycott), Israel, Chile, and the like, that is, those conservative and reactionary regimes renowned for their dependence on the United States in military and economic respects, and who obediently fulfill Washington's will."[103]

Human Rights in the United States

The second legal aspect treated by Soviet propaganda was the claim that the boycott infringed upon the rights of the U.S. athletes as American citizens. The general accusation was that in preventing U.S. athletes from competing in Moscow the United States government was violating the Human Rights Bill, the Fifth Amendment of the U.S. Constitution, and other legal acts.[104] Since *hostages* was a hot word in January 1980 (as a result of the November 1979 seizure of U.S. diplomatic personnel in the U.S. Embassy in Tehran by Iranian "student" revolutionaries), and the release of the U.S. hostages in Iran one of the main goals of U.S. foreign policy, Soviet propaganda made extensive use of the concept of "hostages" in describing various aspects of the boycott, and evoking the sought-after effect. On 21 January 1980 Tass used the concept (in this context) for the first time: "The fact is however, that President Carter (who is known to boast of being a human rights champion) has no use for the rights of others if these run counter to his political ambitions. As a matter of fact, athletes and the sports movement are assigned, in this present adventure of the president, the role of some kind of hostages (again despite the fact that of late Carter has repeatedly denounced the use of hostages for the attainment of political ends)." [105]

The concept was subsequently picked up by all instruments of Soviet propaganda. Spartak Beglov, APN political observer, warned that "thousands of young men and women are under the threat of becoming some kind of 'hostages' in this indecent game."[106] *Sovetskiy Sport* of 26 March 1980 also reported demonstrations by the "French progressive public" against the boycott under the slogan "athletes are not hostages." The boycott was presented as an "eye-opener to many Americans that their country is not as free from the establishment as they used to think."[107] "Astonishment" was exhibited at the fact that "such a thing can happen in 'free' America."[108] Indignation was expressed while presenting the boycott as a "campaign of political pressure... nothing but an act of infringement of the human rights of athletes for the sake of satisfying the selfish ambitions of certain politicians."[109]

This theme of Soviet propaganda intensified in April, when specific and possible reprisals against U.S. athletes and sports officials were described by the Soviet mass media: "It is known that American sports officials have already been taken more than once to various U.S. Government offices where they were subjected to 'arm-twisting.' An official White House spokesman said recently that the State Department had threatened to take away the passports of sportsmen who decide to go to Moscow and thus deprive them of the possibility of leaving the country. It is open to conjecture what methods of influencing American Olympians will be decided upon by the generals at their forthcoming meeting. Other questions also arise: Where will U.S. sports officials be taken after the 'instruction session' in the Pentagon: to the Supreme Court, the FBI, or the CIA? Judging by American press reports the latter two agencies have long been showing a pointed interest in those American sportsmen and organizers of the Olympic movement who intend to boycott the president's demand for a boycott of the Olympic Games in Moscow."[110]

Izvestiya reported "antidemocratic reprisals" in the United States in connection with the Olympic boycott, and termed the situation "McCarthyism." Tass immediately picked up the concept and utilized it, describing the U.S. domestic ramifications of the boycott: "And there is yet another illustration to the theme of freedom of the press, Washington style. Carter has issued a special order prohibiting the American mass media from concluding any contracts connected with coverage of the Olympic games in Moscow.... Matters will not be restricted to a simple scolding. 'Legal action' will be taken against mavericks. To be more precise, those who will risk upholding the ideals of the Olympic movement will be put on trial, and since the issue, according to official Washington's statements, is a 'threat to national security,' the punishment will be commensurate.... In light of the present campaign of hounding American sportsmen, which is McCarthyist by nature, Washington's phrasemongering on the theme of 'defending rights and freedoms' appears especially unseemly and repugnant."[111]

When the U.S. National Olympic Committee decided in favor of a boycott, Moscow termed the decision "illegal" and "unjustified."[112] Despite the fact that earlier Moscow had claimed that according to the U.S. Constitution the U.S. Olympic Committee was the only organ that could decide on participation in the Moscow Olympic Games, no explanation was offered as to what made the U.S. Olympic Committee's decision "illegal." Angela Davis, "the noted U.S. political and public figure and candidate of the U.S. Communist party for the post of vice-president," was widely reported by the Soviet press as condeming the decision of the U.S. Olympic Committee to boycott the Moscow games as "contradictory to the U.S. national interest and the American people, against the cause of peace and the international Olympic movement."[113]

Literaturnaya Gazeta of 23 April 1980 quotes an interview with Benjamin Chavis to the French newspaper *Droit et Liberte*. Claiming that "there are many human hostages in the United States," among them of course the U.S. athletes, Chavis accused the administration of interfering with the country's legal system, applying pressure on the 4th district appeal court to rule against the athletes, who wanted the court to declare the decision of the U.S. Olympic Committee illegal. In addition, Chavis placed support (and opposition) to the boycott on a social basis, maintaining that "the Black and especially the poor do not support the boycott."[114]

Komsomolskaya Pravda showed deep concern for the U.S. athletes, "threatened with severe punishments and even prison" if they decided to compete in Moscow.[115] Quoting Susan Phillips, "coordinator of the movement on saving the Olympic movement," the newspaper stated: "The main task now is to help those athletes who want to go to Moscow and defend them from possible reprisals."[116]

CIA, FBI

The final category of the boycott's legal aspects theme related to the CIA and the FBI. On 3 April Tass reported that the CIA and the FBI "have long been showing a pointed interest in those American sportsmen and organizers of the Olympic movement who intend to boycott the president's demand for a boycott of the Olympic Games in Moscow."[117] Later on many more specific and radical accusations were made. The entire affair followed a long-established pattern of Soviet propaganda: a report in a rather obscure local newspaper (in this case *Moskovskaya Pravda*), followed by a Tass commentary on the report, disseminated throughout the world.

Moskovskaya Pravda of 16 April 1980 accused Zbigniew Brzezinski of organizing a special "anti-Olympic team ... recruited by the CIA and FBI from among the students and alumni of Harvard and Philadelphia Universities." They were to undergo special training and be sent by the CIA and the FBI to Moscow disguised as tourists "to engage in hostile subversive acts against the sportsmen from five continents who will gather in Moscow for the 1980 Olympics."[118] Vladimir Pozner, commenting on the report, added some details: "Volunteers are being picked in the under-thirty age bracket, all of them fluent in Russian or one of the many languages spoken in this country.... A special school, very hush-hush of course, will open in a West European country, most likely England, where 'students'—I put that in quotes—will be given a two-month course on subversive activities during the games."[119]

During the second part of April 1980 the "legal aspects" theme was dominant in the Soviet propaganda campaign. This was no coincidence, since at this time several U.S. athletes approached a Washington court requesting that the decision of the U.S. Olympic Committee be declared illegal. While the court rejected the athletes' plea within a week, the entire episode was extensively covered and commented upon by the Soviet mass media. It was only natural to emphasize the "legal aspects" theme during that period.

Carter and Company

Pinpointing the enemies is a specific technique of every Soviet operational propaganda campaign. Since the "boycott" countercampaign was a typical operational campaign, it had its own villains. The Olympic boycott was proposed by President Carter. This qualified him as villain number one of the "boycott" countercampaign. During the first day of the campaign Moscow spoke of "Carter's attempts to exert pressure on the Soviet Union."[120] This was followed by a commentary disseminated by Tass, devoted almost completely to President Carter. He was accused of "distorting the essence of the developments in Afghanistan," "causing a catastrophe in the Olympic movement," "turning the athletes into hostages—despite the fact that of late Carter has repeatedly denounced the use of hostages for the attainment of political ends," "stepping on laws and rules if they stand in his way," "having no use for the rights of others if these run counter to his political ambitions," "striving to disrupt detente and undermine peaceful cooperation of the peoples," "trying to gain the support of the 'money bags' who finance the presidential campaign candidates," and so forth.[121] The commentary concluded on an historical note: "Carter appears to be willing to leave his mark in Olympic history in the style of Herostratos, i.e., as a man who attempted to disrupt this international sports and youth holiday. If one is to use sports terminology, one can say that the Olympic annals will recall Carter as a man who erected rather than cleared hurdles, and that Carter's decision will, in the long run, doubtless prove to be a goal he scored into his own net."[122]

This was only the beginning. Radio Moscow in English on the same day mentioned the fact that Carter had in September 1979 dropped out of a long-distance race in Washington because of exhaustion (as was widely reported in the West at the time), succinctly adding: "Last September Mr. Carter went rubber-legged and dropped out of Maryland's race. Even if he is not trying to score even with sports after this mishap, President Carter will hardly succeed in making the international Olympic movement go rubber-legged."[123] Later reports and comments accused Carter of organizing the boycott "in order to get reelected,"[124] "acting against the interests of U.S. athletes,"[125] "wanting to thwart the Moscow Olympics,"[126] "pursuing personal ambitions... seeking a split, disunity, and tension... and trying to rally the U.S. citizens around him and distract them from the domestic problems which are tearing the United States apart,"[127] "acting contrary to U.S. legislation,"[128] "getting the U.S. Olympic Committee to boycott the Moscow games by bribing its members,"[129] "lowering an Iron Curtain around the United States—by preventing NBC television from televising the games,"[130] "cutting a poor figure when appealing to Pieter Botha, prime minister of racist South Africa, to support his anti-Olympic plans,"[131] and finally "stage-managing the blackest day in the history of the American Olympic movement by succeeding in literally tearing the American flag from the Olympic flagpole."[132] This is only a fraction of the epithets Soviet propaganda addressed to President Carter. More examples will be discussed when the technique of sarcasm is dealt with.

In addition to personal observations on Carter's goals, aims, and ambitions, Moscow also offered some analysis of his political line: "One of the reasons for the sharp criticism [against the boycott] in the entire world and in the United States is in what many, including specialists in international relations are saying. They say that this White House idea shows political amateurism. A serious politician can hardly think that such a great power as the Soviet Union can be forced through pressure and blackmail to change its policy. Particularly since the Soviet Union's policy rests on international right and international agreement, while Washington's activities directed at a boycott of the Olympic games show that it is caused by personal ambition, personal irritation, and mercenary calculations."[133]

While he was cast as the main villain, Carter was by no means the only one. Other leaders and politicians were frequently attacked by Moscow on a personal basis. British Prime Minister Margaret Thatcher was labeled "hysterical and cynical... blinded by anti-Sovietism and by the desire to play up to the election campaign sentiments of American politicians,[134] and accused of "establishing diplomatic relations with the bloody dictatorship in Chile under the cover of the propaganda campaign against holding the Olympic games in Moscow."[135] Secretary of State Cyrus Vance and Secretary of Defense Harold Brown were accused of "arm twisting,"[136] U.S. Vice-President Walter Mondale and General David Jones, chairman of the Joint Chief of Staff, were accused of "reducing the defenses of U.S. athletes."[137] Zbigniew Brzezinski was accused by Moscow of "organizing a special team of agents and supervising their training to subvert the Moscow Olympic Games."[138]

Leaders of countries that supported the Olympic boycott, such as Egypt's Sadat, Israel's Begin, and others, were also attacked by Moscow as reactionary figures, U.S. servants, and so forth. The bitter personal attacks and the unrestrained vocabulary were an eloquent sign of Moscow's rage and despair, as well as one of the several characteristics that turned the "boycott" countercampaign into a typical operational propaganda campaign aimed against specific enemies and frequently utilizing sharp personal attacks.

Other Themes

The seven major themes of the Soviet "boycott" countercampaign offensive were by no means the only ones introduced by Moscow. Several additional themes of no lesser importance (but perhaps lower intensity) were also constantly stressed.

World-Wide Support of Moscow's Stand

This theme was introduced at the very beginning of the campaign. It faded away after 25 May, when it became apparent that the Soviet estimate of the number of participating countries was somewhat overoptimistic. Still, it was one of the prominent themes until 25 May, especially during the first weeks of the campaign. During that period the Soviet mass media devoted much space to reporting worldwide support for Moscow's position on the issue of the boycott. Among the first to be mentioned were the president of the Swedish Olympic Committee Karl Gustav, who pronounced the proposed boycott "inadmissible political blackmail,"[139] members of the French and British Olympic Committees,[140] the Japanese

Communist party organ *Akahata*,[141] the French Olympic Committee ("accepts invitation to participate in the Moscow games")[142] and French Communist party leader Marchais,[143] the Brazilian newspaper *Jornal do Brasil* ("the boycott will boomerang against the United States and its associates"),[144] the Afghan Olympic Committee ("imperialist circles in the United States are striving to use for their selfish political purposes even the noble idea of the Olympic games"),[145] and many other countries, Olympic committees, progressive organizations, and so on.

When declarations of support increased, Tass started reporting them en bloc. On 23 January it reported the support of the Swedish Olympic Committee, the Swedish Sports Union, the Swiss Olympic Committee, the New Zealand Olympic Committee, and the Iranian National Olympic Committee. On the same day additional statements of support from Bonn, Bogota, Lima, and London were reported. More countries and organizations followed, among them Jordan,[146] Lebanon,[147] Mexico and Brazil,[148] Finland,[149] Denmark,[150] Brussels, Paris, Stockholm and Jakarta,[151] and hundreds of other Olympic committees, front organizations, and sports associations. It was not difficult for Moscow to present a case of worldwide support. In every country, without exception, there were athletes and officials who thought the games should go ahead in Moscow, even when their governments and Olympic committees held a different view. Some of them—willingly or unintentionally—became instruments of Soviet propaganda. It was easy for Moscow to quote one or two athletes or sports officials from a given country and thus create the (inaccurate) impression that the entire Olympic Committee of that country (or even the government) supported Moscow's position. During those first days of the countercampaign, when citing support was so important, almost all Soviet newspapers introduced special sections usually called "We Come to Moscow," "They Will Come to Moscow," "Moscow Awaits Its Guests," and so forth, which reported on preparations of the athletes from the various countries, as well as the last stage of Soviet Olympic preparations.

Limited Support for the Boycott

The theme of support for Moscow was supplemented by the theme of the very limited support for the boycott idea. Also introduced during the first hours of the campaign, this theme was devoted to describing the preparations for organizing the boycott as ridiculous and participation in the boycott was exceptionally limited, "proving" that countries which announced that they would not participate in the Moscow Olympics would do so for considerations other than the proposed boycott, and labeling the countries which had officially joined the boycott "reactionary," "imperialist," and so forth. One of the first Tass reactions to the boycott dealt with the case of Saudi Arabia, which had announced that it would not take part in the Moscow games (intrepreted by Washington as support for the boycott): "As far back as October last year, the National Olympic Committee of that country announced that it would not be able to send its team to Moscow for competitions. A jubilant voice from Washington, amplified by the Voice of America, has now been heard, stating that the U.S. policy, you see, is also shared in Riyadh. Such devices are know to have always been peculiar to the authors of the cold war. They have also been borrowed by the present opponents of friendship and détente."[152]

Trying to minimize the importance of support for President Carter's position, Moscow claimed that "Egypt was the only country of all U.S. allies which responded immediately to President Carter's call,"[153] that Israeli support "was no big deal,"[154] that the governments of countries supporting the boycott "have merged with U.S. capital,"[155] that the countries which supported the boycott were "fascist dictatorships,"[156] that "only six countries have joined the boycott,"[157] and so forth. When it became obvious that support for the boycott idea was more extensive than Moscow expected, this theme vanished almost completely from the campaign and was replaced by the "nothing terrible has happened" theme.

The Games Will Strengthen World Peace

This theme was used in the other Soviet propaganda campaigns related to the Moscow Olympic Games. While during the "preparations" campaign Moscow calmly and repeatedly explained that the games were going to strengthen world peace and cooperation (doing so in a routine way without any urgency or attacking anybody in particular), during the "boycott" countercampaign the tone of the theme became much sharper, and a twist was introduced: it was no longer merely the games themselves that were going to strengthen peace and friendship, but the act of *participation*. Consequently, the boycott was presented as a step against peace, détente, and peaceful cooperation.[158] Soviet front organizations (which were very active during the boycott campaign) were extensively utilized in connection with this theme. The French-Soviet Friendship Society was among the most active. One of its declarations against the boycott, issued in April 1980, summed up the "peace" theme in one sentence: "To come to Moscow and particpate in the games means to not only say 'no' to the boycott, but also 'yes' to sport, 'yes' to détente, and 'yes' to peace."[159]

Tass tried to show that this opinion was shared by foreign sports functionaries: "The leaders of international sports organizations rightly believe that participation in the 1980 Olympics can facilitate a lessening of international tension, that the Olympic games in Moscow will serve the cause of peace, of strengthening friendship and understanding among peoples."[160] In its broadcasts to North America Radio Moscow pursued the same idea: "To prevent American or other sportsmen from going to Moscow means to deal one more blow to the edifice of peace and relaxation of tension."[161] This theme persisted throughout the "boycott" counter-campaign and became one of the major themes during the games themselves.

Sport Has Nothing to Do with Politics

This was a tricky theme. In general, Marxism maintains that everything has something to do with politics. In addition it was the Soviet Union that defined as "naive" the notion that sport and politics were separate. There were no visible difficulties. Moscow merely came out with what it wanted to say. On 21 January, in the first Soviet official reaction to the boycott idea, Vadim Zagladin, first deputy head of the CPSU Central Committee International Department, announced that "sport and politics are different things."[162] Ten days later the Soviet Olympic Committee condemned "the usage of sport as a means of political pressure,"[163] and since then this motto became a integral part of virtually every Soviet commentary or report related to the boycott campaign.

Against Alternative Games

This theme was relevant (and utilized) only during the short period during which the possibility of organizing alternative games was comtemplated by the United States and some other countries. There were two aspects to this theme: to show lack of concern for the idea and simultaneously to condemn it. On 17 March a meeting of countries favoring the boycott was held in Geneva. Not accidentally, many Soviet top sports officials were in Western Europe at that time, voicing their opinions about the idea of holding alternative games. On 16 March Vladimir Popov, Olympiade-80 first deputy chairman, was interviewed by the French radio. When asked about the Geneva meeting he answered: "You see, quite naturally we reject this meeting because it contradicts the specific wording and spirit of the Olympic charter and the regulations and rules of international athletic federations. This is nothing but an additional act in the show some are attempting to set up around the Olympic games in Moscow, a show rooted in speculative political theories. But we are watching this show with utmost calm."[164]

The following day French radio interviewed Yuriy Zhukov, head of the Olympiade-80 Committee International Services Commission, who had this to say about the proposed alternative games: "This idea of organizing alternative games, as mentioned today, has the aim of creating a climate of nervousness around the games. I believe that all attempts at organizing alternative games have no realistic basis....We are perfectly aware of the favorable opinion of international federations as regards the Moscow games. That is why we are certain that the Moscow games will be held and why we continue preparations."[165] Spartak Beglov, one of the APN (*Novosti*) leading observers, spoke on the same theme in one of his frequent commentaries to North America: "It is clear from the start that this idea [the alternative games] runs counter to the principles of the Olympic movement. It serves to undermine this movement and split the international sports community."[166]

The failure of the Geneva meeting was promptly reported by Tass: "The attempt of the opponents of the 1980 Summer Olympic Games to respond to the provocative call of the Washington administration to boycott the games in Moscow and organize 'alternative games' has ended in total failure.... The talks in Geneva took place in conditions of secrecy and behind closed doors, alternating between the British and American diplomatic missions. After two days of barren debate participants in the talks had to admit that they were unable to suggest any alternative to the Moscow Olympics, which, as is known, has the support of most countries and the world sports community."[167] As the idea of holding alternative games lost momentum, the theme faded away and completely disappeared.

Internal Opposition to the Boycott Idea

This theme aimed to prove that even those countries that had announced their participation in the boycott did not enjoy the support of the general public in their countries, least of all their athletes. This subject will be dealt with when the technique of utilizing foreign athletes and front organizations is discussed. Already on 20 January Moscow announced that the boycott was meeting with serious opposition in the United States. Senator Kennedy and "the influential U.S. public organization Women Strike for Peace" were reported as criticizing the president's idea.[168]

From that point on, Moscow consistently reported efforts of U.S. and other countries' Olympic committees and front organizations to overcome the decision to boycott the games. U.S. athletes such as Al Feuerbach and Eric Heiden were repeatedly quoted by the Soviet mass media.[169] Members of the U.S. Olympic Committee were quoted as having said that they had been subjected to pressure by the White House on the matter of approving the boycott: "The matters have already gone so far that the president tells us how to vote, said a member of the Executive Board of the National Olympic Committee."[170] Moscow maintained that "95 percent of the U.S. athletes opposed the boycott."[171]

It was not only the internal opposition in the United States that was reported and commented on by Moscow. Other countries were subjected to the same treatment. Describing the struggle of British athletes against the "pressure of the Thatcher government," Moscow said: "Both in the United States and in many other countries sportsmen are resisting Washington's pressure, intimidation, and dictates with growing determination. They refuse the pieces of silver being offered them as payment for betrayal of the lofty principles of the Olympic movement."[172] British athlete Sebastian Coe was quoted as having said: "I will go to Moscow even if I have to pay for my ticket myself."[173]

In another article the efforts of Australian sportsmen were described: "The majority of Australia's citizens reject the call for a boycott. The arrogant orientation of the United States offends the national honor of the people....It is regrettable that Mr. Frazer is not capable of independent conduct, instead of repeating what the U.S. president is saying and doing."[174] The same article also reported that petitions had been issued and signatures collected by Australian athletes opposing the boycott. A poll was said to have shown that 63 percent of Australia's citizens opposed the boycott.

Izvestiya of 20 February 1980 reported opposition to the boycott in the F.R.G. and described a conference of F.R.G. leading sportsmen in protest of the boycott. The conference adopted a declaration which read: "We reject by all means all calls for boycott, by which President Carter is trying to accumulate political capital in the U.S. election campaign."[175] *Komsomolskaya Pravda* of 7 May 1980 described a protest meeting of Japanese athletes, against "Japan's influential forces and above all the ruling circles, who are ready to sacrifice the interests of sport and the Olympic movement in the name of implementing the 'ally's duty' to the United States, for the benefit of anti-Sovietism and the global strategy of imperialist states."[176] Similar reports from other countries were frequently used. The main goal was obvious: to present the boycott as a venture sustained only through U.S. pressure on its allies and their leaders, and lacking any support on the part of athletes and the general public.

Business as Usual

It was difficult to label this theme. It was what was left of the "preparations" campaign after the boycott had focused the attention of the Soviet propaganda apparatus. A dismal effort was made to exhibit imperturbability and keep the "preparations" campaign alive. It was a pathetic attempt to pretend that nothing had changed and that it was business as usual. Throughout the boycott campaign, here and there, amidst reports of demonstrations against the boycott, declarations, protests, and commentaries condemning Carter, Thatcher, and company, one could also (infrequently) see reports of "Moscow's invitation to the 1980 Olympiade" photo exhibit in Gabon,[177] and the "Olympic Moscow" photo-exhibit in Afghanistan, described by Anatrite Ratebzad, Afghan minister of education, as "yet another vivid manifestation of the friendly relations between the two neighboring countries that will facilitate the further development and strengthening of these relations."[178]

Sport agreements with various countries continued to be reported from time to time, as well as the once so important visits by IOC members.[179] Reports on the progress of the Olympic construction continued to appear (*Sovetskiy Sport* of 30 January reporting completion of the Olympic village's religious facilities "for Christians, Jews, and Moslems, as well as other religions"[180]), but somehow the spirit had gone out of it all. It was painfully obvious that the Olympic boycott had taken the wind out of the sails of the "preparations" propaganda campaign.

INSTRUMENTS

The Soviet "boycott" countercampaign was an operational propaganda campaign. It was prompted by specific and unexpected international developments (the boycott proposal following the invasion of Afghanistan), it sought clearly defined operational and immediate goals (foiling the boycott or at least minimizing its effect and holding the games in Moscow according to schedule), its tone was aggressive and sharp as is usually the case with Soviet operational propaganda campaigns, and it utilized many of the instruments used in other operational enterprises of the Soviet propaganda apparatus.

The Soviet radio and press, classic instruments of Soviet propaganda, were widely used throughout the "boycott" countercampaign, both as propaganda instruments in themselves and as a stage or extension of other more sophisticated instruments, reporting their activity and amplifying their effect. Despite the fact that they very often made an important contribution of their own (commentaries, reports, and so forth), there was nothing peculiar about the way they were used in this particular propaganda campaign. Therefore we shall concentrate on several other instruments, which determined the specific character of the "boycott" countercampaign.

Declarations and Petitions of Support

The purpose of such documents is obvious: they are supposed to demonstrate that the Soviet stand on the issue in question enjoys wide international support, while the rival position is universally rejected and condemned. The Olympic committee of every socialist country and of many nonaligned countries issued declarations condemning the Olympic boycott. One of the first was (naturally) the declaration of the Afghan Olympic Committee. Issued on 31 January 1980 it stated that "the attempts by a number of states and first of all the United States to interfere in matters connected with holding the Olympic games in Moscow fundamentally contradict the very spirit and principles of the Olympic movement. Those attempts are incompatible with the principles of friendship, cooperation, and peaceful coexistence of states."[181] This declaration, like most of the others, was disseminated by Tass and the contents were published by the Soviet press. In addition to national olympic committees, support declarations were also issued by the French Federation of Labor,[182] various youth organizations of the socialist countries, [183] foreign students studying in Moscow,[184] and many other foreign organizations and bodies.

Friendship Societies and Front Organizations

These were clearly associated with the declarations of support. It was through these organizations that the "spontaneous" protests abroad were carefully orchestrated. Such activities took place in many countries, but nowhere were the front organizations more active than in France. In February 1980 the organ of the French Communist party L'Humanite initiated the "committee of French trainers and sportsmen in defense of the Olympic games,"[185] and became the major amplifier of its activities (declarations, petitions, collection of signatures against the boycott, protest meetings). Many of these activities were openly sponsored and organized by the French Communist party and the French Democratic Youth.[186]

In March 1980 the French-Soviet Friendship Society arranged a visit to France by a delegation of high-ranking Olympiade-80 members.[187] The visit happened to take place just when several West European states were in Geneva to discuss the possibility of holding alternative games. The delegation members and especially its leader Vladimir Popov were repeatedly interviewed by the French radio, television, and press (some of their statements have already been quoted in this chapter), thus provided with enough opportunities to present the Soviet position, condemn the U.S. initiative, and praise France for supporting the Soviet stand.[188]

In April the French-Soviet Friendship Society invited the French public to write letters in support of the Soviet position. "About one thousand such letters from workers, peasants, member of the intelligentsia, students, noted sportsmen, and prominent trainers arrived daily."[189] It was also reported that in one month alone (March 1980) the friendship society had organized lectures on the development of sport in the Soviet Union and the Moscow Olympic Games in thirty French cities.[190] During the same month the French-Soviet Friendship Society organized in Paris a photo exhibit called "Greeting the 1980 Olympic Games." R. LeRoi, member of the

French Communist party Politboro spoke at the opening ceremony, stressing that the Moscow Olympic Games had a special significance and praising the French athletes and sports officials on "their stand against the boycott campaign organized by Carter."[191]

Additional meetings were organized and declarations issued in April,[192] the activity gradually subsiding after the French Olympic Committee adopted (as expected) a decision in May on participating in the Moscow Olympic Games. The activities of the French-Soviet Friendship Society and the French Communist party were by no means a separate case. Soviet front organizations throughout the world followed suit, and were instrumental in developing or at least showing opposition to the boycott and generally supporting the efforts of the Soviet propaganda apparatus.

Organizations Especially Created to Resist the Boycott

Most of them were founded in the United States, and were not long-lived (but long enough to be thoroughly reported by the Soviet radio and press). Among them were the Olympic Action Group created at the University of Illinois, "which saw as its main task the mobilization of U.S. public opinion in support of the Moscow Olympics";[193] the United Coalition for the Olympiade-80, "compromised of sportsmen from 28 U.S. cities who want to participate in Moscow even if no Coca-Cola is sold there";[194] the United Forces for the Olympiade, "active in 30 U.S. cities, collecting signatures and issuing petitions urging Carter and the U.S. Congress to relinquish the boycott of the Moscow Olympic Games";[195] and the Committee of Jurists for Freedom of Sport, which was established in San Francisco and attempted to develop legal action against the boycott.[196] There were several other similar organizations.

It cannot be proven that these organizations were founded by Soviet agents. It is not clear who was in back of the organization of these special groups, but it is clear that they played straight into the hands of the Soviet propaganda machine, which amplified and utilized their short existence and limited activity to prove that there was "widespread opposition to the boycott in the United States." This turned them (with or without their knowledge and agreement) into instruments of Soviet propaganda.

Foreign Countries' Athletes and Sports Officials

In every Soviet operational propaganda campaign there are always some idealist, naive persons and prejudiced or interested elements, who unwittingly and often even unwillingly become instruments of Soviet propaganda. The case of U.S. athletes was typical. Their disappointment and bitterness caused by the boycott were legitimate, understandable, and even justified. It would have been strange if there had been no such reaction on their part. Nevertheless, many of them refused to adopt a broader outlook and see the boycott in its proper context, as a protest against the usurpers of national independence and oppressors of human rights, a protest against the state which was claiming to organize an "unprecedented festival of peace and friendship" within a few months. This did not turn them into Soviet agents. Their rights to protest and criticize their government's actions are protected by the U.S. Constitution and comprise an integral part of their basic rights and freedoms as U.S. citizens. However, when their statements and protests became a major source of inspiration and joy for the Soviet propaganda apparatus, which daily amplified their statements and disseminated reports and commentaries on their activites, using them as an example of lack of democracy and denial of human rights in the United States, they became for a while a vital instrument of Soviet propaganda.

Reports and statements connected with opposition by U.S. athletes, trainers, and sports officials to the boycott became an integral part of the Soviet "boycott" countercampaign at its very beginning. Moscow Radio in its 21 January foreign-language broadcasts cited several cases of reaction by U.S. athletes and sports officials condemning the boycott: "Julian Roosevelt, an American delegate to the IOC, has noted that President Carter had done a tremendous disservice to the athletes .... The anti-Olympic campaign by the administration and punitive steps against U.S. athletes, discussed at the State Department, may serve as an eye-opener to many Americans that their country is not as free from the establishment as they used to think. Colonel David Miller, the U.S. committee's executive director, has stated that he is opposed to a U.S. boycott."[197]

This is a typical example of how Soviet propaganda works. There are two facts: Julian Roosevelt termed the boycott a "disservice to U.S athletes," and Colonel Miller "opposed the boycott." In between those two facts, Radio Moscow's foreign listeners also heard about "punitive steps against U.S. athletes," "eye-opener," and "America not being as free as..." The listener is given no indication that the two sports officials had not said this, and that these are Radio Moscow's views. The idea is to make the listener believe that the criticism against U.S. society and the fiction about "punitive steps" came from the two sports officials. Careful examination of the hundreds of reports and comments or similar statements by U.S. athletes and sports officials, carried by Soviet sources, reveals the same pattern: one short question on the need to compete in Moscow—immediately followed by observations on the denial of human rights in America, lack of personal freedom, and general decay—all of which were mixed with the statements by U.S. athletes.

Occasionally there were statements that did not need embroidering.

Such was the statement by U.S. weightlifter Bob Giordano, reported to have said that the "Olympic boycott contradicts the interests of world peace."[198] Giordano was one of the main stars of the "U.S. athletes" instrument of Soviet propaganda. His statements and organizational activities (initiating protests, organizing public meetings) were widely and repeatedly reported in words and pictures.[199] The names of Eric Heiden, Bill Rogers, Al Feuerbach, and other athletes were also frequently used. Some of their actions reported by Soviet propaganda media included press conferences,[200] statements in support of holding the Olympic games in Moscow and participating,[201] picketing,[202] legal action against the decision of the U.S. Olympic Committee to boycott the Moscow Olympic Games,[203] petitions,[204] the well-publicized Carter-Heiden encounter, and so forth.

On several occasions the Soviet press reported that the great U.S. discus thrower Al Oerter had stated that U.S. athletes should compete in Moscow.[205] *Newsweek* of 28 January 1980 carried on page 41 exactly what Al Oerter had said: "The only way to compete against Moscow is to stuff it down their throats in their own backyard."

The same pattern of blurring fact and opinion (Moscow's) following protests by other countries' athletes was reported. Thus reports on the activity of West German athletes[206] were a skilful mixture of statements by F.R.G. sportsmen and Moscow's observations on the characteristics of West German society and policy.

Delegations to the Soviet Union

During the "preparations" campaign such visits were utilized to publicize admiration for the progress of the Olympic construction and preparations. During the "boycott" countercampaign they were aimed at generating support for Moscow's stand. The pattern was predictable: a tour of the Olympic facilities, followed by a press conference at which not only admiration for the facilities was expressed, but also scorn and indignation for the boycott. An interesting case was the visit of a U.S. delegation to the Soviet Union, sometimes described as "tourists"[207] and sometimes as a "delegation of U.S. athletes."[208] One of the delegation's leaders was Philip Shinnick, "a scientist and public figure, creator of the organization Sport for the People which struggles for the development of mass sport in the United States. His opinions do not coincide much with the official viewpoint and therefore Shinnick has it rough. He is persecuted by the FBI, and there have been attempts to arrest him."[209]

Members of the delegation were said to be there "to see the truth and tell about it when we go back to the United States."[210] In an unusually extensive report *Sovetskiy Sport* of 5 May 1980 described the enthusiasm of the delegation after the tour of the Olympic facilities, their questions about life in the Soviet Union, their condemnation of the U.S. boycott, and their sorrow at the fact that somehow they knew so little about the Soviet Union. The following day, the delegation was taken to a meeting with Sergey Pavlov, who briefed its members on the Olympic preparations, Soviet contacts with foreign countries (1,300 delegations of 40,000 athletes in 1979 only), and expressed the standard Soviet view of the boycott. Leading Soviet sportsmen participated in the meeting and answered questions.[211]

The delegation continued from Moscow to Leningrad, only now it was being described as "U.S. and Canadian lecturers and sports journalists."[212] In Leningrad the delegation participated in a meeting with Tass representatives. This time Shinnick made a sharp statement condemning the boycott and U.S. president, "whose position is dictated by his personal interests."[213] Tass immediately amplified the statement, which was included in almost all Soviet broadcasts in foreign languages between 8 and 10 March 1980. On 10 March Tass issued an additional report from Washington on the return of the delegation.[214] Shinnick (this time "the leader of a delegation of U.S. athletes") "made" another statement condemning the boycott and praising preparations for the Moscow Olympic Games.[215] The visit and statements were also reported by the mass media of socialist countries.[216] The entire affair was a typical example of how foreign delegations serve the interests of Soviet propaganda and how their nature is subjected to unexplained changes.

Soviet Athletes

Soviet athletes themselves had a large role in the boycott campaign. First, they appeared in meetings with foreign delegations, scoring the boycott and expressing regret at the fact that some of their rivals would not be coming to Moscow. (Such was the case of the meeting of Soviet sportsmen with the previously described visit of the delegation of the U.S. tourists-athletes-sports journalists-lecturers. Several famous Soviet athletes published lengthy articles in the Soviet press (later condensed and disseminated by Tass). The two most notable were Borzov's article "It Is Impossible to Destroy" *Pravda*, 28 January 1980), and Olga Korbut's "Crime against Sport" (*Komsomolskaya Pravda*, 22 April 1980). Both represented the official Soviet position on the boycott, condemned U.S. policy, and encouraged U.S. athletes to resist the "administration's dictate." Several declarations by athletes of dubious renown were also issued. One of them, protesting the treatment of Soviet skiers at Kennedy Airport en route to the Lake Placid Olympic of February 1980, was signed among others by Tamara Press of the famous Press sisters, who "vanished" after the introduction of sex tests.

Official Declarations and "Open Letters"

Official declarations by the various national olympic committees have already been noted as one of the "boycott" countercampaign instruments. These declarations followed the model of the Soviet Olympic Committee.[217] Using concepts such as "blackmail and hegemonism" to describe U.S. foreign policy in general and the boycott in particular, declarations called the boycott a "preplanned and coordinated hostile act directed against mutual understanding and friendship among nations, against peace and progress," and condemned "the attempts to use sport as a means of political pressure." They called the Moscow Olympic Games "a sports festival in the name of strengthening mutual understanding and friendship of young people in the world, of building a better and calmer world."[218]

On 17 April 1980 all Soviet dailies (and of course Tass) carried an appeal by Soviet sportsmen to their American colleagues. In what amounted to interference in U.S. internal affairs and instigation, the appeal "warmly greeted all U.S. athletes who are struggling against the use of sport as an instrument of political dictate, who decisively oppose the Olympic boycott, and who are struggling for the cohesion and unity of the Olympic movement." "We hope," the appeal read, "that U.S. athletes have not said their last word and that we will see them at the Moscow Olympic Games."[219] In the same category belongs an "open letter" by Aleksandr Koshkin, noted Soviet boxer and Spartakiade champion, to Edwin Green, U.S. boxer, winner of the World Cup compeition.[220] The letter, written in a highly personal tone, recalls their previous boxing matches and expresses the official Soviet stand condemning the boycott—and concludes on a sentimental note: "The boxing tournament of the XXII Olympic Games will be a bright page of world boxing history, but the names of U.S. boxers will not be inscribed in it. The White House has turned them into hostages, victims of militaristic politicians. My sincere sympathy for you, Edwin, and your friends."[221]

Moscow Propaganda's Old Hands

One cannot discuss any Soviet propaganda campaign without mentioning all those collaborators who faithfully and dutifully contribute their share to each campaign: the permanent agents of Moscow's propaganda and policy. While we refrained from describing any U.S. athletes, even the most radical among them, as Soviet agents, charitably viewing them as misguided and naive people who were misused by a sophisticated and powerful apparatus, with this group there is no reason to conceal the true nature of its members: full-time agents of Soviet propaganda. Such are the members of foreign Communist parties and Soviet-sponsored "progressive" and "peace" organizations.

Examples in this category are Georges Marchais and Angela Davis. The French Communist party was very active in the "boycott" countercampaign (its activity was referred to in the section dealing with front organizations as instruments of Soviet propaganda). Even its secretary general Georges Marchais had something to contribute to the campaign. Speaking at the PCF national council in Bobigny on 12 February, he sharply condemned U.S. foreign policy, concluding: "Current developments make me return to the question of the Olympic games. From this rostrum I want to voice my indignation at the inadmissible conduct of U.S. President Carter and his representative Cyrus Vance, who arrived at Lake Placid to try to impose an outrageous dictate on the IOC."[222] Angela Davis, one of the leaders of the U.S. Communist party, was quoted by Moscow as having said that "the decision of the U.S. National Olympic Committee contradicts the U.S. national interest and the cause of universal peace."[223]

Karin Talbot, U.S. representative at the World Peace Council, who was already active during the "preparations" campaign, was also utilized during the "boycott" countercampaign. In April 1980 she visited Moscow and was interviewed by *Novosti,* the interview being disseminated throughout the world. She criticized President Carter roundly, condemning him for stating that no country has the right to deny the freedom of other countries, calling this statement "hypocritical." Then she recalled the murder of Chile's Allende, "organized by the CIA," "the occupation of Puerto Rico by the United States," and "the presence of U.S. troops in South Korea," all of which, in her opinion, were enough reason not to hold the 1984 games in Los Angeles. The attitudes toward Indians and unemployment in the United States were additional reasons for removing the games from Los Angeles, according to Karin Talbot.[224] Justifying the Soviet invasion of Afghanistan (repeating the Soviet version), she analyzed "the real reasons for the boycott" (elections, domestic difficulties, Iran) and called for participation in the Moscow Olympic Games.[225] Similar, although less radical, was the statement by Lord Noel-Baker, another permanent participant in various Soviet campaigns, who also condemned the Olympic boycott.[226]

Those were the main instruments utilized during the "boycott" countercampaign. One could add to this list the frequent interviews with Olympiade-80 officials (some of which were mentioned in this chapter), the invitation to West German citizens to write letters supporting the Soviet stand (the invitation was issued by *Sovetskiy Sport* of 20 June

1980), the photographs of demonstrations in the West supporting Moscow's position, cartoons and letters to Western publications expressing indignation at the boycott. (In a letter to *Time* magazine of 18 February 1980 Spartak Beglov, *Novosti's* political observer, informed the magazine that "the political aim of such a boycott is to divide the unique fraternity of athletes and subvert all other forms of international cooperation.") Nevertheless, the instruments discussed give an adequate picture of the intensity and versatiliy of the "boycott" countercampaign.

TECHNIQUES

While dealing with the themes and instruments of the "boycott" countercampaign we indicated some of the techniques used in the campaign, which are the basic techniques of every Soviet propaganda campaign. Consequently, there is no need to discuss again the obvious techniques of repetition and mixing facts and interpretation. Likewise, there is no need to dwell on the technique of distortion or simply lying. The case of the U.S. delegation which visited the Soviet Union in March 1980, and whose nature varied from one Soviet source to another was a good example of the technique of distortion. Another example will be cited to reinforce this point.

The October 1974 IOC session in Vienna followed a strange procedure in selecting Moscow as the venue of the 1980 Olympic Games. Not only was the voting secret, but the ballots were immediately thrown into the Danube, a fact admitted by Lord Killanin and various Communist sources.[227] Nevertheless, *Pravda* claimed that "Moscow was unanimously chosen as the venue of the 1980 summer Olympic Games.[228] Yuriy Zhukov, head of the Olympiade-80 International Services Commission, said something similar when interviewed in Paris: "The Games, which in 1974 were entrusted to Moscow by the IOC—unanimously, by the way, nearly unanimously—and the events that took place in Afghanistan, have nothing in common."[229]

Let us ignore for the moment the issue of whether the vote was "unanimous" (*Pravda*) or "nearly unanimous" (Zhukov). The question is, How does Moscow know? If it does not know, it is a good example of distortion. If Moscow knows how the voting went (and this author suspects that Moscow knows very well), then it is a very good example of something else, even more unpleasant then distortion. In either case Moscow does not come out smelling sweet. Another technique which does not need much elaboration is that of appealing to sentiments. The cited letter to U.S. boxer Edwin Green from "his friend and rival A. Koshkin," is an appropriate example of this technique, which aims at evoking emotions instead of rational considerations as a means of promoting an idea or implanting a predetermined behavior. Four of the most important techniques involved in the "boycott" countercampaign were polarization, differentiation, flattery, and sarcasm.

Polarization

This technique is characteristic of many Soviet operational campaigns. Its essence is to describe the issue in question in terms of black and white, identifying the "forces of evil" and "forces of good" involved in the dispute, pinpointing the enemies (combined wih name calling), and connecting the positions on the issue in question with much broader and important universal principles and ideas, ususally war and peace, tension and détente, and so forth. Subsequently the position taken on the issue which prompted the propaganda campaign also indicates the entire outlook on other major international issues.

"The forces of evil" (Carter and company) were not only identified at the outset, but were made a special target of personal attacks. Further, it was asserted ad infinitum that the boycott was actually aimed against peace, détente, and international friendship and cooperation, while the Moscow Olympic Games were intended to strengthen those very ideals. Subsequently, boycotting the games meant joining the forces of evil in their attempt to revive the cold war and undermine the Soviet Union's efforts for peace, while participating in the games meant making a contribution to the achievements of these noble goals. Thus "yes" to Moscow was presented as "yes to peace and détente."[230] Part of this technique was the inference that there could be no neutral or halfway position, sides had to be taken, bearing in mind that one's selection indicated one's ideological stand on various international issues and one's attitude toward the declared goals of Soviet foreign policy.

Differentiation

When the characteristics of Soviet propaganda apparatus were discussed, it was pointed out that one of its major advantages is the strict uniformity of every Soviet propaganda campaign. Still, this uniformity, achieved by total control, coordination, and synchronization of everything Moscow says, does not preclude the utilization of the sophisticated technique of differentiation—adapting the propaganda message to specific characteristics, customs, circumstances, and traditions of particular audiences. There were many instances of careful and deliberate differentiation in the "boycott" countercampaign. Broadcasts of Radio Moscow to North America usually stressed U.S. domestic issues (elections, inflation, unemployment, Carter's declining popularity) as the real reasons behind the Olympic boycott.[231] In its broadcasts to other states Moscow usually presented the boycott as an integral part of Carter's foreign policy, aimed against peace, detente, and cooperation.

When the F.R.G. government decided to recommend to its National Olympic Committee that it boycott the Olympic games, Moscow, in its broadcasts to West Germany dwelt extensively on West Germany's dependence on the United States and the U.S. interest:

> It is a fact that the United States grants protection not because the people in Washington are touched by the beauty of the banks of the river Rhine or by the amiability of Bonn statesmen, but for tangible reasons. Specifically, this is required by the interests of U.S. monopoly capital, the global strategy of U.S. imperialism. In other words, the Atlantic partnership so often cited by Bonn these days is not a love match but a marriage based on common sense.... The true motives of the characters in this disgraceful farce are not what they claim to be, the United States does not want the West Europeans to stay away from the Olympic games because it seriously thinks that this could in any way influence Soviet policy...this is... a symbolic though effective act of submission.[232]

After the decision to boycott the games was adopted by the F.R.G. National Olympic Committee, Radio Moscow did not hesitate to remind Germany that this decision "does not serve the aims of good neighborliness and détente, in which West Germany has by no means less interest than any other European country."[233] Thus Moscow subtly reminded the F.R.G. of its vulnerability vis à vis its neighbors (Soviet troops in East Germany), an undisguised threat not addressed at any other West European country.

Another example of the differentiation technique, this time taking into consideration specific religious characteristics and tailoring even the vocabulary accordingly, was evident in Radio Moscow broadcasts in Italy, which often included concepts of a purely religious nature.[234] Another broadcast, this time in Mandarin to China, related the Olympic boycott to Sino-Soviet relations, and clearly could not be used anywhere else. The broadcast was a reaction to an article that had appeared in *Renmin Ribao*, the Chinese Communist party daily, claiming that two-fifths of the IOC member countries would boycott the games:

> The newspaper mentioned that two-fifths of the IOC member countries will not participate in the next Olympic games. But the paper did not mention that the number of countries that will participate in the Moscow Olympic Games is exactly the same number that participated in the Montreal Olympic Games. [Moscow, of course, said nothing about Munich, where about thirty more countries had participated.] The purpose of the Beijing rulers in not allowing Chinese athletes to leave the country is to keep them from attending the current Olympic games, from experiencing the Soviet people's

warmth and hospitality, and from seeing the Soviet people's ease of mind and high living standards. If Chinese athletes see all this they will surely tell their relatives and friends of the spectacular events and friendly atmosphere at the Moscow games. That, of course, is not what the Beijing authorities want. They have long made anti-Soviet slander their specialty and concentrated on activities designed to vilify the true conditions of the Soviet Union.[235]

The frequent and refined use of differentiation illustrates the meticulous planning and coordination of the "boycott" countercampaign, which became one of its characteristics as soon as the original shock and confusion had been overcome.

Flattery

This is a technique seldom used by the Soviet Union. Nevertheless, the "boycott" countercampaign was so important and increasing the number of countries participating in the Moscow Olympic Games so crucial, that on several occasions Moscow resorted to this technique to induce a favorable response in any given situation. France was a frequent target of flattery and cited as an example of "sensible behavior" to other countries. As Vladimir Popov, Olympiade-80 first deputy chairman, pointed out: "The very calm position of principle adopted by France is highly appreciated by ourselves, by the U.S.S.R. in general, and above all by the organizers of the Olympic games."[236] France was also flattered on other occasions, as was Mexico, after the positive decision of its Olympic Committee,[237] and Iran: "As we know, Iranian wrestlers, weightlifters, and soccer players have achieved a well-deserved standing on the international sports scene. Who knows, an Olympic champion might be found among them."[238]

Irony and Sarcasm

This is one of Moscow's favorite techniques in its propaganda campaign. Seldom was this technique used with so much venom as during the "boycott" countercampaign. The usual targets were President Carter, Margaret Thatcher, the leaders of countries supporting the boycott, and Muhammad Ali. Examples of Moscow' opinion of Margaret Thatcher, Sadat, and other leaders have already been cited in another connection. During the first hours of the organized campaign Moscow made President Carter a target of the personal and sarcastic remarks, such as the one about his dropping out of the long-distance run.[239] From this point on there was hardly a commentary or article which did not scorn Carter in a highly ironic and sarcastic manner. The climax was an entire feuilleton disseminated by Tass throughout the world[240] which portrayed Carter and his closest advisors as a bunch of idiots trying to present the boycott as a huge success by fooling around with a computer.

When in February 1980 Muhammad Ali was sent to Africa to generate support for the boycott (and showed himself to be a victim to his inexperience and flamboyance), Moscow had a field day. For several days Soviet mass media savored with undisguised pleasure Ali's "insufficient experience—to put it mildly,"[241] and "the mistakes of the raw-recruit American diplomat,"[242] who "found himself in an embarrassing situation being unable to answer a question by a Tanzanian newsman on 'why he should have let himself be used in attempts to drag Africa into a campaign for the stupid interests of the U.S. administration.'"[243]

Sarcastic remarks were also directed at Coca-Cola and other U.S. companies which cancelled their contracts with Moscow. Several secondary techniques were also employed throughout the campaign. Among them was name calling, introducing specific epithets and phrases aimed at stirring the audience's imagination and evoking certain associations. Describing the U.S. athletes as "hostages" and frequently using concepts such as "McCarthyism," "forces of reaction," and so forth, belonged in this category. Personal contacts was another technique. Many African diplomats and dignitaries were subjected to personal pressure to convince them to support participation in the Moscow games. *Izvestiya* reported a meeting between I. Novikov, Olympiade-80 chairman, and Addis Tedla, deputy chairman of Ethiopia's ruling Supreme Council. After the meeting "the Ethiopian side declared that their full team will arrive in Moscow in July 1980."[244]

Since the end of World War II international sports and politics have inextricably interrelated, mainly through the efforts of the Soviet Union and its socialist allies. Moscow's efforts to acquire the right to host the games, the unprecedented "preparations" campaign, and the games themselves were prompted by overt political considerations and sought clearly defined and political goals. However, it was the Olympic boycott that turned the political issue of the Moscow Olympic Games into a political confrontation, which went far beyond the bounds of the "symbolic confrontation" involved in every propaganda campaign.

Many instances have been cited to illustrate that Soviet authorities regarded participation in the games as amounting to support for peace, international frienship, and détente, or in other words, acceptance of Soviet foreign policy and endorsement or at least toleration of the Soviet invasion of Afghanistan. Many athletes who had invested years of effort, willpower, and training for the Olympics, striving for an edge of a split second or a tenth of a point, did not always comprehend that, but politicians, and especially Soviet authorities, seldom failed to see the real issue behind the Olympic boycott. That is why the outcome of the boycott was so important and charged with so much emotional, ideological, and propa-

ganda implications. That is why each side interpreted the boycott's outcome to suit its goals.

Did the boycott succeed? Let us look at the facts: Some 113 countries
participated in the 1968 Mexico City Olympic Games, 122 in the 1972
Munich Games, and 88 in the 1976 Montreal Games. When on 19 July
1980 the clocks of the Kremlin's Spaski Tower showed 1600 local time and
the delegations began their ceremonial march into Lenin Stadium, only 81
of the IOC's 146 members were represented. Some 16 of them decided to
show partial support for the boycott by marching under the Olympic flag
instead of their country's national flag. This caused great pain to Soviet
television cameras, which had to show the country's name but tried to
avoid showing the flag being carried or the single member of the delegation
marching behind it. It did so by switching to a panoramic view of the
ceremony at the strategic moment in the case of each of these countries.

Many of those who did take part in the ceremonial parade were flown to
Moscow at the expense of the Olympiade-80 Committee. Various international sports officials, among them Count Jean Beaumont, a French
member of the IOC Executive Board, said they thought that about half of
the delegations had come to Moscow with Soviet financial aid. As Count
Beaumont put it—"it gives me the feeling they are being paid to come."[245]
The vast international TV exposure Moscow had hoped for was drastically
limited, especially where it counted most: the American NBC network
completely canceled its dawn to dusk broadcast schedule. Britain's ITV cut
coverage from 170 hours to 40. Japan's ASAHI network reduced its
tentative TV schedule from 240 hours to 40. West Germany announced
that only four TV tranmissions a day totaling just 15 minutes were to be
shown.[246]

Weeks before the opening of the games V. Promyslov, Moscow's mayor,
admitted that the expected number of tourists was reduced to 150,000.
Between 20,000 and 30,000 Americans had been expected. A week before
the games about 2,000 were expected to show up. Canadian bookings
dropped from 3,000 to 400. The number of prospective Japanese visitiors
dwindled from 13,000 to 1,000, of British from 4,000 to 3,000, West
Germans from 12,000 to about 7,000, and French from 5,000 to 2,000.[247]
The absence of the United States, the F.R.G., Japan, and other sports
powers turned many of the sports (most notably swimming, boxing,
basketball, and athletics) into a rerun of the 1979 Spartakiade. There can
be no disputing these facts and figures. The question is—Do they mean the
boycott succeeded or that it failed?

The Soviet mass media were unanimous in declaring the boycott a
"shameful fiasco"[248] and "total failure."[249] This was to be expected. Still,
one should immediately add that there were enough good reasons for

claiming that the boycott had failed. Two of the closest allies of the United States—Great Britain and France—took part in the games, along with Italy, Sweden, Spain, and other West European countries. Washington again proved incapable of rallying effective international support, and thus confirmed in Moscow's eyes (as well as the entire world) that the West is less than united. But then—this too was old news to Moscow. The Soviet propaganda machine overcame its initial confusion and utilized the boycott to develop a tremendous international propaganda campaign, accusing the United States and President Carter of "warmongering," a return to the cold war, destroying détente, and so forth.

The boycott failed to get Soviet soldiers out of Afghanistan or even to cause considerable discomfort to Soviet leaders, let alone to undo the damage done by the invasion. They have to their credit similar ventures in Europe (Hungary in 1956 and Czechoslovakia in 1968) which failed to generate effective reaction, and furthermore the Soviet and East European public were kept mostly in the dark regarding the connection between the invasion of Afghanistan and the boycott.

The games did take place in Moscow on schedule, thousands of athletes participated, and many excellent results were achieved, including numerous Olympic and world records. All this can justifiably be cited as grounds for terming the boycott a failure. But there were other grounds for claiming at least a partial success. First, the serious curtailment of international exposure (TV coverage) and of foreign tourists undermined Moscow's propaganda effort to a certain degree. Only 81 countries took part in the games, despite statements by Soviet sports officials expecting only "6 or 7 countries to boycott the games," and announcing that "more than 120 countries have already confirmed their participation." Eighty-one countries represent about 55 percent of the IOC members. Numerically, one can clearly say that the games fell short of what the Kremlin expected them to be, and the subdued mood of Soviet sports officials during the weeks preceding the games showed that.

Some of the competitions lacked much sports value and contributed to turning the games into a shadow of past Olympics. Various equestrian events, the hockey tournament, and other events were not what one would expect of Olympic standards. The Soviet-American contest, the highlight of every Olympiad since 1952, did not take place and thus destroyed much of the excitement of the Olympics. Refusal by Soviet leaders to clearly admit to their public that the boycott was connected with the invasion of Afghanistan indicates the concern of Soviet authorities that the boycott— imperfect as it was—could later on raise serious questions about Afghanistan, the number of casualties there, cost of the entire adventure, and so forth. No one seriously expected the boycott to bring about a withdrawal from Afghanistan. Nor was it a test of Western solidarity. It was never more than an attempt to discredit Soviet leaders at home and abroad while showing international abhorrence for the invasion of Afghanistan. On those counts, as well as taking into consideration the limited number of participating countries and athletes and the reduction in the number of foreign tourists and TV exposure, one can say that the boycott achieved most of its goals.

Notes

1. Moscow Tass in English (1603 GMT, 7 January 1980), *D.R.* (8 January 1980); Moscow Tass International Service in Russian (1330 GMT, 1 January 1980), *D.R.* (2 January 1980); and many other sources.
2. Moscow Tass International Service in Russian (1330 GMT, 1 January 1980), *D.R.* (2 January 1980).
3. Ibid.
4. "Possible Olympic Boycott Stirs Discussion in United States," *International Communication Agency Wireless File* (10 January 1980).
5. *International Herald Tribune* (17 January 1980).
6. *International Communication Agency Wireless File* (22 January 1980).
7. *International Herald Tribune* (30 January 1980).
8. *International Communication Agency Wireless File* (21 February 1980).
9. Ibid. (14 March 1980).
10. Ibid. (22 March 1980).
11. Ibid. (29 March 1980).
12. Ibid. (9 March 1980).
13. Ibid. (15 March 1980).
14. Ibid.
15. V. Vasiliev, "So wird es auch sein," *Sport in der UdSSr* (no. 1, 1980), p. 11.
16. *Sovetskiy Sport* (19 July 1979).
17. *Komsomolskaya Pravda* (10 January 1980).
18. *Izvestiya* (11 January 1980).
19. Ibid.
20. *Sov. Sport* (13 January 1980).
21. *Izvestiya* (18 January 1980).
22. *Pravda* (24 January 1980).
23. *Sov. Sport* (20 January 1980).
24. S. Bliznyuk, "Peace and Olympism Are Inseparable," *Sov. Sport* (20 January 1980).
25. Ibid.
26. Moscow Tass in English (1317 GMT, 20 January 1980), *D.R.* (21 January 1980).
27. Moscow World Service in English (2100 GMT, 20 January 1980) *D.R.* (21 January 1980).
28. Ibid.
29. Ibid.
30. Moscow Tass in English (2005 GMT, 20 January 1980), *D.R.* (21 January 1980).

31. Moscow Tass in English (1556 GMT, 21 January 1980), *D.R.* (22 January 1980).
32. Paris AFP in English (1314 GMT, 21 January 1980), *D.R.* (22 January 1980).
33. Moscow Tass International Service in Russian (1050 GMT, 6 February 1980), *D.R.* (8 February 1980).
34. Editorial article, "Price of Ambitions," *Pravda* (18 March 1980).
35. Moscow Tass in English (1556 GMT, 21 January 1980), *D.R.* (22 January 1980).
36. Moscow Tass in English (1109 GMT, 31 January 1980), *D.R.* (31 January 1980).
37. Moscow Tass in English (1240 GMT, 9 February 1980), *D.R.* (11 February 1980).
38. Albert Grigoryants, *Izvestiya* correspondent in Bonn, interviewed by Mainz ZDF TV in German (1830 GMT, 23 January 1980), *D.R.* (25 January 1980).
39. Moscow World Service in English (2100 GMT, 20 January 1980), *D.R.* (21 January 1980).
40. Radio Moscow in English to North America (2300 GMT, 27 January 1980), *D.R.* (29 January 1980).
41. *Pravda* (9 March 1980).
42. *Pravda* (18 March 1980).
43. Interview with Sergey Lapin, chairman of the U.S.S.R. State Committee for TV and Radio Broadcasting, Helsinki Domestic Service in Finnish (1550 GMT, 13 March 1980), *D.R.* (14 March 1980).
44. Moscow Domestic TV, Studio Nine (1510 GMT, 19 April 1980), *D.R.* (30 April 1980).
45. Radio Moscow in English to North America (2300 GMT, 9 February 1980), *D.R.* (11 February 1980).
46. *Pravda* (18 March 1980).
47. *Moskovskaya Pravda* (22 March 1980).
48. Radio Moscow in German to West Germany (1627 GMT, 23 April 1980), *D.R.* (24 April 1980).
49. "Wem nützt die Olympiafeindliche Kampagne?" *Sport in der UdSSR* (no. 3, 1980), p. 20.
50. Radio Moscow Domestic Service in Russian, weekly international "Round Table" program (0800 GMT, 6 April 1980), *D.R.* (7 April 1980).
51. *Sov. Sport* (8 March 1980).
52. Moscow Tass in English (1737 GMT, 21 January 1980), *D.R.* (22 January 1980).
53. Moscow Tass in English (1556 GMT, 21 January 1980), *D.R.* (22 January 1980).
54. *Akahara* (23 January 1980), quoted by Moscow Tass in English (0818 GMT, 23 January 1980), *D.R.* (24 January 1980).
55. Moscow Tass in English (1022 GMT, 23 January 1980), *D.R.* (23 January 1980).
56. Ibid.
57. Mainz ZDF TV in German (1830 GMT, 23 January 1980), *D.R.* (25 January 1980).
58. London Press Association in English (1733 GMT, 25 January 1980), *D.R.* (28 January 1980).

59. Radio Moscow in English to North America (2300 GMT, 27 January 1980), *D.R.* (29 January 1980).
60. Ibid.
61. Moscow Tass in English (1240 GMT, 9 February 1980), *D.R.* (11 February 1980).
62. Radio Moscow in English to North America (2300 GMT, 9 February 1980), *D.R.* (11 February 1980).
63. Radio Moscow in English to North America (2300 GMT, 20 March 1980), *D.R.* (21 March 1980).
64. Ibid.
65. Moscow World Service in English (1300 GMT, 14 February 1980), *D.R.* (15 February 1980).
66. Radio Moscow Domestic Service in Russian (1200 GMT, 12 February 1980), *D.R.* (13 February 1980).
67. Moscow Tass International Service in Russian (1430 GMT, 15 May 1980), *D.R.* (16 May 1980).
68. Radio Moscow World Service in English (1300 GMT, 15 May 1980), *D.R.* (16 May 1980).
69. Radio Moscow World Service in English (1600 GMT, 29 January 1980), *D.R.* (30 January 1980).
70. Mainz ZDF TV in German (2000 GMT, 12 March 1980), *D.R.* (14 March 1980).
71. Moscow Tass in English (1035 GMT, 25 January 1980), *D.R.* 29 January 1980).
72. *Moskovskaya Pravda* (22 March 1980).
73. *Pravda* (28 March 1980).
74. Moscow Tass in English (1429 GMT, 3 April 1980), *D.R.* (4 April 1980).
75. Moscow Tass International Service in Russian (2000 GMT, 16 April 1980), *D.R.* (17 April 1980).
76. *Kom. Pravda* (16 April 1980).
77. *Sov. Sport* (16 April 1980).
78. *Krasnaya Zvezda* (13 April 1980).
79. Moscow Domestic Television Service in Russian (1510 GMT, 19 April 1980), *D.R.* (30 April 1980).
80. Radio Moscow Domestic Service in Russian (2000 GMT, 16 April 1980), *D.R.* (17 April 1980).
81. V. Smirnov, interview, "On Schedule and According to Program," *New Times* (no. 22, 1980), p. 28.
82. *Sov. Sport* (22 March 1980).
83. Smirnov, p. 28.
84. *Pravda* (25 May 1980).
85. Moscow Tass in English (1350 GMT, 27 May 1980), *D.R.* (28 May 1980).
86. Moscow Tass International Service in Russian (1627 GMT, 24 May 1980), *D.R.* (28 May 1980).
87. "Roundtable" program, Radio Moscow Domestic Service in Russian (0800 GMT, 1 June 1980), *D.R.* (2 June 1980).
88. *International Herald Tribune* (10 June 1980).
89. Radio Moscow World Service in English (2100 GMT, 20 January 1980), *D.R.* (21 January 1980).
90. Paris AFP in English (1314 GMT, 21 January 1980), *D.R.* (22 January 1980).

91. Radio Moscow in English to North America (2300 GMT, 27 January 1980), *D.R.* (29 January 1980).
92. Radio Moscow World Service in English (1300 GMT, 14 February 1980), *D.R.* (15 February 1980).
93. *Pravda* (28 March 1980).
94. Moscow Tass in English (1007 GMT, 31 January 1980), *D.R.* (31 January 1980).
95. Moscow Tass in English (2029 GMT, 12 February 1980), *D.R.* (13 February 1980).
96. Moscow Tass International Service in Russian (1430 GMT, 15 May 1980), *D.R.* (16 may 1980).
97. *Sov. Sport* (2 April 1980).
98. Ibid.
99. Radio Moscow in English to North America (2300 GMT, 9 February 1980), *D.R.* (11 February 1980).
100. *Sov. Sport* (2 April 1980).
101. Ibid.
102. Moscow Tass International Service in Russian (1918 GMT, 28 January 1980), *D.R.* (30 January 1980).
103. Ibid.
104. *Sov. Sport* (2 April 1980).
105. Moscow Tass in English (1556 GMT, 21 January 1980), *D.R.* (22 January 1980).
106. *Rabotnichesko Delo* (Bulgaria—6 February 1980).
107. Radio Moscow World Service in English (1000 GMT, 21 January 1980), *D.R.* (22 January 1980).
108. *Pravda* (18 March 1980).
109. Radio Moscow in English to North America (2300 GMT, 20 March 1980), *D.R.* (21 March 1980).
110. Moscow Tass in English (1420 GMT, 3 April 1980), *D.R.* (4 April 1980).
111. Moscow Tass in English (1642 GMT, 11 April 1980), *D.R.* (14 April 1980).
112. Moscow Tass in English (1636 GMT, 14 April 1980), *D.R.* (15 April 1980).
113. *Sov. Sport* (22 April 1980).
114. *Literaturnaya Gazeta* (23 April 1980).
115. *Kom. Pravda* (15 April 1980).
116. *Kom. Pravda* (20 April 1980).
117. Moscow Tass in English (1420 GMT, 3 April 1980), *D.R.* (4 April 1980).
118. *Moskovskaya Pravda* (16 April 1980).
119. Radio Moscow World Service in English (0030 GMT, 19 April 1980), *D.R.* (21 April 1980).
120. Radio Moscow World Service in English (2100 GMT, 20 January 1980), *D.R.* (21 January 1980).
121. Moscow Tass in English (1556 GMT, 21 January 1980), *D.R.* (22 January 1980).
122. Ibid.
123. Radio Moscow World Service in English (1000 GMT, 21 January 1980), *D.R.* (22 January 1980).
124. Radio Moscow in English to North America (2300 GMT, 27 January 1980), *D.R.* (29 January 1980).
125. Moscow Tass in English (1209 GMT, 12 February 1980), *D.R.* (14 February 1980).

126. Radio Moscow Domestic Service in Russian (1200 GMT, 12 February 1980), *D.R.* (13 February 1980).
127. Editorial article: "Price of Ambitions," *Pravda* (18 March 1980).
128. Moscow Tass in English (1420 GMT, 3 April 1980), *D.R.* (4 April 1980).
129. Moscow Tass in English (1615 GMT, 13 April 1980), *D.R.* (14 April 1980).
130. Moscow Tass International Service in Russian (1015 GMT, 17 April 1980), *D.R.* (17 April 1980).
131. *Selskaya Zhizn* (13 April 1980).
132. *Krasnaya Zvezda* (15 April 1980).
133. Moscow TV Domestic Service in Russian (1510 GMT, 19 April 1980), *D.R.* (30 April 1980).
134. Moscow Tass in English (1515 GMT, 18 February 1980), *D.R.* (19 February 1980).
135. Moscow Tass in English (1420 GMT, 3 April 1980), *D.R.* (4 April 1980).
136. Moscow Tass in English (1642 GMT, 11 April 1980). *D.R.* (14 April 1980).
137. Radio Moscow World Service in English (0900 GMT, 13 April 1980), *D.R.* (14 April 1980).
138. *Mos. Pravda* (16 April 1980).
139. Moscow Tass in English (1737 GMT, 21 January 1980), *D.R.* (22 January 1980).
140. Ibid.
141. Moscow Tass in English (0818 GMT, 23 January 1980), *D.R.* (23 January 1980).
142. Moscow Tass in English (1009 GMT, 23 January 1980), *D.R.* (23 January 1980).
143. Moscow Tass in English (2055 GMT, 22 January 1980), *D.R.* (23 January 1980).
144. Moscow Tass in English (1022 GMT, 23 January 1980), *D.R.* (23 January 1980).
145. Moscow Tass in English (1833 GMT, 23 January 1980), *D.R.* (24 January 1980).
146. Moscow Tass in English (1018 GMT, 23 January 1980), *D.R.* (25 January 1980).
147. Moscow Tass in English (0856 GMT, 24 January 1980), *D.R.* (25 January 1980).
148. Moscow Tass in English (2017 GMT, 24 January 1980), *D.R.* (25 January 1980).
149. Moscow Tass in English (1317 GMT, 23 January 1980), *D.R.* (25 January 1980).
150. Moscow Tass in English (2145 GMT, 24 January 1980), *D.R.* (25 January 1980).
151. Moscow Tass in English (1624 GMT, 28 January 1980), *D.R.* (29 January 1980).
152. Moscow Tass in English (1317 GMT, 20 January 1980), *D.R.* (21 January 1980).
153. Moscow Tass in English (1737 GMT, 21 January 1980), *D.R.* (22 January 1980).
154. Moscow Tass in English (1035 GMT, 25 January 1980), *D.R.* (29 January 1980).
155. Ibid.
156. Moscow Tass in Russian (1627 GMT, 24 May 1980), *D.R.* (28 May 1980).

157. Radio Moscow Domestic Service in Russian (0800 GMT, 1 June 1980), *D.R.* (2 June 1980).
158. Moscow Tass in English (1556 GMT, 21 January 1980), *D.R.* (22 January 1980).
159. *Nedeliya* (21-27 April 1980), p. 16.
160. Moscow Tass in English (1420 GMT, 3 April 1980), *D.R.* (4 April 1980).
161. Radio Moscow in English to North America (2300 GMT, 20 March 1980), *D.R.* (21 March 1980).
162. Paris AFP in English (1314 GMT, 21 January 1980), *D.R.* (22 January 1980).
163. Moscow Tass in English (1109 GMT, 31 January 1980), *D.R.* (31 January 1980).
164. Paris Domestic Service in French (1200 GMT, 16 March 1980), *D.R.* (18 March 1980).
165. Paris Domestic Service in French (0650 GMT, 17 March 1980), *D.R.* (18 March 1980).
166. Radio Moscow in English to North America (2300 GMT, 20 March 1980), *D.R.* (21 March 1980).
167. Moscow Tass in English (1945 GMT, 18 March 1980), *D.R.* (19 March 1980).
168. Moscow Tass in English (2005 GMT, 20 January 1980), *D.R.* (21 January 1980).
169. *Pravda* (18 March 1980) cited them as an example of U.S. "indignation."
170. Moscow Tass in English (1645 GMT, 12 April 1980), *D.R.* (14 April 1980).
171. Radio Moscow in English to Great Britain and Ireland (2000 GMT, 6 February 1980), *D.R.* (7 February 1980).
172. Moscow Tass in English (1420 GMT, 3 April 1980), *D.R.* (4 April 1980).
173. *Sov. Sport* (3 February 1980).
174. *Pravda* (8 May 1980).
175. *Izvestiya* (20 February 1980).
176. *Kom. Pravda* (7 May 1980).
177. Moscow Tass in English (0947 GMT, 24 January 1980), *D.R.* (25 January 1980).
178. Moscow Tass in English (1815 GMT, 20 May 1980), *D.R.* (21 May 1980).
179. *Sov. Sport* (29 March 1980) reports a sports cooperation agreement with Jordan and a typical visit by several IOC members, who toured the Olympic sites and scored the boycott.
180. *Sov. Sport* (30 January 1980).
181. Moscow Tass in English (1007 GMT, 31 January 1980), *D.R.* (31 January 1980).
182. *Sov. Sport* (3 February 1980).
183. *Kom. Pravda* (18 April 1980).
184. *Kom. Pravda* (7 June 1980).
185. *Kom. Pravda* (26 February 1980).
186. Ibid.
187. *Sov. Sport* (22 March 1980).
188. Ibid.
189. *Sov. Sport* (10 April 1980).
190. Ibid.
191. *Sov. Sport* (5 March 1980).
192. *Nedeliya* (21-27 April 1980).

193. *Sov. Sport* (14 March 1980).
194. *Izvestiya* (19 March 1980).
195. *Sov. Sport* (30 March 1980).
196. *Sov. Sport* (16 April 1980).
197. Radio Moscow World Service in English (1000 GMT, 21 January 1980), *D. R.* (22 January 1980).
198. *Sov. Sport* (1 February 1980).
199. *Kom. Pravda* (8,20 April 1980); *Izvestiya* (6 February 1980); *Sov. Sport* (1 March 1980); and many broadcasts.
200. *Kom. Pravda* (8 April 1980); also Moscow Tass in English (1645 GMT, 12 April 1980), *D. R.* (14 April 1980).
201. Moscow Tass in English (1615 GMT, 13 April 1980), *D. R.* (14 April 1980).
202. *Kom. Pravda* (20 April 1980).
203. *Sov. Sport* (25 April 1980).
204. *Sov. Sport* (1 March 1980).
205. *Pravda* (18 March 1980).
206. *Izvestiya* (20 February 1980); *Pravda* (16 March 1980); *Sov. Sport* (17,21 May 1980); and many broadcasts.
207. *Sov. Sport* (5 March 1980).
208. Moscow Tass in English (1032 GMT, 10 March 1980), *D. R.* (10 March 1980).
209. *Sov. Sport* (5 March 1980).
210. Ibid.
211. *Sov. Sport* (6 March 1980).
212. *Sov. Sport* (8 March 1980).
213. Ibid.
214. Moscow Tass in English (1932 GMT, 10 March 1980), *D. R.* (10 March 1980).
215. Ibid.
216. *Rab. Delo* (11 March 1980).
217. Moscow Tass in English (1109 GMT, 31 January 1980), *D. R.* (31 January 1980); *Sov. Sport* (1 February 1980).
218. Ibid.
219. *Sov. Sport* (17 April 1980).
220. *Sov. Sport* (26 April 1980).
221. Ibid.
222. Moscow Tass in English (2029 GMT, 12 February 1980), *D. R.* (13 February 1980).
223. *Sov. Sport* (22 April 1980).
224. *Otechestven Front* (Bulgaria—9 April 1980).
225. Ibid.
226. *Trud* (Bulgaria—18 March 1980).
227. K. Casta and K. Ullrich, *Olympisches Moskau* (Berlin 1979), p. 3.
228. Editorial, "Price of Ambitions," *Pravda* (18 March 1980).
229. Paris Domestic Service in French (0650 GMT, 27 January 1980), *D. R.* (29 January 1980).
230. *Nedeliya* (21-27 April 1980).
231. Radio Moscow in English to North America (2300 GMT, 27 January 1980), *D. R.* (29 January 1980).
232. Radio Moscow in German to West Germany (1627 GMT, 23 April 1980), *D. R.* (24 April 1980).

233. Moscow Tass International Service in Russian (1430 GMT, 15 May 1980), *D.R.* (16 May 1980).
234. Radio Moscow in Italian to Italy (1730 GMT, 19 May 1980), *D.R.* (21 May 1980).
235. Moscow Peace and Progress in Mandarin to China (1430 GMT, 4 June 1980), *D.R.* (9 June 1980).
236. Paris Domestic Service in French (1200 GMT, 16 March 1980), *D.R.* (18 March 1980).
237. Smirnov, quoted by AFP in English (1529 GMT, 1 February 1980), *D.R.* (4 February 1980); Radio Moscow in English to Great Britain and Ireland (200 GMT, 6 February 1980), *D.R.* (7 February 1980).
238. Radio Moscow in Persian to Iran (1100 GMT, 18 April 1980), *D.R.* (21 April 1980).
239. Radio Moscow World Service in English (1000 GMT, 21 January 1980), *D.R.* (22 Janaury 1980).
240. Moscow Tass in English (1738 GMT, 25 May 1980), *D.R.* (28 May 1980).
241. Radio Moscow Domestic Service in Russian (1330 GMT, 8 February 1980), *D.R.* (12 February 1980).
242. Ibid.
243. Radio Moscow in French to Africa (1700 GMT, 5 February 1980), *D.R.* (13 February 1980).
244. *Izvestiya* (15 March 1980).
245. R. Martin, "Russia's Struggle to Salvage the Olympics," *International Communication Agency Wireless File* (no. 126, 9 July 1980).
246. Ibid.
247. Ibid.
248. *Pravda* (30 June 1980).
249. *Lit. Gazeta* (25 June 1980).

8

The Games

The final weeks before the games were an interlude during which no specific propaganda campaign was introduced or developed. Therefore perhaps, elements of all propaganda campaigns related to the Olympic games were evident. Despite the fact that the "boycott" campaign turned the "preparations" campaign into an obsolete memory, some long-forgotten features of this campaign reappeared for a short while. Despite the fact that all the important decisions related to the boycott had been made and there was no real reason to continue this campaign—it was still much in evidence. Finally, despite the fact that the games were to start only on 19 July, the first indications of the "games" campaign were noticeable even before the first foreign athletes arrived in the Olympic village.

On 25 June virtually the entire Soviet party and state leadership attended the ceremony of the opening of the Olympic village. The entire Soviet press on 26 June, as well as all foreign-language Soviet broadcasts of 25 and 26 June carried extensive reports on the ceremony. The entire affair was accorded the status of an official state event, beyond any sensible limits characteristic of such an occasion. Phrases such as "working heroism," "selflessness," "working enthusiasm," were freely applied to describe the builders' work. Needless to say, no Soviet newspaper failed to remind its readers that this was the best Olympic village ever. Similar ceremonies took place at the opening of the press center[1] and other Olympic facilities.

The "preparations" campaign was wrapped up in a series of interviews of the Olympiade-80 top brass, who repeated one more time what they had been saying for several years. I. Novikov, Olympiade-80 chairman, stated that the games would give a new impetus to the cause of peace and friendship, and strengthen détente, mutual understanding, and cooperation. The basis of all this, according to him, had been laid during the preparations. Thus even before they began, "the games made their contribution to implementing the historic decisions of the Helsinki conference and had become an important stimulus to developing sports, scientific, commercial and economic relations, as well as mutually beneficial international cooperation."[2]

S. Pavlov, chairman of the Soviet Olympic Committee, promised that "foreign athletes, trainers, and sports officials will be cordially welcomed in Moscow, regardless of their political views, social position, and religious convictions. We want them to see Soviet reality with their own eyes and effectively evaluate the truth about the Soviet land, and about the work, life, and hopes of the Soviet people."[3] A New Times editorial[4] once again quoted Lord Killanin praising the preparations "with which he had been familiar for several years." S. Pavlov had an additional opportunity to summarize everything he had said in the last five years, in his 14 July speech at the luncheon in honor of Lord Killanin. He praised the preparations and urged IOC members to be active in their efforts against those forces "which want to destroy the Olympic movement and prevent the holding of the Olympic games—this unique festival of youth, physical perfection, and brotherly contact of people from all continents."[5]

The "boycott" countercampaign was still pretty much in evidence. Of course, many of its elements had completely disappeared. There was no longer any reason to flatter anyone. The chips had fallen. There was also no longer any sense in repeating that participation meant supporting peace and détente and boycotting the games—reviving the cold war. Once again, that decision had already been made by the various national Olympic committees. Since the Soviet propaganda machine had successfully turned a defensive campaign into an attack of substantial dimensions against the "warmongering of U.S. imperialism" and President Carter, there was no reason not to keep a good thing going. The "boycott" campaign continued both during the final weeks before the games and throughout the competitions themselves. It became somewhat more limited and restrained, mainly describing the despair of the athletes of these countries that had decided to boycott Moscow. A favorite concept during that time was that of "betrayal." Both Japanese[6] and American[7] athletes were quoted saying that they had "simply been betrayed." It was maintained that "pressure had been applied to English, Swedish, and New Zealand athletes to refrain from participating in the Moscow Olympic Games."[8]

Various authorities were quoted saying that the boycott had failed. One of them, James Riordan, an English scholar of Soviet sport, claimed in an article (which according to him had been rejected by many magazines and published only by *Morning Star*, the organ of the Communist party of Great Britain, and subsequently reprinted by *Sovetskiy Sport*) that the Soviet Union had brought about the democratization of world sport. He criticized the Western press for supporting the boycott and accused those who were condemning the Soviet action in Afghanistan of not refusing to compete against American athletes "during years of American invasion of Indochina, the Dominican Republic, and Cuba."[9] His conclusion was that the boycott was morally wrong and had completely failed.

Several weeks before the games Soviet sports authorities indicated that athletes from the countries boycotting the games could approach the IOC with a request to be permitted to participate in the Moscow Olympic Games on a personal basis.[10] There is no record of any sportsmen having made such a request. When the foreign athletes started arriving in Moscow, some of them were used in the closing stages of the "boycott" countercampaign. Alberto Mercado, a 17-old Puerto Rican boxer, was quoted saying: "My country's economy depends completely on the United States. They pressed our government, which in turn pressed us to boycott the games. They succeeded only partially. That is why our delegation has only five members."[11] Slowly, as more athletes arrived in Moscow, the "games" campaign gradually took precedence.

On 1 July *Sovetskiy Sport* reported, with pictures, that foreign athletes were eagerly buying Soviet records and newspapers. The same newspaper described the great interest being shown in Soviet films, which incidentally were screened in the Olympic village from 9 AM until 11 PM.[12] On the following day—2 July—*Sovetskiy Sport* reported that foreign athletes were speaking their first words in Russian. Later on *Komsomolskaya Pravda*[13] described a training session of Senegalese athletes, in which instructions had been given in Russian. As time passed, more reports appeared on the growing popularity of Soviet music[14] and books[15] among foreign athletes. The Olympic village library offered Russian books in forty-five languages.[16] More statements by foreign athletes followed, thanking the organizers "from the bottom of their hearts,"[17] expressing their happiness to be in the Soviet Union,[18] describing their enthusiasm about overcoming the boycott.[19] The first meetings with Soviet heroes of labor and leading cultural figures,[20] and visits to museums and exhibitions[21] began to take place. The tone and trend of the "games" campaign was set before the beginning of the actual competitions.

Also evident before the beginning of the games was the fact that Soviet authorities were not going to permit any interference with the "games" campaign—exclusiveness being one of the preconditions of a successful propaganda campaign. When the enormous facelift of Moscow's gray and shabby aspect was completed, turning Moscow into a huge Potemkin village, there appeared several strange and sour indications that the games would not be an event in which representatives of democratic countries could feel comfortable. Early, in December 1979 foreign journalists were warned by Soviet authorities to refrain from political comments.[22] F.R.G. television reporters were the first to learn that this was by no means an empty threat. Soviet authorities censored a film of the rehearsal of the Olympic opening ceremony, which apparently included some political remarks.[23]

Another such indication was a *Sovetskaya Rossiya* article[24] which accused the CIA of making fervent preparations for the games, which included preparing agents in special "Olympic schools," producing "false-bottomed suitcases, panties, and other underwear with secret pockets, confectionery packs, crackers, candies, and cookies and coffee jars filled with leaflets and pamphlets printed on tissue paper." The CIA was also accused of planning the disruption of the games, threatening the athletes, conducting propaganda warfare, and so forth. Rumors were intentionally spread in Moscow that CIA agents would leave half-empty Coca-Cola bottles after poisoning the contents.[25] Once Soviet citizens had been properly warned, foreign journalists taught the realities of free expression in the Soviet Union, and foreign athletes taught their first Russian words, the games could begin, and the "games" propaganda campaign could go full speed ahead.

Many weeks before the beginning of the Moscow Olympic Games it was already clear that the propaganda campaign which was to serve as sound track would be different from the one originally planned. Several long years of preparations, tremendous efforts, and unprecedented investments were programmed to end in a short, but exceptionally intensive and effective campaign. It was to last only as long as the foreign athletes and guests were in Moscow, but its results were expected to be permanent. Since the eyes of the world were to be glued to the television sets for more than two weeks, Moscow expected during that period to be the capital of the world, the focus of the planet's attention and most of all, an object of admiration and adoration and an example to be imitated and followed.

Unfortunately for the organizers, things did not turn out that way. The boycott spoiled, at least partially, the planned show, reducing both the number of participants and (what probably hurt even more) the size of the potential TV audience. Thus two of the main arguments of claiming that the Moscow games were the greatest became nonexistent. Worst, the boycott compelled the Soviet propaganda apparatus not only to set up the unexpected and unplanned "boycott" countercampaign, but also to devote time, space, and effort to this subject during the games, thus spreading the "games" campaign a bit thin by dividing the propaganda effort in several directions.

There were also factors which dulled the programmed gleam of the "games" campaign. Thousands of foreign journalists crowded into Moscow during the games. Their reports often contradicted the official themes of Soviet propaganda, describing the gloomy lives of Moscow's citizens, the omnipresent hords of uniformed and civilian police, the limitations and restrictions on one's movements, and the lack of really spontaneous reactions and warm atmosphere. All this made the "games" campaign a propaganda enterprise of doubtful effect.

Originally, the "games" campaign was to have two major themes: the victories of Soviet athletes as proof not only of their superiority, but of the superiority of the entire Soviet social system; and familiarizing tourists and athletes with Soviet culture and life style, in an attempt to develop further interest in and a positive attitude toward the U.S.S.R. which would be utilized in future Soviet propaganda campaigns. The games as an instrument for strengthening peace and international cooperation was expected to be an integral part of the second theme. In reality, however, there were four major themes to the "games" campaign.

The first was the continuation or rather the remnants of the "preparations" campaign. The games were supposed to be the culmination of this campaign, proof that everything said and promised during the last five years was true. It was a far cry from the planned triumph. First of all only 5,923 athletes from 81 countries showed up in Moscow,[26] less than in Montreal, Munich, and even Mexico. Second, how many times can one repeat that the facilities are "the best," the organization is "the best," the press center "belongs to the twenty-first century," and that "never before..." etc.? There was a clear feeling of deja vu. True, the Soviet and East European mass media dutifully went through the motions. The newspapers introduced special sections dealing with nothing but statements by foreign athletes and guests praising everything connected with the games, usually concluding that these were the greatest games ever. For the nth time one could read the opinion of Frank Taylor, president of the Association of Sports Journalists,[27] Franz Muhri, secretary general of the Austrian Communist party,[28] IOC members such as A. Kumar (India) and R. Bose (The Netherlands),[29] journalists such as the Italian Enrico Krispi[30] and hundreds of other names familiar from the "preparations" campaign, repeating the same superlatives published hundreds of times by the Soviet mass media between 1974 and 1980. At least one of them (the American Armand Hammer, a very old hand of Soviet propaganda) went as far as declaring that the Los Angeles games "will be nothing like Moscow."[31]

Daily summaries of carefully selected reaction from the foreign press were also published. Not one single Soviet newspaper printed even the mildest criticism of the games. It was clear, however, that the "preparations" theme had lost much of its urgency. The reports were mechanical, joyless, and the statements sounded familiar from endless repetition. The quotations from Benin television, the Mexican newspapers, and Venezuelan radio seemed as though they were mainly intended to convince the hosts that theirs was the greatest Olympiad ever. Even the frequent comparison with the Lake Placid games, highlighting the great difference between the "poorly organized and impoverished winter Olympics"[32] and "The Greatest Ever," had already been used many times in the past. The remnants of the "preparations" theme did not seem to make a great contribution to the "games" campaign.

The second theme, a much more important one, was the continuation of the "boycott" campaign. If one had any doubts about the success of the boycott, the constant preoccupation of the Soviet mass media with this subject during the games themselves was clear proof of its success. The general idea was to show that the boycott had not diminished interest in the games, and had only hurt the boycotting countries. This of course pinpointed the areas in which the boycott was most successful. Of the expected 300,000 tourists only about 150,000 eventually showed up, and only a fraction came from the West: 8,000 Finns, 7,000 West Germans, 1,500 Americans, and a few hundred Britons.[33] Many Western countries drastically reduced their TV coverage of the games. Consequently, Soviet propaganda had to concentrate on these areas. This was done by interviewing tourists from the boycotting countries and reporting on the indignation in these countries, evoked by the very limited TV coverage.

Sovetskiy Sport reported the visit of a group of Japanese tourists and quoted them as saying: "we come as supporters of peace, friendship, and cooperation to the holiday of sport and the symbol of people's friendship and peace."[34] While many similar statements made by tourists from countries boycotting the games were quoted, the stars were two Americans, Edward Lamb and Nick Paul. Edward Lamb was presented as an "88-year-old industrialist, banker, writer, and attorney."[35] Stating "Mankind owes you!" Lamb declared that he was visiting the Soviet Union for the eighteenth time. Condemning the boycott, he said that the only thing awaiting Americans in Moscow was friendship and kindness—as nowhere else.[36]

Nick Paul was the tourist who waved the U.S. flag in Lenin Stadium during the opening ceremony. Many Soviet newspapers quoted his statement: "We waved the U.S. flag in Lenin Stadium to declare that not all Americans support the political game of President Carter. We wanted to declare that U.S. citizens are also attending the opening ceremony of the 1980 Olympic Games and that they are greeting the games from the bottom of their hearts. We wanted to show the indignation of many simple U.S. citizens who think that the U.S. president sacrificed the U.S. sportsmen for his election campaign."[37] Nick Paul also shared his impression of "Moscow's ideally clean streets and sweet air," and compared them with New York's dirt and pollution, concluding in a clearly anti-Semitic vein (something which seldom troubles Soviet authorities and never fails to impress them): "Our politicians prefer to send money to the Israeli Zionists instead of cleaning the streets."[38]

A great effort was made to demonstrate that lack of proper TV coverage had not reduced interest in the games in countries in which coverage was limited. *Pravda* claimed that "the manipulation of Western public opinion by not televising the games did not decrease interest in the games."[39] As proof, the newspaper pointed out that many F.R.G. citizens went to East Berlin, where they could watch G.D.R. telecasts of the Olympic games.[40] *Pravda* repeated the story, giving more background, and claiming this time that many F.R.G. citizens had gone to areas bordering the G.D.R., Austria, and the C.S.S.R. to watch these countries' TV coverage of the Moscow games.[41]

There was an attempt to show that the only damage the boycott inflicted was on the sportsmen of the boycotting countries. While U.S. athletes were once again extensively and repeatedly quoted as condemning the boycott[42] and political interference with sport, the "boycott" theme this time had an unmistakable star—the F.R.G. decathlon world record holder Guido Kratschmer. *Sovetskiy Sport* (20 July) quoted him as saying that "the farce of the White House failed ... the real sportsmen are in Moscow." A week later Kratschmer surfaced in person in Moscow. *Komsomolskaya Pravda* of 28 July reported that the F.R.G. magazine *Stern* had paid his travel expenses, while the Bulgarian party daily *Rabotnichesko Delo* of 2 August quoted Kratschmer as saying: "Here I sit in the honor guests' box of Lenin Stadium, having received my tickets as an Olympiad-80 guest." Kratschmer repaid his host faithfully: "I wanted to participate but Carter's pressure on the F.R.G. killed my hopes. Believe me, it is a personal tragedy for all F.R.G. sportsmen. There is nothing superior to the Olympic games."[43] Calling the "freedom games" in Philadelphia "terribly organized, boring, and weak," he once again described the situation of F.R.G. athletes as "tragic,"[44] his conclusion being—"we have lost everything."[45]

Statements by sportsmen from other countries that could be interpreted as condemning the boycott were widely quoted. For instance Duncan Goodhew, the British swimmer who beat U.S.S.R. and G.D.R. swimmers in the 100 meters breast stroke event, was quoted as expressing sorrow that it was the Olympic flag that was raised and the Olympic anthem played in his honor, instead of the British flag and national anthem.[46] This statement was picked up by many East European newspapers.[47] Special comments aimed at American audiences continued throughout the games. In a special radio commentary to North American audiences, Valentin Zorin termed the boycott a "complete failure," describing the satisfaction of U.S. tourists in Moscow, the records set during the Olympic games, the despair of athletes from the boycotting countries, Washington's inability to foist its will on many Latin American countries, and Moscow's "friendly atmosphere."[48]

The Bulgarian daily *Otechestven Front* had a strange way of describing U.S.-Russian friendship throughout history, against the background of the Olympic boycott. After (once again) describing in gloomy colors the despair and bitterness of U.S. athletes (under the headline "The Lost Class of '80"), the newspaper concentrated on the relations between the United States and Imperial Russia during the eighteenth and nineteenth centuries. The newspaper maintained that as long ago as 1776 Russia had confronted England with an ultimatum, demanding that London lift the sea blockade of America. "The English government yielded to the ultimatum, and the young state could breathe freely."[49] The newspaper went on to describe the development of U.S.-Russian relations in the nineteenth century, quoting President Jackson as saying after signing the 1832 commercial treaty with Russia: "This treaty strengthens our mutual friendship."[50] The inevitable comparison with the present followed immediately: "This was at the beginning of the nineteenth century. At the end of the twentieth century the thirty-ninth U.S. president had forgotten the words of his predecesor. In the Kremlin they are still remembered and the U.S. flag will be raised in Moscow at the closing ceremony."[51] Incidentally, it was not. After the U.S. administration refused to allow it, the Los Angeles flag was used as a compromise.

The third theme, the victories of Soviet sport, was expected to be the climax of the Olympic propaganda campaign. One of Moscow's main reasons for struggling to acquire the right to host the games was its desire to prove the superiority of its social system by means of its athletes' victories. However, it was exactly this aspect of the games that destroyed much of what the impregnational propaganda was attempting to achieve, namely, building good will toward the Soviet Union. Out of 203 sets of medals, the Soviet Union won 80 gold, 69 silver, and 46 bronze medals.[52] No country has ever achieved such overwhelming predominance at the Olympic games. Yet the way in which some of those medals were won disgusted foreign athletes and audiences.

Millions of TV viewers throughout the world saw Soviet hammer thrower Yuriy Sedich throwing the hammer a distance of 81.80 meters, a new world and Olympic record. Some also noticed that in doing so he clearly overstepped the throwing circle. Austria's television on 4 August showed in slow motion the foul. It also showed the Soviet referee, standing one meter away from Sedich, watching his foot overstepping the barrier, and nevertheless rising the white flag. A successful attempt. A new world record. A gold medal.

Several Western reporters noticed that whenever Soviet javelin thrower Danis Kula was throwing, Soviet officials supervising the competitions opened the stadium gates behind Kula, thus creating a wind canal which helped him throw his javelin to 91.20 meters. A new Olympic record. Another gold medal. Incidentally, the point of whether the stadium gates were actually opened and why gave rise to a heated dispute after the games. The Soviet stand was that the gates had not been opened, and if they had, it was in order to admit trucks carrying supplies to the stadium. This was also the position of Adrian Paulen, chairman of the Internal Amateur Athletic Federation (IAAF), in an interview published in several East European newspapers, including Bratislava's *Pravda* of 1 August 1980. Numerous Western journalists, however, maintained that the gates were indeed opened, and no trucks were seen in the area.

Australian triple jump athlete J. Campbell jumped 17.50 meters, some 15 centimeters more than Soviet jumper Jaak Uudmae, and enough to win the gold medal. The referee raised the red flag. The athlete's persistent request for explanation did not help him much. There was no footprint over the line, so there could be no foul. Later on it was explained that in the second step of his triple jump Campell had ostensibly dragged his foot on the ground. Red flag. Another gold medal for the Soviet Union.

The Soviet public in Lenin Stadium was frequently hostile toward foreign competitors, particularly when a Soviet athlete looked as though he or she was on the verge of losing the gold medal. This could also be observed in some of the team ball games. But nowhere was it more obvious than in the case of the pole vault competition. Everything possible was done to disturb Polish pole vaulter Wladislaw Kozakiewicz. Yet despite the whistling, noise, and derogatory cries Kozakiewicz vaulted to a new world and Olympic record. Triumphantly he made the only too well known Italian gesture with his arms, the continental equivalent of "up yours..." and turned to all four directions of the stadium to make sure that there was no misunderstanding. This of course did not prevent the Soviet press and most of the East European press from endlessly praising the fairness and friendliness of the Soviet public.[53]

Soviet diver Aleksandr Portnov had a comfortable points lead when disaster struck and he botched a dive, ending up almost on his back.

Shock, confusion. No gold medal? No way. The referees decided that Portnov had been disturbed by the Soviet (!) public, something which had affected his concentration. Against all logic, fairness, and rules, he was permitted to repeat his dive. This time it was perfect. First place. Another gold medal.

The most blatant injustice was done to Romanian gymnast Nadia Comaneci, the triple Olympic champion of Montreal. She needed a 9.95 grade on the beam—one of her best areas—to become absolute Olympic champion again. She did very well. There was no doubt that she would get the (deserved) 9.95. The jury deliberated for more than forty minutes. No decision. Yuriy Titov, Soviet president of the gymnasts federation, and Ellen Berger, G.D.R., head of the female technical commission of the international gymnasts, went to the jury. After a heated discussion the jury complied with the dictate. The Romanian head of the jury Maria Simonescu, refused to press the button which showed the score on the screen. No problem; Kolog Nomus, the Soviet referee pressed it. 9.85. The Soviet gymnast Davidova won. Another gold medal.

On the following day, 25 July, the entire Romanian press was outraged. *Scinteia*, the party organ, devoted 2,000 words to the event. "A flagrant violation of sports ethics and the Olympic spirit," "fraud," "unfair verdict," "an Olympic title snatched from Nadia's hands"—these were only some of *Scinteia's* expressions. Bucharest *Romana Libera* of 26 July joined in: "fraud," "injustice," "disregard of appeals," plus many other words describing Olympic injustice, lack of objectiveness, and so forth, embellished its pages. As usual in such cases, injustice and fraud were accompanied by hypocrisy. Ellen Berger, the official responsible for Comaneci's not winning the gold medal, presented her with the silver medal. She also kissed Comaneci while awarding it to her. *Scinteia* dramatically commented: "Late last night, at the end of the gymnastics competition, when Ellen Berger ... kissed Nadia on the winners' platform, one wondered if there existed any gesture that would console the hurt soul of a young athlete, a gesture that could wipe out the stains thrown with such defiance on the clean Olympic spirit. No, there are no such gestures. The lips that uttered an unfair verdict were not able to kiss away those stains. The hand that had taken away her gold medal and was now shaking the hand of the athlete entitled to it, could not wipe those stains away either."[54] The Austrian large circulation independent daily *Kronen Zeitung* of 26 July printed the picture of Berger kissing Comaneci with the caption: "The kiss of Judas." It is hard to see Davidova's gold medal making any friends for the Soviet Union. Especially in Romania.

Sovetskiy Sport of 4 August claimed that 9,292 drug tests were conducted during the games (Austria's *Kurier* of 10 August claims that only

2,486 tests were conducted). There was not even one single incidence of a positive test. In other words, an Olympic gathering of nonusers. This of course only meant that the testing systems were one step behind the science of doping. So many of the G.D.R., U.S.S.R., and Bulgarian female athletes looked like sure contenders in the Miss Ana Bolica contest, so many of them displayed a physique and muscles resembling those of their countries' wrestlers and weightlifters, and so many of them had been banned in the past for using illegal drugs (the Bulgarian Totka Petrova and the Russian Olga Rukavishnikova, to mention only two)—that the entire show of negative tests looked ridiculous.

The Soviet and East European press (with the exception of the Romanian press and some Yugoslav newspapers such as Belgrade's *Borba* and *Politika* of 31 July and 1 August) vehemently denied any fraud or unfair judging, calling the whole claim "provocation and propaganda."[55] Still, some measures were taken to reduce the damage. For the first time since 1952, when the Soviet Union first participated in the modern Olympic games, the Soviet mass media did not print the table of medals won by countries, something it regularly did and loudly publicized during and after previous Olympics. Vladimir Popov, Olympiade-80 deputy chairman, suddenly discovered that "there is nothing about team classification in the Olympic charter. It is the participation that counts and not the results."[56] As usual, Moscow had no difficulty in finding a Western figure who publicly admired the lack of team classification. This time it was D. Follows, chairman of Great Britain's Olympic Association: "I greet the fact that the Soviet television and press stress the success of individual athletes and not countries. This presentation of the competition fully corresponds with the Olympic spirit."[57] The fact that it was the Soviet Union who invented team classification and for twenty-eight years had used it as ultimate proof of the superiority of its sport was immediately forgotten. So much for victories as propaganda. This particular aspect of sports propaganda, usually the most effective weapon of this propaganda, became a liability during the Moscow Olympic Games. True, the Soviet Union won more medals than any other country ever before. This, however, only inflamed emotions and irritated even some of the Soviet Union's East Eurpoean allies, failing to increase friendship toward the Soviet Union among Western participants and guests.

The fourth theme of the "games" campaign was acquainting foreign guests and athletes with the Soviet Union's achievements, its culture, social system, and historical heritage, in an attempt to impregnate them with admiration and good will toward the Soviet way of life. The games took place under the motto "Oh, Sport, You Are Peace!" On 19 July, the day the games opened, *Ivestiya* had this motto printed in fifteen different languages on its sports page. On the following day the headlines of most Soviet newspapers dealt with the same subject: *Pravda's* headline was "The Torch of Peace and Friendship Burns Over Moscow!" while *Komsomolskaya Pravda* titled its report of the opening ceremony "Greetings! Holiday of Sport and Peace!"

Many exhibitions devoted to the subject of peace opened during the games. The opening of the central one, "Sport—Ambassador of Peace" was attended by E. Tyazhelnikov, CPSU Central Committee Propaganda Department head.[58] Another opening, this time of an exhibition of children's paintings called "I See Peace," was sponsored by V. Shevtchenko, chief of the Olympiade-80 propaganda department.[59] Foreign athletes and tourists were strongly encouraged to visit these and similar exhibitions.

While Soviet authorities put up a live barrier of militia between visiting athletes and the ordinary population, no effort was spared to organize special meetings with carefully selected groups and individuals. Many delegations were "adopted" by various industrial plants or Moscow districts. The Bulgarian delegation was "adopted" by Moscow's Kuybishev district industrial plants.[60] On 23 July they were taken to a meeting with Pavel Volodin, CPSU Kuybishev district secretary, who briefed them on the success of the district's industrial plants.[61] On 30 July the athletes were taken to the Khromatron plant where accompanied by Volodin they held a friendship meeting with the workers, at which speeches were exchanged.[62]

Western tourists and journalists received the same treatment. After one such visit, on 30 July, French journalist J. Pettijean expressed his admiration: "I never dreamed that the workers had such sport palaces, and their places of work were so bright and colorful. I spoke with your workers. They are wonderful, simple, and sincere people. Real working people!"[63] American journalists were quoted making similar statements.[64]

It was through such meetings, the Soviet and East European press maintained, that "hundreds of thousands of guests could sense the Soviet people's love for peace and the fruits of the Soviet peaceloving foreign policy, based on the Decree on Peace and the Peace Program."[65] Newspapers enthusiastically reported the great interest evoked by Lenin's museum and the exhibit of Soviet economic achievements and space research, "the most attractive points for the foreign guests."[66]

Young foreign tourists from the United States, France, Greece, Spain, and other countries, who had come to Moscow with the Sputnik youth tours, were subjected to even more intensive treatment. Not only were they "adopted" by the Kirov district industrial plants, but they were also taken to meetings with Komsomol leaders, people's representatives, and Soviet journalists. In addition special "international clubs" were established for them, in which they discussed current events and held discussions with Soviet representatives.[67]

Athletes who preferred to remain in the Olympic village were not forgotten. First there was the library with books in forty-five languages. In the village there was also an "international club," frequently visited by various Soviet personalities, cultural and political figures, who also participated in political discussions with the athletes. On 27 July cosmonauts G. Beregovoy and Y. Kozlovsky visited the village and met with the foreign athletes.[68] The journalists from African countries were also a favorite target. Frequent meetings with Soviet journalists were organized for them,[69] at which they were informed about Soviet success in many areas.

Several spectacular propaganda events were organized on the eve of the games and during them. One such event was the Soviet "peace initiative" which began a month before the games with the announcement of a limited troop withdrawal from Afghanistan. Then, when F.R.G. chancellor Helmut Schmidt visited Moscow, Brezhnev announced he would be willing to discuss nuclear force limitations in Europe with the United States. A Soviet proposal on reducing the NATO-Warsaw Pact conventional weapons in Europe followed.[70] Although the timing of these proposals was obvious and their purpose clear, they attracted press headlines on the eve of the games and scored the Soviets some points in the "peace efforts" game.

The most spectacular propaganda event was the launching of Soyuz-37 with the joint Soviet-Vietnamese crew (Viktor Gorbatko and Pham Tuan). Soviet space research featured largely in the Soviet propaganda effort during the games. During the opening ceremony the huge film screen of Lenin Stadium repeatedly showed the faces of Leonid Popov and Valeriy Ryumin, the Salyut-6 crew, as well as their greeting to participants in the Olympic games: "Let the Olympic flame of friendship always burn, let rivalry be confined to the sports field only."[71] As mentioned, Soviet cosmonauts visited the Olympic village and foreign tourists were brought to the space exhibit. The climax was the launching of the spaceship with its joint Soviet-Vietnamese crew on 24 July. The same day, at his daily press conference with foreign journalists, V. Popov greeted the Vietnamese journalists, athletes, and Olympic officials on the success of Soyuz-37.[72] The event was widely reported and commented on by the Soviet and East European mass media, its relevance to the games being explained in the following manner: "Only a country with a great industrial, scientific, technological, intellectual, and moral potential could organize such unrepeatable Olympic games. Many people asked themselves: how is it possible simultaneously to organize such huge games of a Soviet scale and scope, and launch such a complex cosmic flight with an international crew in which there is a representative of the yellow continent.... This became an exceptional example for the thousands of foreign journalists and tourists, who could learn the truth about the U.S.S.R."[73] A French journalist was quoted as adding: "The international Soyuz-37 crew is an example of Soviet assistance to developing countries."[74]

Was all this effective? Impregnational propaganda is a long-term undertaking, its results developing gradually over the years. Nevertheless, the Soviet mass media, as usual, had no difficulty in producing hundreds of statements by foreign guests, athletes, and officials that in themselves illustrated the success of Soviet impregnational propaganda. Afghan athletes in Moscow declared that they "feel at home."[75] Ethiopian Minister of Culture Tesfaye Shewayeh was quoted by Tass as saying: "Acquaintance with the Soviet masters of art, who portray the historical way of the first worker-peasant state in the world is of great significance in strengthening the consciousness of our people, who are beginning their march along the road of socialism."[76] Athletes from Ecuador promised "to tell the truth about Soviet life" when they returned home.[77] S. Feiler, secretary general of the Olympic Committee of Swaziland, declared that he was trying to "buy as many records and books as possible in order to acquaint as many people as possible with Soviet life."[78] French tourists were quoted as saying that French youth was misinformed about the Soviet Union, and that cooperation with the Soviet Union is the only way toward progressive transformation and world peace.[79] Georges Marchais, secretary general of the French Communist party, added: "I am boundlessly happy that French tourists have learned the truth about the U.S.S.R. with their own eyes. Every new day in Moscow will be a new revelation. Socialism—this is the wonderful future of France!"[80]

Soviet authorities did not try to conceal that they were conducting a propaganda campaign aimed at enhancing Soviet prestige and proving the superiority of the Soviet way of life. On the contrary, they showed amazement that this should be the subject of accusation or reprimand: "What is wrong with enhancing prestige? What is wrong with Frank Taylor and Armand Hammer praising the organization of the Olympic games?"[81] In Moscow, Lord Killanin had one of his last chances to officially display his naivete, this time clearly bordering on stupidity, when he compared Soviet Olympic propaganda with "similar propaganda" conducted by other Olympic cities: "Every Olympic city tries to show its best sides. This is how it was also in Munich and Montreal. Therefore it is only natural that Moscow is striving to demostrate the wealth of its sport and the generosity of its arts and culture.... I would like to remind you that Moscow was awarded the right to host the Olympic games not because of political considerations, but because of its contribution to sport." Little wonder there was no Soviet newspaper which did not print this amazing statement.

Notes

1. *Sovetskiy Sport* (29 June 1980).
2. I. Novikov interview, *New Times* (Russian—no. 28, 28 November 1980), p. 25.
3. S. Pavlov, "A Holiday of Peace, Friendship, and Mutual Understanding," *Sport in der UdSSR* (no. 6, 1980), p. 7.
4. Editorial, "The Nobel Ideas of Olympism," *New Times* (Russsian—no. 29, 18 July 1980), p. 1.
5. Moscow Tass in English, 1655 GMT (14 July 1980), *D.R.* (16 July 1980).
6. *Sov. Sport* (28 June 1980).
7. *Sov. Sport* (4 July 1980).
8. *Sov. Sport* (19 June 1980).
9. *Sov. Sport* (14 June 1980).
10. V. Smirnov interview, *New Times* (Russian—no. 26, 27 June 1980), p. 29.
11. *Pradva* (2 July 1980).
12. *Pravda* (27 June 1980).
13. *Komsomolskaya Pravda* (13 June 1980).
14. *Sov. Sport* (5 July 1980).
15. *Sov. Rossiya* (10 July 1980).
16. Ibid.
17. *Sov. Sport* (6 July 1980).
18. *Sov. Sport* (8 July 1980).
19. *Sov. Sport* (12 July 1980).
20. *Sov. Sport* (11 July 1980).
21. *Sov. Sport* (11 July 1980).
22. *Kurier* (Austria—29 November 1979, 20 December 1980).
23. *Kurier* (19 July 1980).
24. B. Antonov, "On a Subversive Mission," *Sov. Rossiya* (13 July 1980).
25. *International Herald Tribune* (29 July 1980).
26. I. Marinov, Olympic Dimensions 1980," *New Times* (Russian—no. 30, 25 July 1980), p. 25.
27. *Rabotnichesko Delo* (Bulgaria—1 August 1980).
28. *Pravda* (25 July 1980).
29. *Sov. Sport* (17 July 1980).
30. *Sov. Sport* (1 August 1980).
31. *Sov. Sport* (22 July 1980).
32. *Sov. Sport* (17 July 1980).
33. *Time* (11 August 1980), p. 28.
34. *Sov. Sport* (19 July 1980).
35. *Sov. Sport* (2 August 1980).
36. Ibid.
37. *Pravda* (25 July 1980).
38. Ibid.
39. *Pravda* (25 July 1980).
40. Ibid.

41. *Pravda* (28 July 1980).
42. *Sov. Sport* (1 August 1980); *Pravda* (30 July 1980).
43. *Sov. Sport* (28 July 1980).
44. *Kom. Pravda* (28 July 1980).
45. *Rab. Delo* (2 August 1980).
46. *Sov. Sport* (24 July 1980).
47. *Rab. Delo* (25 July 1980).
48. Radio Moscow in English to North America, 001 GMT (27 July 1980), *D.R.* (28 July 1980).
49. *Otechestven Front* (Bulgaria—25 July 1980).
50. Ibid.
51. Ibid.
52. *Pravda* (5 August 1980).
53. *Rab. Delo* (26 July 1980).
54. *Scinteia* (Romania—25 July 1980).
55. Bratislava *Pravda* (CSR—1 August 1980).
56. *Der Spiegel* (4 August 1980).
57. *Sov. Sport* (28 July 1980).
58. *Sov. Sport* (15 July 1980).
59. *Sov. Sport* (16 July 1980).
60. *Rab. Delo* (20 July 1980).
61. *Rab. Delo* (24 July 1980).
62. *Rab. Delo* (31 July 1980).
63. *Sov. Sport* (31 July 1980).
64. Ibid.
65. *Otechestven Front* (1 August 1980).
66. Ibid.
67. *Sov. Sport* (28 July 1980).
68. *Pravda* (28 July 1980).
69. *Izvestiya* (30 July 1980).
70. F. Halpin, "The Olympic Flame and Afghanistan," International Communication Agency *Wireless File* (16 July 1980). pp. 10-11.
71. *Sov. Sport* (20 July 1980).
72. *International Herald Tribune* (29 July 1980).
73. *Otechestven Front* (4 August 1980).
74. *Sov. Sport* (27 July 1980).
75. *Izvestiya* (23 July 1980).
76. *Sov. Sport* (25 July 1980).
77. *Pravda* (24 July 1980).
78. *Sov. Sport* (15 July 1980).
79. *Sov. Sport* (27 July 1980).
80. Ibid.
81. *Rab. Delo* (27 July 1980).

9

Conclusion

The seas are quiet when the winds give o'er;
So calm are we when passions are no more.
For then we know how vain it was to boast
Of fleeting things, so certain to be lost.

Edmund Waller

We have described and analyzed the Soviet propaganda campaign devoted to the 1980 Olympic Games, revolving around one major subject—sport. In dealing with the various aspects of this campaign one has had the opportunity to observe the Soviet propaganda apparatus in action, recognize its main strengths and weaknesses, and identify the main rules and considerations which both prompt and direct its activity. It is time now to draw several conclusions regarding the general activity of the Soviet propaganda apparatus and the Olympic campaign.

One cannot help being impressed by the fundamental and unshakable belief of Soviet authorities in the power of propaganda. It is hard to blame them. Propaganda and agitation were the main and certainly the most effective weapons of the arsenal used in the October 1917 Revolution. Marx, Engels, Plekhanov, Lenin, Trotsky, Bukharin, and many other theoreticians of world and Soviet communism discuss in their writings the use of propaganda and prescribe its frequent use. Every regime based on a strict and rigid ideology, claiming to possess the answers to all past, present, and future problems, as well as the prescription for arriving at a bright future, has to rely on propaganda, as an instrument for both spreading its ideology and weakening the defenses of its enemies.

Hence the central place propaganda occupies in Soviet foreign policy. It precedes, accompanies, and follows every single Soviet step in the international arena. Serving as the sound track of Soviet policy, it supplements each of its moves and often serves as a substitute for any real moves. Since there can be no international development that does not lend itself to being made the subject or target of Soviet propaganda, and since propaganda is the main instrument of Soviet foreign policy, the intensive propaganda campaign surrounding Olympic preparations and the games was expected and in many ways even predictable in its form and course.

The importance attached to propaganda by Soviet authorities has led them to create a worldwide apparatus that can be activated by Moscow at any given moment and quickly galvanized into producing a noisy and widespread campaign.

It is a major mistake to view Soviet radio, press, films, books, and various political statements as the only instruments of the Soviet propaganda machine. Foreign politicians and public figures, front organizations, Communist party leaders and members, and various "progressive" elements are integral, vital, and indispensable parts of this apparatus. When one deals with a single Soviet propaganda campaign the activity of these other elements can easily be overlooked, or interpreted as bona fide political support—or protest. But when several campaigns are analyzed, it is impossible to escape the conclusion that their permanent presence, their "firm and principled position" (on the side of Moscow, of course), and the speed and ease with which they can be activated by Moscow are all parts of a standard and frequently rehearsed procedure. Many of them participated in each of the four related campaigns discussed in this study, their statements and remarks varying only slightly (if at all) from one campaign to another.

The existence of this tremendous apparatus is both a strength and a weakness of the Soviet propaganda apparatus. It is a strength because no other country has at its disposal such a sophisticated and world-embracing apparatus, one that is at the same time subjected to the strict rules of uniformity and obedience imposed by Moscow. There can be little doubt that this apparatus gives tremendous resonance to Moscow's words and guarantees what seems to be worldwide support of Moscow's position on any given issue. But this apparatus can (and sometimes does) turn into a liability. For several decades people and organizations have trained to say more or less the same things against the same factors and to support the same side. Regardless of the issue, regardless of where or when it takes place, once the Soviet position has been announced, they automatically begin to go through the motions. Protest meetings, declarations of support and condemnation, signature collecting, and so on—they are all automatic, lack real spontaneity and genuine persuasion, and often evoke a feeling of deja vu. It is a drilled and mechanical activity, and when something unexpected happens, when an unusual campaign, perhaps a defensive one, needs to be organized, this part of the Soviet propaganda apparatus is at a loss. The same is true of the general Soviet propaganda apparatus.

The Soviet propaganda process is long and cumbersome. While dealing with this process it has been stressed that it originates in the main political decision-making organ, which sets the goals of the country's foreign policy. It has also been stressed that the propaganda effort is subjected to these goals and expected to contribute to their implementation. The main decision-making organ issues appropriate instructions to the top propaganda department, which in close cooperation with representatives of the decision-making organ adopts decisions related to the professional side of the propaganda campaign—mostly what is to be siad, how, by whom, to whom, and how often. Subsequent instructions are sent to the propaganda instruments (radio, press, front organizations) and the professional propagandists. Then—and only then—the propaganda messages are issued.

This complicated process is even more pronounced in the Soviet Union, where the principles of personal responsiblilty and obedience subject every political move to the decisions of the Politburo. This is where the real power and responsibility are vested and where every important decision— on any subject—originates. Whatever action is to be taken, it has to originate or at least be approved beforehand by the Politburo. Every single word used by the Soviet propaganda machine has to conform with Politburo decisions and with the principle of centralism, which guide and control the propaganda process, and at the same time restrict and subject it to heavy personal responsibility and strict discipline. This is another aspect of Soviet propaganda which is often overlooked. The reason is obvious: most Soviet propaganda campaigns are carefully planned and smoothly executed operations. They begin only *after* the political decisions relevant to the campaign have already been adopted by the Politburo, and appropriate instructions have been issued by the top propaganda department and inculcated by the propaganda instruments.

When an unexpected and sudden development on the international scene necessitates the introduction of an unplanned propaganda campaign, or when an urgent shift in the ongoing campaign is to be executed, the Soviet propaganda apparatus displays its main weakness: it is not programmed to react quickly, let alone instinctively. It has to wait for the appropriate decisions to be made by the Politburo and instructions to be issued by the propaganda department. Until then, the propaganda apparatus is paralyzed. Nothing can be done or said. Nobody is willing—or can—assume responsibility for unauthorized action, original thinking, or independent initiative.

This characteristic of the Soviet propaganda apparatus was clearly demonstrated during the first stages of the boycott campaign. One could observe the helplessness and temporary paralysis of the Soviet propaganda apparatus. Indecisiveness and confusion prevailed. The Politboro took its time studying the issue, and the propaganda apparatus was immobile. It was like a huge car which could not start its motor on a cold morning. More than two weeks after the boycott idea surfaced, the Soviet propaganda apparatus produced only hestitant, sporadic, and obviously confused and uncoordinated reaction. The unexpected had happened! The Soviet Union had become the target of a sudden propaganda campaign. The motor was cold and could not start. However, if the propaganda apparatus was temporarily out of order, the political decision-making machine was visibly active. Only after the 16-17 January meeting of the CPSU Central Committee members with representatives of the socialist countries' Communist parties, and the 22-23 January meeting of the Olympiade-80 Organization Committee with Evgeniy Tyazhelnikov, CPSU Central Committee Propaganda Department head, appropriate decision were adopted and relevant instructions issued. Only then the real action started. Once the decision on a massive countercampaign and its major themes was adopted, the old enemy was pinpointed, and the old and familiar concepts and slogans were introduced—the propaganda machine was in familiar waters. The old and tested vechicles and techniques of propaganda, ready as old veterans always are, were activated. The defensive campaign turned into an offensive against the perennial butts of Soviet propaganda: U.S. imperialism, U.S. warmongers, the U.S. administration and its allies, Zionism, and so forth. The wheels were set in motion. The engine was purring like a satisfied cat. Nevertheless, the whole affair served as a visual demonstration of the involvement of the Soviet political apparatus in defining goals and targets of the propaganda process, as well as of the vulnerability of the Soviet propaganda apparatus in unplanned and unexpected situations.

Despite its importance and relative effectiveness, Soviet propaganda is never utilized as a single instrument of international politics. Its always accompanies practical political steps or is supplemented by personal pressure, manipulation, and so forth. This was especially evident during the "games" campaign. While the victories of Soviet sportsmen were supposed to serve as vehicles of propaganda per se, manipulation of results and various kinds of pressure on foreign athletes were employed as auxiliary instruments facilitating the effect sought by propaganda. Personal contacts and pressure were also integral parts of both the "boycott" countercampaign and the campaign to acquire the hosting rights.

Since the Olympic propaganda campaign epitomizes the general activity of the Soviet propaganda machine, this conclusion applies to all Soviet propaganda campaigns. It has been frequently stressed throughout this study that propaganda facilitates the implementation of political goals, and international propaganda facilitates the implementation of foreign policy goals. The achievement of these goals is never sought by propaganda means only. The obvious conclusion is that whenever the Soviet Union initiates and develops a major international propaganda campaign, this fact should serve as an indication that the goals sought by the propaganda campaign are also being sought by other means. The emergence of a Soviet propaganda campaign should not be seen as a routine activity of the Soviet propaganda apparatus, but as a reliable indication of Soviet interest in that matter, and of the activation of other means promoting Soviet interest in said matter.

Official Soviet sources declared the 1980 Moscow Olympic Games an unqualified success in several areas. The fact that the games took place in Moscow on schedule was viewed by Moscow as one of its main successes. Despite the fact that during the "boycott" countercampaign Soviet authorities showed great confidence and ostensibly and repeatedly stated that the games would take place as scheduled, it seems that this self-confidence was not real and that Moscow had some nightmares regarding the possibility of moving the Olympic games from Moscow or even cancelling them. When it became apparent that the boycott simply aimed at avoiding complicity in the Soviet aggression in Afghanistan, and not at forcing the Soviet Union to withdraw from Afghanistan or preventing further murder, *participation* in the games became for Soviet authorities an act of indentification with their position on Afghanistan, and a protest against the U.S. position on the same matter. Consequently, after the games, the fact that they took place as planned was hailed as a great achievement and one of the organizers' main successes.[1]

The numerous articles and commentaries praising this particular aspect of the Moscow games displayed several common denominators. While they all defined the boycott as a total fiasco, it was nevertheless repeatedly pointed out that the struggle against the Moscow Olympic Games started immediately after the October 1974 IOC session, which decided on Moscow as the site of the 1980 Olympic Games. According to Sergey Pavlov, this decision was greeted by the "forces of reaction, imperialism, Zionism, and supporters of the cold war, as well as by various anti-Soviet organizations, with unconcealed malice."[2] The obvious implication was that the Soviet invasion in Afghanistan was not the real reason behind the Olympic boycott.

Ignoring the fact that Begin became Israeli prime minister only in June 1977, Pavlov included him, along with former British Foreign Minister Owen and "some U.S. congressmen" among those who had opposed the Moscow Olympic Games immediately after the October 1974 IOC decision.[3] "Devilish efforts"[4] against holding the Games in Moscow is how Pavlov defined the struggle of these persons against the Moscow Olympic Games. Soviet sources did not conceal Moscow's urgent steps to ensure the holding of the games, nor their gratitude to those Western athletes who chose to participate. In his official report to the General Assembly of the International Sports Federations I. Novikov, Olympiade-80 chairman, stated: "We financed the transportation of athletes from forty developing countries to Moscow. This was our contribution to international solidarity."[5] *Pravda* defined participation in the Moscow Olympic Games as a "contribution to peace,"[6] and described in this context the participation of Austrian equestrienne Sissy Teurer, who defied the decision of the Austrian Equestrian Federation to boycott the games and took part in the competition, winning a gold medal in the process, as an "act of civil heroism."[7] Another source stated that by participating the athletes "clearly demonstrated their desire for good will, mutual understanding, and friendship among nations."[8] After all this it was only natural to rejoice at the fact that the games took place in Moscow, and define this fact as an "undoubtful achievement for the forces of peace and détente,"[9] and a "victory of peace and cooperation."[10]

The high level of the competitions and the unprecedented victories of Soviet athletes were viewed by Soviet authorities as another great success. This is an ambiguous point which requires clarification. There is no doubt that the Soviet athletes scored a great victory. They have 80 gold, 69 silver, and 46 bronze medals to prove it. It is also true that athletes of some West European states, especially Great Britain, Italy, and France also competed successfully and that 36 world and 74 Olympic records were broken, something which attests to the high level of the competition. Credit for these achievements went not only to the athletes but also to "the CPSU, its Leninist Central Committee, and the Soviet government, who are constantly demostrating their concern for the development of sport and physical culture in the U.S.S.R.... and consider this a component part of communist construction."[11]

The very long (540 names!) and revealing list of those who were rewarded by the Soviet government on their achievements in the Olympic games and their contribution to the achievements of others[12] indicates who else was considered instrumental for these achievements: along with the athletes and their trainers there were also sports officials (among them S. Pavlov—The October Revolution Order and V. Popov—the Friendship among Nations Order), CPSU Central Committee Propaganda Department officials (S. Arutyunyan, consultant at the CPSU Central Committee Propaganda Department and N. Rusak, A. Pashin, and V. Kudryavtsev, instructors at the CPSU Central Committee Propaganda Department), and an unusual number of medical doctors and laboratory heads. Among them was Zoya Mironova, department chairman at the Moscow Central Institute of Traumatology and Orthopedics, who was awarded the Lenin Order—the highest Soviet award, and T. Absalyamov, R. Piloyan, V. Monogarov, and other laboratory heads in Moscow, Kiev, and other cities.[13]

The victories of Soviet athletes and the high level of the competitions had other aspects which were either treated subjectively or completely ignored by the Soviet mass media. The subjective treatment was reserved for undermining the importance of the absence of many excellent foreign athletes who were boycotting the games. On this point too Soviet sources were unanimous: "The absence of a number of states did not have a detrimental effect on staging the Olympiad."[14] S. Pavlov even ventured a measure of prophesy. After repeating the standard position that "the absence of the U.S. team did not hurt the games,"[15] he added: "In any case the U.S.S.R. and the G.D.R. would have been first anyway."[16] He prophesized further that "even if the games had taken place on U.S. territory, U.S. athletes would have not been able to achieve the degree of success achieved by Soviet athletes."[17]

Soviet sources completely ignored the fact that the achievements of many athletes, especially those of the developing countries, were far below the usual international level, sometimes bordering on the embarrassing. The "achievement" of the 5,000-meter runner from Benin who ran his heat exactly two minutes and one second behind the winner, another runner from Benin who ran the 1,500-meter in 4:15.3, the Vietnamese girl who ran the same distance in 4:38.6, the Lao girl who ran the 100-meter in 14.62[18] and many similar "feats" of hundreds of swimmers, weightlifters, and so on, were simply ignored by the Soviet press. It was painfully obvious that in their effort to increase the number of participants the organizers had brought to Moscow "athletes" who did not belong in any competition of such high level. If the sports aspect of their participation was discreetly ignored, these athletes were prominently featured in the numerous Tass reports and newspaper and radio comments praising every conceivable aspect of the games. It was apparent that the presence of these athletes in Moscow had nothing to do with the purely sports aspect of the games and did not contribute anything to the level of competitions. This of course did not disturb *Pravda*, which claimed that "the excellent results attested to the fact that the Olympics in the capital of the Soviet state evoked special interest among the world's young people who prepared for it in an unprecedently intensive and responsible way."[19]

Another area in which the games were deemed a great success by Soviet authorities was the realm of everything surrounding the games which was not a part of the actual competition. There were no surprises in this area. Since success was promised years in advance, the organizers did not have much choice but to declare that everything—the facilities, the atmosphere, the Soviet public, the spirit of the competitions, etc., was as successful as promised. For months after completion of the games the Soviet mass media continued to print self-extolling articles, commentaries, and statements by foreign athletes and officials praising every single aspect of the Moscow games. Praise for the organization of the games and the quality of the facilities was deserved. They were really excellent. But the endless repetition and especially the praising of every obscure detail reached absurd proportions. *Komsomolskaya Pravda*[20] and *Krasnaya Zvezda*[21] proudly stated that Herr Bindert, chief cook of the 1972 Munich Olympic Games who had been invited as consultant, had said there was nothing he could teach the Olympic-village cooks and that everybody could learn from them. Other sources praised the fact that there were no traffic jams during the games,[22] and many other aspects of similar relevance. The organizers placed a special book in the Olympic village sometimes called "book of reactions"[23] and sometimes "book of gratitude,"[24] in which foreign athletes inscribed their impressions of the Moscow Olympic Games. This book was one of the main sources utilized by Soviet newspapers and radio after the games.

In their passion to praise everything connected with the games, Soviet sources did not hesitate to commend even the Soviet public, which did everything possible to prevent the rare victories of foreign athletes. Sergey Pavlov said: "All sportsmen stressed the exceptional objectivity of the Moscow Olympic Games public."[25] V. Popov added in the same vein: "The public was extremely fair and sincerely supported the representatives of foreign states."[26] In describing the general atmosphere of the games, Soviet sources unearthed the cliches coined during the "preparations" campaign. Brezhnev himself pronounced the games a "holiday of sport and friendship... which facilitated the strengthening of friendship, mutual understanding, and peace among nations."[27] This obligatory phrase was repeated verbatim by all Soviet articles and commentaries devoted to the Olympic games. The "calm, businesslike, benevolent, and hospitable atmosphere,"[28] the "friendship meetings with Soviet youth,"[29] "the lesson to those who thought they could maintain today positions of threat and hegemony,"[30] "normalizing the international atmosphere and strenthening the cause of peace and detente,"[31] and "a blow on the cold war,"[32] were some of the most frequently repeated phrases. *Pravda* visualized even broader achievements: "The Moscow games confirmed the fact that the Olympic movement aims at strengthening international confidence and good will. This conforms the final act of the Helsinki Conference, whose fifth anniversary coincided with the 1980 Olympic Games. The XXII Olympic Games made their contribution to strengthening mutual understanding and friendship among nations."[33] The general conclusion was that "by withstanding the intrigues of those who are trying to sow mistrust and enmity among peoples, the Olympiad in Moscow had fulfilled its high and humane mission."[34]

The final and probably most important aspect of the Moscow Olympic Games' success—as seen by Moscow—referred to the political value of the games as a booster of the Soviet image and a promoter of good will toward Soviet society and Soviet life. The 1936 Berlin Olympic Games were the first modern Olympic games to be organized by state authorities—by placing all state resources and facilities at the disposal of the organizers. The Moscow Olympic Games surpassed the Berlin precedent. Official Soviet sources presented the organization of the games not only as a state task of supreme importance, but also as a "high and noble mission of the Soviet people."[35] There is little if any exaggeration in this. The political implications of the Moscow games were well known years in advance. As the first Olympic games to be held in a socialist country they were supposed to demonstrate the advantages of Soviet society, improve the Soviet image, and serve as a reason for a worldwide and intensive propaganda campaign aimed at developing interest in the Soviet Union and good will toward the country and its people.

After the games, Soviet authorities did not conceal their satisfaction with the achievement of these goals. "The Moscow Olympic Games will live forever because they demonstrated the huge possibilities of socialist society—the only one capable of organizng such a complex and responsible project in such a brilliant and unique way."[36] Many statements by foreign athletes and officials were quoted in an obvious attempt to reinforce this conclusion. *Krasnaya Zvezda*, reporting the visit in the Olympic village of Mr. Huberrot, chairman of the Organizational Committee of the 1984 Los Angeles Olympic Games, quoted him as saying: "I am shocked! Frankly, we cannot construct such a village!"[37] The newspaper hastened to explain and strengthen this statement: "Yes, this isn't surprising. The Moscow Olympic village reflects in a nutshell the social achievements of our people and the advantages of the planned socialist economy."[38]

The euphoria of the Soviet mass media surrounding the "holiday of peace" and the "festival of friendship and cooperation" will continue for years to come. Satisfaction with the Moscow games' results is total. Were the games really the success presented by the Soviet mass media? Did they really fulfill the expectations of the organizers? Let us concentrate on two main areas: the role of the Moscow games in promoting the Soviet image abroad, and their relevance to the association between sport and politics. Image building is a fine art. To a large extent it resembles sleight of hand: it works only if the audience does not see or is not aware of what is happening. In short—image building succeeds if no image is seen to be built. Soviet authorities overlooked this rule. Their promotional effort was massive and obvious, and the unpleasant aspects of Soviet society, too evident to hide.

The Soviet regime is an autocratic system. Despite its democratic facade (elections, parliament of sorts, constitution) Soviet leaders have no illusions as to the real nature of their political system. Haunted by the realization of the regime's illegitimacy, they are constantly searching for new forms of recognition and new demonstrative acts of acceptance and even admiration on the part of the world public. In some peculiar way the repeated admiration, the praise of everything Soviet, adulation of the Soviet way of life—by foreigners—is viewed by the Kremlin leaders as a safe substitute for free elections, human rights, and basic freedoms. It is what they consider the seal of acceptance.

The Moscow Olympic Games were programmed to be the greatest, conclusive, and all-convincing seal of approval and the ultimate evidence of the regime's legitimacy and supremacy. In order to ensure this, authorities took several measures aimed at purging Moscow of its "dangerous" elements (mostly dissidents), isolating foreign guests by preventing any possibility of spontaneous and unplanned contact with Soviet citizens, and strictly organizing their stay in the Soviet Union. Additional measures aimed at preventing contact between foreigners and the local population included the scare campaign opened by the organizers on the eve of the games, warning Soviet citizens of American spies and provocateurs, Zionist propagandists, and CIA agents. Wild rumors were freely disseminated by authorities, one of them, for instance, maintaining that foreign athletes were going to put poisonous powder in public telephones.[39] The Olympic arena was made into a fortress. The sportsmen lived in isolation behind a control apparatus the world had rarely seen before. Veterans among sportswriters said they had never experienced anything similar. Their briefcases with typewriters and photographic equipment were handled as if they contained bombs and hand granades.[40]

The organizers obviously desregarded the paradoxical situation which could (and did) develop, namely, the contradiction between the totalitarian practice of isolating foreigners and preventing any real and spontaneous contact with the local population on the one hand, and the attempt to impress them with the advantages of Soviet life on the other. In attempting to neutralize everything which could interfere with their propaganda effort, including isolating the foreign guests from any factor (such as Soviet citizens) which could distract their attention from the official line, Soviet authorities effectively displayed some of the most unpleasant aspects of Soviet life. The consequence was inevitable: Soviet authorities learned that the sophisticated and independent-minded Western tourist is no easy prey. He might be vulnerable in some areas, perhaps on his home ground, when Soviet propaganda can direct his attention to his country's problems and weaknesses. There is little, however, that Soviet propaganda can offer him inside the Soviet Union. On the contrary, the positive attitude previously created abroad by various instruments of Soviet impregnational propaganda can easily be neutralized. Many foreign athletes and journalists who were in Moscow during the Olympic games will remember forever various sad pictures of Soviet daily life and not the games' highlights. Characteristic in this context are the words of Kenneth Turan, who covered the games for *Inside Sports*:

> Yet the memories of specific events dissolve before the impressions made by the Soviet system. It was almost as if Moscow was the event, and the Olympics the excuse for holding it. And try as they would to make the games a showcase for the best features of their system, it was inevitable that the Soviets would have to expose the most humbling flaws as well. So if one image had to be picked out of the sixteen days, it was an image that had nothing to do with sport. It was a scene that repeated itself daily, and involved those Russians lucky enough to have passes into the Rossia, the press hotel. Every day without fail, they lined up at he hotel's small snack bars, standing patiently for long stretches of time like serfs at the castle door, waiting without complaint to buy literally by the dozens the jams from Hungary, the glossily packaged drinks, the fresh fruits and so on, that were totally unavailable elsewhere so that they could be provided here in abundance to foreigners who needed impressing.[41]

If the organizers really succeeded to impress somebody, it was the athletes from Third World countries. They really had a good time. Brought to Moscow at the expense of the Olympiade-80 Organizing Committee and losing (in most cases) painlessly and hardly unexpectedly to their opponents, they efficiently disposed of their duties and were left with plenty of free time to enjoy the Olympic village and the cultural attractions so lavishly provided by the organizers. Yet the question remains—Were *they* the main target of Soviet propaganda? It seems that it was the Western athletes who were the prime target. As far as they were concerned, Moscow succeeded in turning them, or at least most of them, into ardent patriots of their own countries.

Even the victories of Soviet athletes, which were expected to be per se visual demonstrations of the superiority of the Soviet social system, did not fulfill the organizers expectations. On the contrary, they learned that these victories could be a source of irritation, chagrin, and what is much worse—even ridicule among the Soviet Union's own allies, let alone the Western world. What contributed to this was the realization of the sinister manipulations involved in securing the victories of Soviet and East European athletes, and the repeated recurrence of injustice, prejudice, and hostility toward foreign athletes competing against Soviet athletes on Soviet territory—all in the name of preventing them from beating the hosts. When one sees the masculine-looking women athletes of the Soviet and East European teams or the mechanical monster dolls of the Soviet and G.D.R. gymnastics teams, looking hypnotized, hungry, and sad, one comprehends that physical health and sanity do not count in the Soviet Union and Eastern Europe when the all-important Victory is at stake— and one is puzzled, offended and disgusted. True, the Soviet Union won 80 gold medals at the 1980 Moscow Olympic Games, a feat never before accomplished by any other country. Did these medals induce many foreign countries, tourists, or TV viewers throughout the world to fall in love with the system that produces such athletes, or goes to such extremes to ensure their victories? It seems that the opposite is true. The reaction of the Romanian and Yugoslav party press to what the Belgrade *Borba* called "national greediness for Olympic and world records"[42] was a good example of the effect achieved by the unprecedented victories of Soviet athletes. Another Yugoslav newspaper—*Politika*—went even further in stating: "What has perhaps left a bitter aftertaste of the Moscow Olympic Games is the nearly hysterical race for sports results at any price and for medals at any price, a race that shows tendency to use achievements in sports as evidence of the supremacy of an individual or a community over another individual or community. When that happens, that is no longer sport!"[43]

The reaction of the Mexican press to this insane race for medals was indicative of the tremendous damage this race caused the Soviet image abroad. Reporting the "clear partiality of the Soviet judges" the Mexican newspaper *El Nacional* stated: "The one who lost prestige with such behavior is not Mexico, which has been swindled out of two medals, but the U.S.S.R. which, as host of these Olympics, has given itself over to the blatant hunt for trophies, not giving a hoot about altering the results and giving awards to those who did not deserve them. This is the first time such an unusual thing has occured in such famous and important events. The

Soviet Union in its insane desire to gather medals has broken all boundaries of shamelessness and evil. They have not considered the consequences for their system of government, already as totalitarian as it is dictatorial, which these wrongs against other peoples and nations can have. The reputation of the Soviet Union will come out of these Olympics more tarnished than ever."[44] So much for the Moscow Olympic Games as an image booster. Let us turn now to the area of sport and politics as expressed by the Moscow Olympic Games.

The Moscow Olympic Games served as conclusive proof that sport and politics are connected, and that sport in fact *is* politics, that major international competitions are major business enterprises, and that all top world athletes, no matter what country they are from, are professionals. Let us start with the last part of this statement. The importance of sports victories has been discussed at considerable length in this study. While the Soviet Union was the first to grasp the tremendous political implications and ramifications of a major sports international victory, it did not remain alone for a long time. While all states are aware today of sport's political value, none matches the efforts of the U.S.S.R. and the East European countries to produce better athletes. Since socialist states consider a sports victory an affair of state importance, their athletes are trained and treated as state assets. It becomes increasingly difficult for athletes of other states (who do realize the political value of sport but do not do much to utilize this value by patronizing their athletes) to compete successfully against Soviet and East European athletes, unless they maintain a training regime which no amateur can afford. The fierce international competition requires exceptional skills, top form, and outstanding results, which can hardly be produced by simple amateurs. Continuous training, medical treatment, and financial compensation accompanying the sports life of a totally dedicated athlete can only be provided by a state or by wealthy sports organizations and sponsors.

True, 36 world and 74 Olympic records were broken during the 1980 Moscow Olympic Games. None of them by an amateur! They were broken by professional athletes, trained and paid by their states (and subsequently bestowed awards for their service to the state), or by "amateurs" devoting their active sports life to major competitions, competing and training continuously and receiving large (and usually secret) payments from the organizers of the major competitions or from the producers of sports equipment and advertising agencies, often as a down payment for future services.

It is not the intention of this study to laud or condemn this practice. After all, there is hardly anything wrong with achieving top professional quality and high proficiency in one's performance—regardless of what this performance is. International sports competitions will hardly evoke any interest if no high professional level of competition is exhibited. The concept of professionalism should not be used derogatorily when appled to athletes. But everybody, and first of all the IOC, should stop the hypocritical lip service to amateurism in world top sport and admit that all top athletes, including of course the top Olympic athletes, are professionals. The Moscow Olympic Games were a meeting of some of the world's best professional athletes, who earned their bread by exhibiting high professional skills, something for which they had been thoroughly prepared.

Another hard fact of life, which long ago ceased being a secret, is the close association of sport and business. The Olympic games are the world's greatest market of sports equipment. Misha, the Olympic mascot, and the official emblem of the Moscow Olympic Games were printed on thousands of different articles, thus indicating that the company producing the article was an official supplier to the Moscow Olympic Games. Cameras, watches, clothes, everything conceivable was promoted with the Moscow games' official symbols. Since the Moscow games were so important and instrumental for promoting sales, it was not surprising to see owners and officials of large sports equipment companies involved in the Moscow propaganda effort during the "preparations" and "boycott" campaigns. The huge sum paid for televising rights by NBC (with an eye on even bigger profit from advertising during the games) serves as additional proof of the close association of sport and big business. In the final account, this is another factor which promotes the professionalization of amateur sport and the Olympic games, by turning them into a major promotional enterprise.

The Moscow Olympic Games did not reveal for the first time the fiction about amateur sport or discover the association of sport and business. Those "secrets" had been known for years by everybody. There were two areas in which the games made an original contribution: the sudden change in Soviet attitude toward the relation between sport and politics, and the origins of the sports boycott prompted by political considerations. Both involved two major deceptions by the Soviet Olympic propaganda campaign (mostly the "boycott" countercampaign) related to sport and politics. Goebbels is reputed to have said: "if you repeat a lie many times, people are bound to start believing it." The huge volume and great variety of instruments of the world wide Soviet propaganda apparatus allow a further development of this thought: when a lie is repeated endlessly by a myriad of instruments, agents, and officials, its volume silences the truth. Throughout the "boycott" countercampaign the Soviet propaganda apparatus stressed two main motifs: (1) sport and politics are separate and should not be mixed; and (2) the United States invented sports boycott as a political instrument.

In 1979 the Novosti press agency published a booklet called *Soviet Sport in Questions and Answers*. It was translated into several languages (as part of the "preparations" campaign) and dealt with the question of sport and politics in the following manner:

> Question: In many countries the opinion prevails that sports are incompatible with politics. What is the Soviet attitude to this matter?
> Answer: The slogan "Sports have nothing to do with politics," which is popular in the West, is not supported in the Soviet Union. This slogan cannot be accepted in our country for the very reason that the Soviet state and Soviet people consider sports as the most important means of improving relations among peoples, for developing and consolidating friendly relations, and as a means of reaching mutual understanding. To put it briefly— we consider sports as a means of serving peace. Whenever Soviet representatives support, for example, the expulsion of the South African and Rhodesian racists from the Olympic movement, we can certainly call this a political action. This, however, is a political action in the interest of peace, a policy serving the promotion of the Olympic ideals, which do not allow any discrimination in the sports area. When members of the Soviet soccer team refused to play in the stadium of Santiago, where the blood of Chilean patroits had been shed, this was certainly a political action as well. It was a policy of struggle and protest against the fascist regime.This policy is close and understandable to all decent people throughout the world. Sport is playing a specific and special role under the conditions of détente and consolidation of world peace. The trend toward effectively developing cooperation among sports organizations from countries with different political and social systems has intensified recently.... Sportsmen are ambassadors of peace. This fact is more and more frequently acknowledged whenever meetings of athletes from various countries proceed with statements of nationalistic character, without expressions of mutual distrust, in short, whenever such meetings proceed in an atmosphere of sincerity and mutual trust.... We cannot take it seriously when somebody speaks of sport existing without any relation to politics.[45]

This revealing statement was published in February 1979, long before anybody thought of an Olympic boycott, but this fact should not obliterate it from one's memory. Yet the Soviet propaganda apparatus reversed this statement and indignantly turned "sport has noting to do with politics" into one of the major themes of the "boycott" countercampaign. The voice of those who tried to remind the Soviet Union of the fact that their propaganda apparatus used to promote the reverse view only months before, was lost against the background of the noise produced by the numerous Soviet propaganda instruments. The United States was blamed for utilizing the idea, formerly introduced by the Soviet Union. The entire affair served as an example of the fact that in propaganda the truth seldom matters, and that it is the volume, strength, and intensity of the propaganda apparatus, as well as constant repetition, that determine the outcome.

The second deception related to the claim that the United States had invented the sports boycott as a political instrument. Indignantly deploring the U.S. Olympic boycott, the Soviet propaganda machine completely ignored the fact that in Olympic sport it is the Soviet Union that invented the word *boycott*. The Soviet Union was not expelled from the Olympic movement after the October Revolution. The communist regime pulled out of the "bourgeois" event immediately after 1917 and did not return until 1952. We have already mentioned the Soviet refusal to compete against U.S. athletes (Vietnam), Chilean soccer players (the overthrow of Allende), Israeli chess players (the general policy of Israel), and of course, South Africa and Rhodesia (apartheid). It was the Soviet Union who threatened to boycott the 1968 Olympic Games unless South Africa was excluded, and the IOC acquiesced. Nevertheless, during the "boycott" countercampaign the Soviet Union succeeded in creating the impression that the sports boycott was another sinister idea of "certain U.S. circles." Another triumph of volume and noise over the truth.

A definite conclusion on the effectiveness of the Olympic propaganda campaign is impossible at this point. Impregnational propaganda sows the seed, and it is future operational propaganda campaigns that harvest the fruit. Several results, however, are evident: Soviet authorities were forced to change their plans after the boycott was announced. Compelled to develop an unplanned campaign and continue it throughout the games, they divided their attention in several directions causing the "games" campaign to lose some of its momentum and effectiveness. As it turned out, the political significance of the Soviet victories was to be played down (and the table of medals won by the countries totally abandoned), which deprived the "games" campaign of its sweetest moments. Many Western and even socialist countries' tourists and athletes left Moscow bitter, disappointed, and troubled by what they had seen. Therefore, while it is impossible to assess the long-range effectiveness of the total Olympic propaganda campaign, it seems that it fell short of what Moscow had expected.

Notes

1. V. Popov, "16 Days Which Astounded the World," *Ivestiya* (9 August 1980); S. Pavlov, "A Real Holiday of Sport and Friendship among People," *Komunist* (no. 14, September 1980), pp. 76-77.

2. Pavlov, p. 76.
3. Ibid.
4. Ibid., p. 81.
5. I. Novikov, "Report to the General Assembly of the International Sports Federations," *Sov. Sport* (17 October 1980).
6. *Pravda* (4 August 1980).
7. Ibid.
8. Editorial, "Ambassador of Peace," *Pravda* (5 August 1980).
9. V. Bolshakov, "The Olympic Flame Burns," *Pravda* (23 August 1980).
10. *Otechestven Front* (Bulgaria—5 August 1980).
11. Pavlov, p. 85.
12. *Sov. Sport* (26, 27 September 1980).
13. Ibid.
14. Weekly "International Observers Roundtable," Moscow Domestic Service in Russian (0800 GMT, 10 August 1980), *D.R.* (11 August 1980).
15. Pavlov, p. 84.
16. Ibid.
17. Ibid.
18. *Los Angeles Times* (3 August 1980).
19. *Pravda* (5 August 1980).
20. *Komsomolskaya Pravda* (8 August 1980).
21. *Krasnaya Zvezda* (8 August 1980).
22. "Olympisches Moskau—ein Erlebnis!" *Mitteilungsblatt der Österreichisch—Sowjetischen Geselschaft* (no. 6, August-September 1980), pp. 3-4.
23. *Komsomolskaya Pravda* (8 August 1980).
24. *Krasnaya Zvezda* (8 August 1980).
25. Pavlov, p. 79.
26. Popov; *Izvestiya* (9 August 1980).
27. "Brezhnev's Greeting Message to All Those Involved in the Preparation and Conduct of the Moscow Olympic Games," *Pravda* (17 August 1980).
28. "Roundtable," *D.R.* (11 August 1980).
29. "Olympisches Moskau," pp. 3-4.
30. Novikov; *Sov. Sport* (17 October 1980).
31. Popov; *Izvestiya* (9 August 1980).
32. Bolshakov; *Pravda* (23 August 1980).
33. *Pravda* (4 August 1980).
34. "Roundtable," *D.R.* (11 August 1980).
35. Popov; *Izvestiya* (9 August 1980).
36. *Rabotnichesko Delo* (Bulgaria—5 August 1980).
37. *Krasnaya Zvezda* (8 August 1980).
38. Ibid.
39. *The Economist* (12 July 1980).
40. *Aftenposten* (Norway—16 July 1980).
41. Kenneth Turan, "The Naked Olympics," *Inside Sports* (30 September 1980), p. 147.
42. *Borba* (Yugoslavia—3 August 1980).
43. *Politika* (Yugoslavia—4 August 1980).
44. *El Nacional* (Mexico—31 July 1980).
45. S. Popov and A. Srebnitskiy, *Sowjetsport in Fragen und Antworten* (Moscow, 1979), pp. 62-63.

INDEX